God's final n
Second ed

Bernard Pa

To Tiger Woods
God Bless.

There are many professing Christians who are so misguided on the matter of truth in relation to God's law and God's love as to make a mockery of the death of Jesus on Calvary.

There is so much error being taught such as the devilish doctrine of eternal torment in hell-fire, and that God's law of Ten Commandment were nailed to the Cross as to make the gospel of Christ look ridiculous.

The mark of the beast is not a figment of the imagination but a real danger that will face all of those who refuse to heed the last call of God to worship Him in truth.

It is widely believed that at the relevant time it will be an easy thing to refuse to have the mark of the beast. However, the mark of the beast is not a visible sign to accept or reject but a subtle intrusion upon the mind by Satan the arch deceiver.

There are real issues at stake when confronted by the Spirit of truth. In these circumstances, it is important to be aware of present truth whether from this or any other source before the return of Jesus.

CONTENTS:
SECTION ONE
Chapter 1	Is God there?	Page 4
Chapter 2	Darwin or the Divine	Page 11
Chapter 3	The Great Deception	Page 24
Chapter 4	Comma from Calvary	Page 38
Chapter 5	God's Law	Page 41
Chapter 6	Sign & Mark	Page 49
Chapter 7	The Spiritual Sabbath	Page 61
Chapter 8	Perfection	Page 83
Chapter 9	Circumcision and two Covenants	Page 95
Chapter 10	Two Resurrections & Return of Elijah	Page 102

SECTION TWO
Chapter 11	Prophetic time Scale	Page 107
Chapter 12	Papacy in Prophecy	Page 111
Chapter 13	Destiny Foretold	Page 115
Chapter 14	Cleansing the Sanctuary	Page 121
Chapter 15	Choice	Page 128
Chapter 16	Judgement of the Saints	Page 130
Chapter 17	Rites, Jacob and the 144,000	Page 133
Chapter 18	Fit man	Page 145
Chapter 19	Anti-Type differs from Type	Page 149
Chapter 20	The Plagues	Page 154
Chapter 21	Time of the end	Page 157
Chapter 22	One Hour & the Ten Kings	Page 170
Chapter 23	U S A. and the World Order	Page 175
Chapter 24	Come out of Her My People	Page 181

SECTION THREE
Chapter 25	One God in Plurality	Page 185
Chapter 26	One Spirit	Page 192
Chapter 27	Eternal & Immortal	Page 195
Chapter 28	Church Doctrine Bible Doctrine	Page 199
Chapter 29	Personality and Character	Page 206
Chapter 30	Anointed Cherub	Page 217
Chapter 31	This Generation	Page 225
Chapter 32	The 2520 Curse	Page 230
Chapter 33	The Seven Thunders	Page 242

SECTION ONE
Chapter 1
Is God there?

It is possible to make a god out of anything or anybody but, the pertinent question is, does there exist an all-powerful divine God? The answer to this question is that no human being has any positive proof that would necessarily be convincing one way or another.

The next question is does it matter what we believe? In the matter of belief in an all-powerful God, in the first instant, the desire to seek an answer is initiated by choice. Basing our answer on the fact that the evidence is that whatever choices we make can be relevant to future events it seems that it does matter.

Accepting the evidence that through the execution of our choice we could in some respects fashion the future, it must surely be of the uttermost importance to make the right choice. This is especially true if our eternal welfare is at stake.

Much emphasis of conviction has often been applied by both sides in the controversy involving belief in the Bible account of creation versus evolution.

Those who believe in evolution will claim that the survival of man is based upon our genes.

It is said that genes provide the selfish motivation and determination to survive. Those who propagate this theory are faced with the problem of explaining how a selfish organic substance produces beauty, unselfishness and the sheer complexity of human behaviour.

Fundamental to this theory of evolution there is a real dilemma. It is the existence of good. There are those who are willing to acknowledge evolution but not its apparent corollary that unselfishness is a distortion of our true selfish nature.

A second theory in connection with the term evolution is a strong suggestion that with the passage of time everything improves on the road to an eventual state of perfection. However, this theory is also without any basis in fact because when left to the ravages of time even the most cultivated object has a tendency to deteriorate.

Those who do not believe in a divine God will find adequate evidence to bring satisfaction that such a God does not exist. Being thus content with these conclusions there are often many who find no reason to seek further. For those of a less conclusive persuasion there still remains the question regarding the existence of a divine Being.

In search of an answer to this fundamental question there is ample evidence to prove the wonder in the make up of the human body, indicating a divine purpose in the formation of man.

How is it possible to explain the marvellous biological construction of the eye other than the existence of an all-powerful Being who is responsible for creation?

In spite of the overwhelming evidence to the contrary some evolutionists would still claim that over an extended period of time it is possible for inanimate ugliness to evolve into beautiful life. Applying this hypothesis it would need to be conceded that a bag of nails thrown into a garden, with no intelligent influence, could one day become a handsome ticking time-piece.

However, when considering the argument in favour of a creative divine Being, we are left with an even bigger conundrum.

Assuming that the origin of the species is creation, it would need to be conceded that the one greater than creation would be the Creator.

The question then presented would be how did such a superior divine Being come into existence. This question then has the effect of tipping the balance of truth back to the horizontal. We are back to square one.

In a quest for an answer to the original question we are left with no sensible alternative other than assume that there does exist a divine Being, and seek for confirmation or otherwise in the professed word of God.

Those who believe in creation claim that the Bible is a proclamation from God and a revelation of the divine will. If this is true there is no worthwhile purpose in seeking truth other than through divinity. It would then logically follow, that only the Divine could satisfy the hunger of the soul.

In the absence of conclusive proof, if we are convinced regarding the superior quality in the portrayal of the living word of God as set out in the Bible, it becomes essential to acquire an understanding of this word.

It should take pre-eminence over all other claims on our time or the demands of lesser writings. It is through the study of God's word that the human mind begins to become in tune with the will of the Divine.

One truly amazing discovery from the Bible is that there is even proof of its authenticity in the fulfilment of prophecy. We do not know how it is possible for God to foresee the future but, speaking metaphorically, there is in Scripture oceans of proof to show that He can.

For just one example, in Genesis 15:13, 14 it is shown that an infinite God of creation is able to see the end from the beginning. He saw in advance how the descendants of Abraham would be slaves in Egypt and yet after 400 years would leave the land *"with great substance"* (Verse 14).

Because our finite minds are puny by comparison to the infinite it would be compounding our ignorance if we were to dismiss the truth of Scripture simply because it is sometimes beyond our comprehension.

God controls the destiny of man so from this aspect alone He would have knowledge far beyond the scope of human intelligence.

Also to be considered is the fact that with the help of computer programmes, man is able to create charts foretelling with a great deal of accuracy the answers to questions that were once impossible to calculate.

Is it not possible that according to the will an infinite mind is capable, by miniaturising or expanding, of portraying a grand panorama of world history on a mental chart? Then by inserting the relevant constituent elements portraying events, this same infinite mind would be able to know in minute detail the eventual outcome of every action and every thought.

Regarding the Bible account of salvation it is inconceivable that any ordinary man would have the motivation or the spiritual dimension that would enable him to portray anything so grand, sublime, yet as simple as God's plan for saving souls.

Without the presence of Divinity how could a man for no apparent reason possibly find the initiative to think out with such detail a plan that is so simple yet also involving such complexity as that of salvation?

And even if it were remotely possible, there would still be no sensible achievement in spending so much time in developing such a plan for no logical reason.

Without the presence of Omniscience and a promised Saviour, it would be futile for man to devise a plan to defeat sin as portrayed in the Bible. In these circumstances, the whole structure involving the plan of salvation just falls apart.

If there were no God and no divine law there is no way of measuring sin, or any reason for man to invent a divine Being.

Without God, from where would originate the desire and power to invent a divine Being in order to be convicted of sin, and to conquer sin that can only be revealed and defeated by a divine Being?

Added to which, the very existence of evil in the world speaks of a huge rebellion against something or someone. So, contrary to popular belief the existence of absolute evil gives credence to the Bible claim of absolute good.

An indication of the effect of God's word on His servants can be found in the book of Jeremiah 15:16 where it says:

"Thy words were found, and I did eat them; and thy word was unto me the joy and rejoicing of mine heart: for I am called by thy name, O Lord God of hosts."

In contrast to the joy felt by those whose lives are in tune with God's word, who experience the delight which it brings, it speaks in Jeremiah 6:10 of those that will not listen to God's word because *"they have no delight in it."*

If Scripture is really the word of a divine God then it is the wise thing to be influenced by what it says. Psalm 119:105 further declares: *"Thy word is a lamp unto my feet, and a light to my path."*

In Psalm 119:41 is the record of God's servant making the following prayer:

"Let thy mercies come also unto me, O Lord, even thy salvation, according to thy word."

Presented before us is evidence from Scripture that the word of God is a joy and a lamp to those who seek to live in harmony with its teachings.

Alternatively, we have read that those whose lives are at variance with the divine will have no delight in the word of God. Thus it is that God, through the joy that He bestows, is the power who is responsible for leading one to delight in the truth.

Association with the word and fellowship among the saints can often measure the degree of conviction among believers. Thus it is spiritual communication that enlightens the mind to bring fulfilment to the thirsty soul. This is the reason why genuine Christians hold a strong conviction of God's presence as opposed to the lack of belief by those who are not spiritually persuaded.

Thus continued fellowship with the word of God feeds a desire that further stimulates spiritual awareness of a loving Being that can only be adequately described as divine.

Evidence that knowledge of the Creator God can only be spiritually discerned is found in the following quotation taken from 1 Corinthians 2:14:

"But the natural man receiveth not the things of the Spirit of God: for they are foolishness unto him: neither can he know them, because they are spiritually discerned."

If our minds are staggered by the sheer subliminal complexity in the make up of man then we must be similarly impressed by the subliminal simplicity of God's plan of salvation set out in the word of God.

On studying the Bible one soon becomes impressed by the style of writing and the authority of the message it expounds.

By the presence of the Holy Spirit of God there is a power in the word. It is the word itself that enlightens the human mind spiritually so that the unconverted heart experiences a change enabling it to desire and acquire knowledge of a divine Creator God.

We have the truly amazing situation where the Spirit of God leads men to seek knowledge of divinity and salvation. All that is necessary for man to do is to make a positive response.

It is this same Spirit that makes it possible for mankind to live in harmony with the holy law of God.

As a summation of the original question regarding the existence of a divine Creator God we can come to this conclusion: If the Spirit of God changes the way of thinking so that one's thoughts are holy, then the Spirit provides all the proof that is needed to know that there does exist a Creator God. On the other hand, if the Spirit of God has not changed one's way of thinking, then there still remains a need to prove that God does exist. Such proof or conviction is made possible through the word of God.

What then is God's plan for His people? Is it not to bring joy and peace to the saints?

It is plainly set out in the first chapter of Genesis that God created the world and all life, including man. Yet man chose to rebel against God and His law.

We are told in Romans 6:23 that the wages of sin is death. To bring death to His people was against the desire of a loving God. Yet because of love for His subjects, God could not set aside His law of love. To do so would have brought perpetual misery to the human race.

Even without God's pronounced death sentence on the unrepentant sinner, the depravity of human nature would have still signalled eventual death.

In order to overcome the problem of death, God gave Himself, in His Son, to die in the place of the fallen human race.

This means that all who are prepared to accept this sacrifice that has been paid on behalf of sinners, will live.

However, accepting Jesus as a Saviour also means being prepared to allow the Holy Spirit of God to change our human nature so that our lives might be in harmony with the divine purpose.

If we just partly believe that there does exist an all-powerful God in command of the affairs and destiny of man, it would be extremely unwise to live our lives in deliberate ignorance of the divine plan. This may be the reason that under inspiration the following words are recorded in Psalm 14:1:

"The fool hath said in his heart, There is no God, They are corrupt, they have done abominable works, there is none that doeth good."

The claim made above that those who deny the existence of God are corrupt and no good may appear to be a harsh carte blanche judgement against non-believers.

However, if we were to seriously reflect on the spiritual teachings from the word of God, the plain language throughout is that without God we are nothing. This means that to reject the Holy Spirit of God is to reject the only source that offers any defence against the spirit of rebellion.

In 2 Corinthians 2:15,16 there is clear and compelling evidence that describes the spiritual gap that exists between the servants of Christ and the anti-Christ. Paul likened the saints as *"sweet smelling incense offered by Christ to God, which spreads among those who are being saved and those who are being lost."*

From the verse above we see that the same evidence testifying to the presence of Christ, and also the same opportunity to be saved, is made available to all. However, as can be seen from the following verse 16, the lost do not take the same view of Christ, as do the saints:

"For those who are being lost, it is a deadly stench that kills; but for those who are being saved, it is a fragrance that brings life." (Good News Version).

If it is accepted that there truly is a divine plan for humanity, it is surely in our interest to begin a spiritual journey through God's word in search for the truth.

As far as the infinite mind is above the finite so is the God of creation above created beings. So, if honestly seeking truth, the only hope for mankind is to appreciate the infallibility of God's Spirit and that the Word is an expression of the divine will.

There are times in the life of everyone when there is experienced the impressive influence of God's Holy Spirit as He pleads to dwell within the soul. No one has been denied the opportunity to secure the gift of salvation and eternal life that comes through sanctification and acquisition of the nature of Christ.

In order to reap the benefit of any worthwhile enterprise, a measure of sensible preparation is always essential. This is especially true regarding the matter of choice in relation to one's eternal destiny. Appreciation of the gospel truth and a holy sensible preparation leads to salvation and eternal life. Wasting time in procrastination leads to the despair of eternal death.

Chapter 2
Darwin or the Divine

There is a controversy taking place between two great powers. The supreme power belongs to the God of creation, but God cannot simply annihilate Satan the other power and author of rebellion. It is first necessary to establish in the minds of all who are prepared to listen that a Spirit of love motivates God, while it is the spirit of selfishness and evil which motivates the arch deceiver.

It would be a simple matter for the Creator of all life to furnish irrefutable evidence of His existence. Faced with such overwhelming proof even those who have no desire to follow the way led by Jesus Christ would be left with no alternative other than to bow to the Holy will. But therein would be no Holy Communion between God and His people. God desires that His people choose to follow the example set by Jesus Christ because of a moral conviction not out of coercion.

In order to save people from their sins that they might become holy citizens in His kingdom of righteousness God has initiated simple conditions of naturalization.

However, under the command of their leader Satan, there are forces at work planting obstacles that are causing humanity to stumble as they seek to follow the pathway of salvation.

From the very beginning of the great controversy between good and evil, God has been seeking reconciliation with humanity.

In its simplicity God's plan of salvation is easy to understand. It is not God's will that His relationship with humanity be cluttered by unnecessary ritual or marred by the organised involvement of large bodies for political reasons. Salvation comes through individual choice.

Because they see no clear evidence to confirm the existence of a Creator God, non-believers often make the claim that there is no such God. However, there is much more evidence in the intricate design of the Universe to support a belief in creation when compared with the lack of evidence in support of any alternative conviction.

For those who have no desire to seek a spiritual relationship with God, certain knowledge of His existence could impose on their lives an unnecessary burden. Alternatively, for those who profess such a relationship, conclusive evidence of God's existence could inspire an arrogance that would stint spiritual growth.

Relief from the influence of intellectual certainty of God's presence ensures complete freedom of choice and the absence of pressure when seeking a relationship with God.

In the knowledge of God there can be no absolute and conclusive evidence of His existence when such knowledge could breed a false sense of security that might rob one of the initiative to seek a spiritual relationship with God built upon faith.

There is no method other than faith that would better serve the purpose of reconciliation with a God of love. An expressed belief in the loving purpose of God is the beginning of a spiritual journey in faith that concludes with a perfect character in harmony with Christ. There follows a spiritual conviction leading to salvation giving more joy and assurance than a mere intellectual conviction born of physical evidence.

Thus it is that in order to bring salvation, a manifestation of God's love finds a full expression by withholding from man a full revelation of His glorious presence until the saints are bathed in glory at the last trump.

In the controversy between good and evil Satan does not intend to allow the question of God's existence to develop in such a way as to reach a spiritual level. It is for this reason that he has invested so much time and effort in an attempt at deceiving people about the origin of the species.

The Holy Bible declares that God created the earth and man in six days. In order to cast doubt on the word of God, Satan has fostered the belief that man evolved. He has encouraged the belief that mankind had a slimy beginning before slowly advancing to become intelligent beings with lofty ideals of morality. With no evidence of a missing link in the supposed chain of evolution theory we are left with a hypothesis without logic.

It stands to reason that if it took a number of years for basic slime to reach the lofty stage of humanity that there would be evidence of beings at different stages of evolutionary development. There would be evidence of a stage when there were beings that were part man and part beast. There is, of course, no such available evidence.

In order to defend and justify a cherished official position within Christendom, there are those of a weak spiritual conviction who make pretence of reconciling the theory of evolution with the Bible account of creation.

Because of their weak spiritual conviction, and in defence of their cherished positions, they make the claim that God uses poetic language in order to explain evolution.

There is a vain attempt at reconciling a belief in evolution with a belief in creation, and in the process project God as giving a poetic but confusing account of how the world began.

It is an insult to a God of love and His plan of salvation to suggest that mankind's salvation depended upon its evolving position in its progress to intelligent appreciation of the gospel.

With the passage of time one attempted erroneous theory follows another as Satan continues in his aim of promoting confusion and deception.

Just recently the discovery was made in the South of England of human fossilised remains with a projected age of over 200,000 years. This find was the cause of much excitement when it became apparently clear to deceived minds that man had his existence so deep in the past.

Making the false assumption that mankind had its existence so deep in the past, means that no consideration has been given to the fact that such a conclusion is in direct contradiction with population number of the world today.

When confronted with the claim that mankind had its beginning so deep in the past, it surely must be obvious in any reasonable assessment based upon this assumption that the earth would now be declaring a population that would be unsustainable by the earth's present resources. This issue will receive more attention later.

When making such fossilised discoveries there is often no account taken of the effect that the flood of Noah's time had upon the earth.

Little regard for the effects of the flood can lead to conclusions that can be confusing, unreasonable and unreliable.

It is noted that on the occasion of the discovered fossils, that they were found at a lower level of stratum than expected on the cliff face of a seashore.

The logic behind the reasoning that allegedly determined the great age of the fossils is the low level of location on the cliff face. It being reasoned that the lower the level of discovery the older the fossil.

The weakness of such a theory becomes immediately apparent when the chaos of a world flood is brought into the equation. Using this theory of location in order to date fossilised remains is rendered useless if the story of the flood is believed.

For example, using the present dating method, if it were possible to locate some now filled deep valley that pre-dates the flood of Noah's time, any fossilised findings would give a misleadingly different reading to the same aged fossils found on a mountain top or washed onto the plains below.

The formation of rocks is a constituent part of our planet, and the claim is commonly made that they provided a time clock that reliably declares the age of the earth.

One reason why this theory of an old earth is commonly propagated is because of added discoveries made by a Scottish geologist named James Hutton (1726-94). He developed the theory that the history of rock formation occurred in cycles. Under the influence of weathering over a period of time rock formations are said to break down into sediment.

Then by being subjected to immense force the sediment experiences a mass transportation to accumulate in a new place. The moved sediment then consolidates to become a new type of rock. This is then said to become buried under the formation of new rock until, heated to its melting point, it flows back to the surface as lava. Lava cools into rock that can then be broken down by weathering. The whole cycle is then repeated.

Because of the theory of slowly moving different layers of rock formation, there arose the theory supporting the possibility that the earth was far older than had previously been thought. The theory arose that the different layers of mass were constantly changing and recycling. The resulting conclusion led to the often-repeated claim that our planet is very old.

Another reason for the theory of an old earth is because of discoveries made by the geologist named William Smith (1769-1839).

During the execution of his work of mapping coalmines, etcetera, which involved cutting out large areas, he became aware that the order in which rock units were laid never varied whatever the geographical extent. It was logically concluded that the rock units at the base of the columns were older than those above. This is said to have begun an age of enlightenment.

The originator of the theory that leads modern geology is said to be Sir Charles Lyell (1797-1875). His main contribution is the concept of "uniformitarianism". This proposed that past events occurred at the same rate as they do today.

It was reasoned that the same process of sediment deposition as is occurring today, formed the accumulations of deep units of sedimentary rock.

Because of the slow geological processes, and the large size of rocks formed, it pointed to the belief that the earth was very old. It is said that

Lyell was the first person to come to the conclusion that the earth was billions of year old.

There is another more recent theory of Plate Tectonics developed by the German meteorologist, Alfred Wegener, who published *"The Origin of Continents and Oceans"*. Alfred Wegener came to the conclusion that continents were subjected to movement and proposed the theory of continental drift.

Alfred Wegener held the view that continents were not fixed in position but that they slowly moved across the surface of the earth.

However, Alfred Wegener could not propose a suitable mechanism by which the continents moved. It is said that for this reason his ideas were largely ridiculed or ignored.

As part of the ongoing cold war between the East and the West in the 50s, both the U.S.A. and Russia set up sensitive vibration detectors in order to monitor atomic tests by both sides. Thousands of earthquakes were logged. Nearly all occurred in distinct lines across the earth. Thus developed the concept of plate tectonics, related to, but not to be confused with continental drift. For some, this is further evidence of evolution.

Based upon the above conclusions, the theory has developed that the earth is very old. Habitation of organic matter and the human race are seen as very recent dwellers in and on the earth that is said to be billions of years old.

Having briefly considered an account of how the earth's supposed clock is reckoned to reveal its age, there is absolutely no need to allow this very unreliable clock to shatter any convictions regarding the history of the earth as proclaimed on divine authority in the book of Genesis.

The growing rings of trees testify to their age that in the Garden of Eden, could have indicated an age in excess of five hundred years old at the time of creation week. However, because the growing rings of the trees in the Garden of Eden could have declared an age of hundreds of years this would not disprove the six days creation story of Genesis.

Just as there were fully-grown mature trees in the Garden of Eden, so were Adam and Eve fully-grown and mature rulers in the kingdom that God had prepared for them.

There is nothing strange in the fact that Adam and Eve were created as mature adults. Neither is it strange that the garden wherein they dwelt was beautiful in its maturity.

The earth was also mature and fully dressed with the wonder and majesty that can only be revealed in its maturity. The diet of fruit and the vegetables that Adam and Eve needed to eat also had to be in a ripened state of development.

In like manner, when assessing the age of the earth in relation to the time of creation, one should not be confused with the apparent age of trees and rock, when compared with the actual age as proclaimed by God.

If one were to become the first resident in a recently built house, it would be described as new. Yet the timber used could have come from an apparently five hundred year-old tree. The bricks could have been manufactured from clay that had lain in a quarry since creation.

The house itself might have taken more than a year to build. However, it would still be described as a new house in spite of all the above observations.

If one were to purchase a new watch with its hands indicating an advanced time this would not be a true record of its age. Also, the apparent date that the materials of the watch were manufactured does not date the age of the watch.

The same truth regarding dating is also relevant to the earth. I do realise that this is an over simplified analogy, but the principle is the same as the supposed world clock presented above.

It can be difficult for some people to believe in the Bible account of creation. The power needed to speak the world into existence is so incredible as to be almost beyond human comprehension. Yet when the same power of creation is released and set in reverse by a nuclear explosion it is more acceptable as a reasonable hypothesis.

In six days God was responsible for the whole of creation. It is the power innate within matter that holds creation within its bounds.

It is not in the scope of man to create such an awesome source of power as is needed for creation. When man triggers a nuclear explosion, he has not been responsible for the constituent particles of matter that enables the explosive chain reaction to take place.

It is the creative power of God within matter that is kept by God within its bounds that enables man to cause destruction by setting this power in reverse.

The same logic that explains the functioning of nuclear bombs and nuclear energy can also explain creation. The tremendous power that is caused by man through a nuclear explosion is a clear demonstration of the awesome power that was needed for God's creation.

To the limited intelligence of man it might appear to be an unreasonable hypothesis to believe that in the beginning, God spake the world into existence. However, although less dramatic, there are many examples where by the power of the voice, glass has been shattered when exposed to musical notes delivered at a certain pitch. Neither is it considered so unusual for people to operate a computer at the command of the voice, and also to be able to open a locked safe in the same way.

By those who believe in creation, the world is widely believed to be approximately six thousand years old with a population of between six and seven billion.

However, the time that the population of the world began dates from the time of the flood in Noah's time. From Adam to the birth of Noah, was one thousand and fifty six years. Noah was six hundred years old when the flood came to the earth. This means that four thousand years plus have passed since the flood.

I believe that these generally accepted facts form the basis for believing that the world was brought into existence by a Creator God, and makes nonsense of the theory claiming evolution.

There were eight souls on the earth at the time of Noah and the flood. In less than a lifetime this figure could quite easily reach into the hundreds. As the population increased so would the population numbers accelerate to form a population explosion to eventually reach the number that it is today.

If the theory of evolution is to be believed, don't you find it a strange coincidence that the number of years since the emergence of man upon the earth makes such a good match with the number of the present day population and the earth's resources?

If the age of the world could be numbered in billions of years, for evolutionists, it would surely be reasonable to believe that the emergence of mankind could have occurred much earlier than it has.

Mankind could, for example, have emerged twenty thousand years earlier than the record now shows. Should this have been the case the world conditions would most likely now be in chaos.

This would also be true if mankind had emerged upon the earth just ten thousand years earlier or even just five thousand years earlier. What an awful situation there would be if the need for water exceeded the supply. This is just one example of possible catastrophe if the population number did not balance to match the earth's resources.

We are told in Genesis 2:5,6 that in the beginning God did not cause rain to fall upon the earth but a mist rose from the earth to water the ground.

Although no rain fell upon the earth before the flood, in the beginning the earth was watered by the same water that is resourced today. The amount of available water remains constant neither increasing nor decreasing. In spite of man's ingenuity he is unable to create more water to meet the additional needs of an ever-expanding world's population.

In these circumstances, it is difficult to imagine that anyone could believe that the earth evolved, and that it was just coincidence that the emergence of mankind took place at just the right time over a period of billions of years to harmonise with the conditions presently prevailing upon the earth.

Had human kind appeared on the scene at a significantly earlier date than it has, it would now be unlikely that there would be any living evidence of their existence.

Alternatively, a scenario, where descendents still existed from those who emerged at an earlier date, would have produced a vastly different situation than the one that prevails today.

Because of the earth's limited resources, at best there would be evidence of the survival of the fittest from a burdened civilisation.

Just recently there was a programme on T.V. when the commentator enthusiastically expounded an argument in favour of Charles Darwin's theory of the origin of the species. In this commentary, time was measured in millions and billions of years.

In support of the theory of evolution there was presented evidence of a fish fossil that had been discovered in a limestone quarry in Bavaria. This particular fish fossil revealed evidence of feathered wings and tail with claws at the ends of its wings. It did not have a beak but jaws with teeth indicating that it was part reptile and part bird. This fossil, which was named archaeopteryx, is claimed to provide evidence of the missing link between reptile and bird.

Those who believe in evolution believe that eventually such inefficient examples of a particular species became extinct to be replaced by more efficient and advanced examples.

One such advanced example given of progression of the species is a bird named hoatzin, and is to be found nesting in the swamps of tropical South America. The young chicks of this bird would be under threat from the cayman (alligator) lurking in the water beneath their nests if it were not that they are able to hold on securely to the branches by means of claws at the end of their wings, similar to that of the archaeopteryx. Evolutionists claim that it is because of a mindless process of evolution that the chicks have modified forelegs with claws that improve their chance of survival.

Thus, evolutionists claim that an unintelligent species of life is able to make an intelligent natural selection leading to modification of its physical make-up in order to meet a specific need. Surely, it more sensible to believe the Bible version of creation and that God is the one responsible for the intricate diversities to be seen in nature.

It is that those who believe in creation and the existence of God often suffer the derision of evolutionists because of their apparent naivety, yet there is very little logic in the alternative argument projected by those who believe in evolution. For example, evolutionists ignore the fact that there is no living evidence of a missing link between the kingdom of beasts and the kingdom of man. The best that can be offered is obscure fossil evidence of a low form of life that bears no resemblance to mankind. It needs a gigantic leap in faith to believe that without the existence of an intelligent designer that animals would evolve to a certain level and then to become extinct without leaving any living evidence that they ever existed.

The marvel of the human eye is presented by those who believe in creation as evidence of an intelligent designer. Yet even on this fact, evolutionists would cast doubt. It is shown how different forms of life have different levels of ability to discern light and dark.

Evolutionists will explain how a complicated organ such as the eye can begin in a simple form before becoming a perfectly functioning eye. It is said how in its most simple form, some species have nothing more than light-sensitive spots. It is shown how if these spots develop they could throw a shadow to reveal the direction of light. If the spot got deeper and started to close, it is claimed that the light would form blurred images. Mucus formed by the cells could then harden to form a proper lens. In this way an argument can be made in support for the evolving of an eye. This kind of theory gives rise to the belief that sight can begin with nothing more than a light discerning spot before the development into a fully focussed and functioning eye.

For example, flatworms have a small pit containing light spots able to detect the shadow of a predator. A snail's limited vision enables it to find food. An octopus has a lens with a detailed vision. The weakness of this argument for the progressive development of an eye from a simple beginning becomes immediately apparent with the knowledge that there is no evidence of any lower level of species, such as the flatworm, or the snail, ever reaching the stage of developing a fully functioning eye.

The above examples reveal different levels of complexity in the formation of sight, and is said to demonstrate support for evolution.

Thus it is that the above observations are produced by both sides in the controversy between those who believe in creation and those who believe in evolution as sound arguments in favour of each.

Those who believe in evolution insist that an intelligent designer is not required in the formation of life, maintaining that each low level species of life progresses to a higher level of existence before becoming extinct. All of this progress is said to be taking place without any level of intelligence, and all with no evidence of any convincing missing link. Yet the vision of the lowly ranked flatworm and snail does not improve with time. And all other species of life remain the same. The fish stay in the sea. The earth-bound animals stay on the land. Neither, with the advancement of time, is man able to fly, neither is he able to run significantly faster.

Evolutionists believe that it is possible for an unintelligent form of life species to acquire a mysterious power from an unknown source in order to change its physical form required to meet a specific need.

Even though laboratory experiments have proved the possibility of a big bang being responsible for creation, in most circumstances sensible people would associate a big bang with the destruction of matter triggered by friction applied to an explosive agent such as nitro-glycerine etc.

Such a big bang would most likely leave in its wake, disorder and chaos. Yet in spite of the order and wonder that is evident throughout the Universe, evolutionists often promote the big bang theory as an explanation for such an awe inspiring demonstration of time and motion that the Universe displays.

There is so much wonder displayed by the creation of the Universe as to make nonsense of arguments in favour of evolution. What about the incredible way that the moon moves in space as it makes its monthly journey round the earth? At the same time, the earth makes its year-long journey through space as it journeys around the sun, and on it way it turns on it axis once every day.

In addition to this amazing process, incredibly the earth tilts towards the Sun to give the world its four seasons. The Bible gives evidence that God's creation was not limited to the planet Earth. In Genesis 1:14-17 is the record of God making the sun, the moon and the stars. In Psalm

105:19 it also says that God *"created the moon to mark the months."* In Daniel 2:21 it says that God *"changeth the times and the seasons."*

It should be noted that the Bible gives evidence of the month being measured by the movement of the moon before man had any knowledge of its journey around the earth. Surely, it can be seen from the above reference to *"times and the seasons"* that it is God who is in control of the Universe. As it journeys through space is it not by the power set in motion by a creator God, that the earth tilts year after year with unchanging precision towards the sun to give the earth its four seasons?

The only sensible explanation for the existence of the Universe is to recognise that it began with an intelligent design, and was created by God and is sustained by the same creative power.

Applying a measure of analytical fairness and common sense to the argument involving creation versus evolution, we are left with two alternative conclusions. The one is that a divine God created the earth and all forms of life. The other conclusion is that the earth came into existence without any reasonable explanation. This was then followed by the unexplained emergence of life forms that in effect began the process of creation originating from itself. In the final analysis we either believe that God created us or in some mysterious way and without our knowledge or volition we created ourselves.

Even if there were a life form to begin with how can we explain a cause and effect that would ensure the evolution of thousands of different life species to a specified completion, and then stop?

On every issue involved in the great controversy between Christ and Satan, there is the same old battle of truth versus error. Even for those who have no desire to follow the spiritual teachings of Christ, there is a measure of satisfaction to be found.

God will send a strong delusion so that those who love to be in harmony with rebellion will believe a lie.

Evidence of God's answer to those who refuse to be spiritually guided can be found in 2 Thessalonians 2:7-11, and reads:

"For the mystery of iniquity doth already work: only he who now letteth [will let], until he be taken out of the way. 2:8 And then shall that Wicked be revealed, whom the Lord shall consume with the spirit of his mouth, and shall destroy with the brightness of his coming: 2:9 [Even him], whose coming is after the working of Satan with all power and signs and lying wonders, 2:10 And with all deceivableness of unrighteousness in them that perish; because they received not the love

of the truth, that they might be saved. 2:11 And for this cause **God shall send them strong delusion, that they should believe a lie."**

The clearest evidence of God's existence and His claim of creation versus the theory of evolution comes from the conviction of genuine Christians. Spiritual maturity ensures an incisive awareness of fundamental truth and humanity's need for a Saviour.

As always, the battle taking place for souls is in the minds of men. The more that Satan controls man's thinking the greater is his success. Satan leads all who so choose to follow along a path strewn with confusion, despair and eternal loss.

In His quest to bring peace and eternal joy, God pleads for the attention of sinners. In Isaiah 1:18 it is put this way:

"Come now, and let us reason together, saith the LORD: though your sins be as scarlet, they shall be as white as snow; though they be red like crimson, they shall be as wool."

Satan is satisfied if by spreading confusion he secures just a little of man's attention. It is enough to bring him success. By contrast, God needs all of man's attention in order to save his soul. From Jeremiah 29:13 we learn:

"And ye shall seek me, and find [me], when ye shall search for me with all your heart."

Giving consideration to the reality and pleadings of God's Spirit is the first step of a spiritual journey that builds a character in harmony with eternal life.

There can be no depth of character in the shallow waters of disbelief or in the selfish preoccupation of self.

In spite of trials facing His people, God will not allow Satan or discouragement put asunder what by His Spirit He has made one. God will clothe His people with His Spirit enabling them to become spiritual giants that will dwarf all satanic obstacles to the land of spiritual Canaan.

Satan, with millions of fallen angels, is indulging in frenzied activity to create as much havoc as possible in the minds of humanity. It is important to their cause of rebellion for Satan and his followers to gain as much support as possible.

The battle for souls is spiritual but if the controversy can be kept on an intellectual basis then Satan is guaranteed success.

It is not necessary to be clever in ways of the world to search out the secrets of God. Quite often the opposite is true. In Luke 10:20,21 is an example where Jesus gave thanks to His Father that what was hidden from the formally educated was revealed to those who were unlearned.

The key word that unlocks the word of God is desire. Even if the seed of desire to overcome sin is as small as a mustard seed, watered by God it will grow to conquer all sin. Those who never allow the Spirit of God to initiate a desire for righteousness will never know the truth.

"But God hath chosen the foolish things of the world to confound the wise; and God hath chosen the weak things of the world to confound the things which are mighty." (1 Corinthians 1:24).

Closing this subject with a final simple truth, it is an obvious fact that with the exception of Adam and Eve, mankind begin life as a baby. With the knowledge that babies need help to survive, how do evolutionists explain the unaided survival of a baby? Or is there to be another projected contradiction claiming that mankind did not progress from a baby but began life as an adult?

Chapter 3
The Great Deception

From the very beginning of the great controversy between Christ and Satan, the arch deceiver has projected by all possible means a great lie. Under the crafty influence of Satan, organisations and countless individuals have perpetuated the false doctrine that the soul of man cannot die.

This heinous falsehood leads to the outrageous claim that those who neglect to pay lip service to God will suffer the consequences of continual and eternal conflict in hell-fire.

It baffles any reasonable mind that folk could be so misguided and gullible to even contemplate such nonsense. In one breath the virtue and wonder of God's love is portrayed. Then without pause of self-conscious realisation that it sounds ridiculous, the same people will often preach gloom and doom for those who reject this message of fear and hell-fire.

In the gospel of John 4:24 it says: *"God is a Spirit"*. This means that to be sons of God is to be born of the Spirit.

According to the apostle Paul such a birth is to be *"renewed in the spirit of your mind. And that ye put on the new man, which after is created in righteousness and true holiness."* (Ephesians 4:23,24).

The fruit of the Spirit is love (Galatians 5:22).

In character a born again Christian is love. In consideration of this fact, it is inconceivable for a Christian to ever be guilty of an unkind action resulting in torment to a fellow man.

Yet what would be an impossible action for a Christian to take is often considered not to be unreasonable for God. Thus often more is expected of those created in love than the Creator of love.

For example, it is not uncommon to find that there are people claiming to be Christians who believe that at death some cursed souls are consigned to everlasting or eternal torment in hell-fire.

It is believed that God is capable of a doctrine that has more in harmony with Satan than a God of love. In spite of this wide spread belief, there is no evidence of such a doctrine in Scripture.

Far from a possible torment, the dead, both wicked and good, rest in an unconscious sleep until the resurrection day.

One reason for misunderstanding regarding length of time in connection with the terminology *"for ever"* and *"everlasting"* often comes about because of not taking into account the context in which these words are used. The example in Leviticus 25:46 is a recording of how the Israelites were told that they could take strangers as *"bondmen for ever"*.

Yet, of course, this did not mean that there would be bondmen for eternity because at death the relationship would come to an end.

Another example of a similar situation can be found in 1 Samuel 1:22 where it is recorded that *"Hannah went not up; for she said unto her husband, I will not go up until the child be weaned, and then I will bring him, that he may appear before the Lord, And there abide for ever."*

When Hannah dedicated her son Samuel, it was said to be *"for ever"* but this length of time could not extend beyond the lifetime of Samuel.

The term forever denotes an age or ages, and could mean a limited or unlimited length of time. For mankind, life and consciousness began by the breath of God and it ends at death. In Genesis 2:7 it says:

"And the Lord God formed man of the dust of the ground, and breathed into his nostrils the breath of life; and man became a living soul."

In consideration of the unfortunate connotation that has developed with the word "soul" it is wise to consult a concordance for a more accurate translation of the above verse.

From the word *"Nephesh"* we get the translation that *"man became a living being, creature or animal"*. Thus it can be seen that there is nothing mysterious in the mythical connotation that has developed in connection with the word soul.

The above interpretation finds harmony with Ecclesiastes 3:19 where it shows that the same manner of death overtakes both man and beast.

"For that which befalleth the sons of men befalleth beasts; even one thing befalleth them: as the one dieth, so dieth the other; yea, they have all one breath; so that a man hath no pre-eminence above a beast: for all [is] vanity."

There are few who would unreasonably suggest that a dead animal goes to heaven. So why would anyone deny the truth of Scripture by believing that a dead person goes to heaven when Scripture clearly states that a man has *"no pre-eminence above a beast"*?

In the book of Job 14:10 there is this record:

"But man dieth, and wasteth away; yea, man giveth up the ghost, and where is he?"

The answer to the question above is found in Ecclesiastes 12:7 where is this record:

"Then shall the dust return to the earth as it was: and the spirit shall return to God who gave it."

There can be no mistaking the Bible account of the state of the dead. A dead body will return to the earth as it was before God gave it life.

Of the dead, Psalm 146: 4 further says:

"His breath goeth forth, he returneth to the earth; in that very day his thoughts perish."

There is no reasonable excuse for misunderstanding the verse above. It states plainly that in death, *"thoughts perish."*

The dead are no longer in any position to further influence the destiny of the living as indicated below:

Ecclesiastes 9:5: *"For the living know that they shall die: but the dead know not any thing, neither have they any more a reward; for the memory of them is forgotten."*

The Psalmist David knew the truth regarding the state of the dead as proved by the following quotation taken from Psalm 6:5: *"For in death there is no remembrance of thee: in the grave who shall give thee thanks?"*

There are those who profess to be able to communicate with the dead. They are either deceived or make elaborate pretence of hearing knockings and other signs claimed to be of the dead. It is not strange that Satan should give the false impression of noises coming from the dead in an attempt to refute the truthful account of silence declared by God.

The following evidence of Psalm 115:17 is proof that in death there is only silence: *"The dead praise not the Lord, neither any that go down into silence."* But this does not prevent the false claims that communication with those that are dead is still possible.

The Bible describes those who go to the grave as in a state of unconscious silence but the holy word indicates that this condition is not meant to be permanent.

In the gospel of John 11:11 Jesus spoke of the death of Lazarus, but said: *"Our friend Lazarus sleepeth; but I go, that I may wake him out of sleep."*

By claiming that Lazarus was sleeping Jesus was revealing that a person was not considered to be permanently dead until made that way at the final death of the wicked at the end of the world. Until that time all who die as followers of the Lord are sleeping in Christ.

Whether in Christ or not, the state of the dead is clearly set out in the word of God.

The following are yet further examples taken from the "Good News" version of the holy Bible instead of the King James otherwise used.

In Psalms 88:10-12 it says:

"Do you perform miracles for the dead? Do they rise up and praise you? 11 Is your constant love spoken of in the grave or your faithfulness in the place of destruction? 12 Are your miracles seen in the place of darkness or your goodness in the land of the forgotten?"

In his prayer the above comments came from a servant of God who knew the truth about the state of the dead.

In addition, read the following quotation taken from Isaiah 8:19, 20:

"But people will tell you to ask for messages from fortune-tellers and mediums, who chirp and mutter. They will say, 'After all, people should ask for messages from spirits and consult the dead on behalf of the living', 20 You are to answer them, 'Listen to what the Lord is teaching you! Don't listen to mediums-what they tell you will do you no good'."

For those who claim to be servants of Christ and spiritual mediums, the verse above presents them with a message of truth. It is plainly teaching that it is against God's will for anyone to attempt communication with the dead.

There are many professing Christians who are ill informed in the matter of Bible doctrines. Some will offer the account of the medium (witch) of Endor as a basis for belief in the conscious state of the dead.

The background to this story is found in 1 Samuel chapter 15 where is the account of Samuel giving instructions from the Lord. King Saul was told that he was to destroy utterly the wicked Amalekites, and leave no one alive.

With the help of God, Saul succeeded in defeating the Amalekites. However, Saul did not carry out the Lord's instructions given through the prophet Samuel.

Contrary to the Lord's instruction Saul decided to spare the life of the wicked King Agag, in spite of killing all of the people.

Also, contrary to the Lord's instruction concerning the battle with King Agag, in 1 Samuel 15:9 is the record that Saul also kept: *"the best sheep and cattle, the best calves and lambs, or anything else that was good; they destroyed only what was useless or worthless."*

In verses 10,11 is the record showing the Lord's displeasure with King Saul, and God said that He was sorry that He had made Saul king.

In chapter 16:1 it says:

"The lord said to Samuel, 'How long will you go on grieving over Saul?' I have rejected him as king of Israel."

These were the circumstances surrounding King Saul's experience with the medium (witch) of Endor.

Chapter 28 of 1 Samuel gives an account of the death of Samuel.

It also recounts that King Saul, in harmony with holy law, *"had forced all the fortune tellers and mediums to leave Israel."(See* verse 3).

Now without the support of Samuel, when *"Saul saw the Philistine army, he was terrified, and so he asked the Lord what to do."* (Verses 5, 6).

"But the Lord did not answer him at all, either by dreams or by the use of Urim and Thummim or by the prophets." (1 Samuel 28:6).

It was in this state of dejection that Saul sought the services of a medium in spite of holy teaching that mediums were not a true source of knowledge.

1 Samuel chapter 28 tells how Saul succeeded in securing the service of a medium of Endor.

When asked to call up a spirit of the dead, the medium expressed her fear at being requested to break the law of the land instigated by King Saul.

Not recognising the disguised king in the dark she explained about the king's law against mediums, and asked:

"are you trying to trap me and get me killed?" (Verse 9).

Once he had reassured the woman, Saul asked her to recall Samuel from the dead. As recorded in verse 14 it was then that the medium described the appearance of an old man wearing a cloak.

Saul was convinced that the figure that now appeared was the dead Samuel, and spoke as if it were a fact.

When studying this account of Saul and the medium, it is wise to apply some common sense. We have read from Scripture that the dead know nothing. Therefore, it is not possible for the dead to communicate with the living or the dead.

An added dimension to the question of who really appeared to Saul is the character of Samuel. When alive, Samuel was a faithful servant and prophet of the Lord.

It was not in Samuel's nature to disobey God. We know this from reading Samuel 15:22 where is the record of Samuel saying it is better to obey God than to sacrifice.

This chapter of 1 Samuel 15 recounts God's rejection of Saul, and also the Prophet Samuel's rejection of Saul in obedience to God.

We can conclude with certainty that when alive, Samuel was a good man. For example, if he had gone to heaven are we to think that this made Samuel less than good, and able to disobey the God he had obeyed in life?

Are we to believe that God was counted less by Samuel after he had died and supposedly in the very presence of God?

There are so many anomalies in the conclusion that it was Samuel who appeared to Saul as to make the whole concept quite ridiculous.

The simple truth of this story is this: Satan and his fallen angels are the only ones able to communicate through mediums and such like. It was not the dead prophet Samuel who appeared to Saul but Satan who took on the likeness of Samuel.

There is no reason to wonder at the actions of Satan and his servants as they employ all kinds of subterfuge in an effort at deceiving those who could be honest seekers of truth. In 2 Corinthians 11:14,15 are the apostle Paul's comments in this respect as follows:

"Well no wonder! Even Satan can disguise himself to look like an angel of light! So it is no great thing if his servants disguise themselves to look like servants of righteousness. In the end they will get exactly what their actions deserve."

Conspiring further in the deceptive and hideous doctrine that teaches of the living dead is the subterfuge applied by Satan that is recorded in 1 Samuel chapter 28, verses 18,19. There it speaks of Satan in the form of Samuel, tormenting Saul with these words:

"You disobeyed the Lord's command and did not completely destroy the Amalekites and all they had. That is why the Lord is doing this to you now. He will hand you and Israel over to the Philistines. Tomorrow you and your sons will join me, and the Lord will also hand the army of Israel over to the Philistines."

When reading any part of Scripture it is important that we don't allow ourselves to be led from the pathway of logic and consistency.

We have been presented with truth regarding the state of the dead. The dead, both the saints and the wicked, lay in the grave until the resurrection when the judgement will reveal the reward of eternal life for the saints and eternal death for the wicked.

In the above verses Satan is portraying a picture of the dead Samuel being called back into the land of the living. Saul is correctly informed of his broken relationship with God and his coming death in the battle to follow with the Philistines.

As a result of this broken relationship with God, Saul had no defence to resist Satan who engineered his death and that of his sons, Jonathan, Abinadab and Melchishua in the coming battle with the Philistines.

Revealing further the inconsistency of this account of Saul's experience with the apparition, the supposed Samuel told Saul that *"Tomorrow you and your sons will join me."* (Verse 19).

If the saints go to paradise at death then it would be logical to believe that the faithful Samuel would receive such a reward. Are we being told in the verse above that the faithless King Saul, who had been rejected by God, was to join Samuel in a supposed paradise? Samuel was dead and in his grave. Proving the absurdity of believing otherwise, the above reference speaks of the wicked Saul joining the godly Samuel in paradise.

It is not possible to hold any communication with spirits after death of the body. Scripture is implicit in its instructions on this matter. There is no knowledge, neither is there any pain once death has overcome the body.

It is from the false basis of belief in a live spirit after death that one can possibly be led to the horrible devilish assumption that there exists a place called purgatory or hell-fire where there are said to be living souls in torment.

Any belief that projects an eternal torment has no support in Scripture. Reverting to the King James Version of the Bible, as previously quoted we learn from Genesis 2:7 that in the beginning;

"the Lord God formed man of the dust of the ground, and breathed into his nostrils the breath of life and man became a living soul." And *"shall the dust return to the earth as it was: and the spirit shall return to God who gave it."* (Ecclesiastes 12:7).

Just as mankind has no knowledge of any life before birth so will there be no knowledge or remembrance of life after death. We all have our existence in the mind of God. After death there is no life until the resurrection day.

The punishment for the unrepentant sinner is an everlasting or eternal one, but it is not everlasting life or everlasting or eternal torment. It is the punish**ment** that lasts forever not the punish**ing**.

In Romans 6:23 we are told, *"the wages of sin is death."* This death of which Paul speaks is to be everlasting or eternal.

There is no continual pain for those who reject the grace of God. It is not possible to be dead and to suffer. Job says of man: *"He cometh forth like a flower, and is cut down: he fleeth also as a shadow, and continueth not."* (Job 14:2).

Again it can be seen that Bible truth should dispel all doubt regarding the end of man in death. In death, man is like a shadow that continueth not. For the wicked this will mean for eternity.

Because of rejecting life they are to be like a shadow that continueth not.

It is difficult to imagine that even the vilest person would derive any pleasure in seeing souls suffering in torment throughout eternity. To dispel any error of belief regarding the eternal fate of the wicked, there is the following record taken from 2 Peter 3:7:

"But the heavens and the earth, which are now, by the same word are kept in store, reserved unto fire against the day of judgment and perdition of ungodly men."

This fire of which Peter speaks will leave no bodies of suffering in its wake. For we are further told in verse 10:

"But the day of the Lord will come as a thief in the night; in which the heaven shall pass away with great noise, and the elements shall melt with fervent heat, the earth also and the works therein shall be burned up."

These words of Peter do not indicate any life remaining for the wicked at the end of the judgement. There are those who are willing to concede that the mind of a decomposed or consumed body is not capable of consciousness, but will then claim that the soul is conscious after death.

As an answer to this claim, and that there be no reason for any misunderstanding, in Matthew 10:28 there is the following account of the state of the wicked dead which applies equally to the body and soul:

"And fear not them which kill the body, but are not able to kill the soul: but rather fear him which is able to destroy both body and soul in hell."

In Ezekiel 18:4 there is also the record that *"the soul that sinneth, it shall die."*

If eternal torment were a possible punishment awaiting the wicked, why would eternal reward always be linked to life, and eternal punishment linked to death? Why would judgement speak of death if death meant a life of torment for the wicked?

Hell is not to be thought of as a place of everlasting or eternal torment. It is no more than a final grave for those who choose not to belong to God's kingdom of peace. Scripture does not teach that the wicked will be suffering for eternity. In Proverbs 2:22 it says:

"But the wicked shall be cut off from the earth, and the transgressors shall be rooted out."

The choice before all is life or death. There is no in between twilight existence of pain.

In John 3:36 it offers both alternatives when saying:

"He that believeth on the Son hath everlasting life: and he that believeth not the Son shall not see life but the wrath of God abideth in him."

It can be seen that the wicked are not threatened with a life of torment but are told they shall not see life of any kind.

As even further evidence regarding the state of the dead, it is clearly stated by the apostle Paul in 1 Thessalonians 4:15-17 that he did not believe that people go o heaven when they die.

In fact, Paul sought to dispel the error of believing that on the day of the Lord the living saints would go to heaven before the risen saints. He would not have been preaching this if the saints already dead were alive in heaven. Nothing is said to give one the false impression that there are saints who have died but are now alive in heaven.

Paul is on recorded as saying: *"What we are teaching you now is the Lord's teaching: we who are alive on the day the Lord comes will not go ahead of those who have died. There will be the shout of command, the archangel's voice, the sound of God's trumpet and the Lord himself will come down from heaven.* ***Those who have died believing in Christ will rise to life*** *first; then we who are living at that time will be gathered up along with them in the clouds to meet the Lord in the air. And so we will always be with the Lord."* (Good News version).

It says above that those saints who have died will rise to life before the living saints join them. Nothing is said to indicate that these saints are already alive in heaven.

To say that the soul of man cannot die is to claim that man is immortal. However, the apostle Paul tells us as recorded in 1 Timothy 6:15,16 that it is only God who *"hath immortality."* It says in 1 Corinthians 15:53,54 that it is at the time of the resurrection that the saints are blessed with immortality. Only through the power of Jesus Christ is it possible for mankind to gain immortality. This is plainly taught in the gospel of John 11:25 where Jesus is on record as saying:

"I am the resurrection, and the life: he that believeth in me, though he were dead, yet shall he live."

The mendacious teaching that proclaims that the soul continues to live after death of the body is so widespread as to have had the effect of causing millions of misguided souls to believe a lie. Illogical belief is expressed in the absurd doctrine that there will be dead souls suffering for eternity in hell-fire.

In the New Testament of the Bible there are examples describing the fire that is to take place in connection with the final judgement of God at the end of the world. Sometimes, as in Matthew 5:20, this judgement is linked with the terminology *"hell fire"*.

In Revelation 20:10 the final judgement is described in association with the lake of fire. Verse 10 gives an account of the devil being cast into the lake of fire, and suffering *"day and night for ever and ever"*.

It is an easy thing to misunderstand the true meaning of the above account in connection with the devil and eternity. There are serious students of Scripture who honestly believe that in the final judgement the devil and his angels are not to be completely destroyed.

In spite of the previous examples regarding the terminology *"for ever"* used in the Bible, there are many who still believe that the devil, with his servants, will live in torment throughout eternity.

However, this false assumption is the cause of introducing discrepancies and contradictions in the word of God. If there were no end to the devil there could not be an end to sin, but in Nahum 1:9 we have the assurance that *"affliction shall not rise up the second time."*

The reference to *"ever and ever"* mean no more than a prolonged length of time that will not be curtailed before the task of purification is completed.

Thus depending on the context in which it is being studied, the term *"for ever"* could mean various lengths of time ranging from an extended but limited length to that of eternity.

Speaking of the final death in Revelation 20:14,15 it says, *"death and hell were cast into the lake of fire. This is the second death. And whosoever was not found written in the book of life was cast into the lake of fire."*

It can be seen from the verse above that there is no life for those who are cast into the lake of fire.

From 2 Peter 3:10 we have read *"and the elements shall melt with fervent heat, and the earth also and the works that are therein shall be burned up."*

Then shall emerge *"a new heaven and a new earth: for the first heaven and the first earth were passed away."* (Revelation 21:1).

The above evidence clearly demonstrates that the final judgement will bring eternal death for the wicked and eternal life for the saints. It is a serious error to believe that sin, or the author of sin and his army of rebels, will be allowed to mar the peace of heaven and eternity.

It has been established from Scripture with irrefutable evidence that communication with the dead is impossible. Yet in spite of this overwhelming evidence there are people who will quote one text in a misguided support of a doctrine known as baptism of the dead. It is wrongly believed that it is possible to secure the consent and co-operation of the dead in the matter of baptism.

The section of Scripture used in this connection is found in 1 Peter 4:5,6, and reads: *"Who shall give account to him that is ready to judge the quick and the dead. For this cause was the gospel preached also to them that are dead, that they might be judged according to men in the flesh, but live according to God in the spirit."*

If the above reference is studied using common sense, it will be seen that Peter is simply explaining that the gospel of Christ had been just as available to those who were dead, in the same manner as it is now available to those alive in the flesh.

The ultimate objective of all who choose to follow God is to *"live according to God in the spirit."*

Before the return of Jesus, both the dead and the living saints must first be subjected to judgement in order for Jesus to bring the reward of eternal life to both the living and the dead saints. It is not wise to take one text out of context and make a false doctrine.

In Matthew 8:21 is the record of a disciple asking the Lord to suffer him *"first to go and bury his father"*. In verse 22 is the following answer: *"But Jesus said unto him, Follow me; and let the dead bury their dead."*

In the verse above, Jesus is not saying that a physically dead person is able to bury another dead person. Therefore, Jesus was making reference to the spiritually dead.

If Peter really was referring to the gospel being preached to those who were actually dead. Then he must have meant dead spiritually.

Our Bible study has proved the unconscious state of the dead. Yet there remains one section of Scripture that could lead to confusion in any final assessment on this subject. The section being referred to can be found in Luke 16:19-31, and reads as follows:

"There was a certain rich man, which was clothed in purple and fine linen, and fared sumptuously every day: 16:20 *And there was a certain beggar named Lazarus, which was laid at his gate, full of sores,* 16:21 *And desiring to be fed with the crumbs which fell from the rich man's*

table: moreover the dogs came and licked his sores. 16:22 And it came to pass, that the beggar died, and was carried by the angels into Abraham's bosom: the rich man also died, and was buried; 16:23 And in hell he lift up his eyes, being in torments, and seeth Abraham afar off, and Lazarus in his bosom. 16:24 And he cried and said, Father Abraham, have mercy on me, and send Lazarus, that he may dip the tip of his finger in water, and cool my tongue; for I am tormented in this flame. 16:25 But Abraham said, Son, remember that thou in thy lifetime receivedst thy good things, and likewise Lazarus evil things: but now he is comforted, and thou art tormented. 16:26 And beside all this, between us and you there is a great gulf fixed: so that they which would pass from hence to you cannot; neither can they pass to us, that [would come] from thence. 16:27 Then he said, I pray thee therefore, father, that thou wouldest send him to my father's house: 16:28 For I have five brethren; that he may testify unto them, lest they also come into this place of torment 16:29 Abraham saith unto him, They have Moses and the prophets; let them hear them 16:30 And he said, Nay, father Abraham: but if one went unto them from the dead, they will repent. 16:31 And he said unto him, If they hear not Moses and the prophets, neither will they be persuaded, though one rose from the dead"

The first point to establish when reading the above section of Scripture is that Jesus was relating a parable. It was a method used by Jesus in order to convey a lesson and was not meant to have a literal interpretation.

When addressing the people, Jesus needed to take into account the measure of knowledge and understanding enjoyed by those that listened, and adjust His message accordingly. For example, Abraham was regarded as the patriarch of Israel and the terminology *"Abraham's bosom"* would have been immediately appreciated.

Verse 22 says that the beggar *"died and was carried by the angels to Abraham's bosom"*. We, of course, know that this could not literally be true because Abraham's bosom would not be large enough to accommodate the population of saints in heaven. Besides which, Abraham is dead until the resurrection day.

Verse 23 and 24 speak of the rich man in hell speaking to Abraham who was a long distance away, and requested that the beggar dip his finger in heavenly water and cool his tongue.

We now have an impossible picture of the beggar in heaven dipping his finger in water of heaven and wetting the tongue of the rich man in hell.

35

Yet heaven is so far away as to make such an act impossible, and hell is so hot and near as to render such an act useless.

If taken literally, the crowning absurdity of the parable is the story of the unkind and wicked rich man suddenly developing a kind compassionate character. In the torment of hell he displays a concern for his live brothers, and a supposed desire to warn them of his torment. Thus in life rich with goods he was mean but in hell and death he became kind.

In this section of Scripture Jesus is using a parable in order to convey an important lesson, and there is no more to the story than that. Jesus is calling all to repentance because salvation's destiny belongs to the living not the dead.

If the dead are incapable of thought then the implications are profound. It means that it is not possible for one to have a relationship with Jesus at death. Also, communication with the dead is impossible. This would include canonised saints and Mary the mother of Jesus.

Any kind of belief in unnecessary torment is the doctrine of Satan. This includes the erroneous teaching that there could be a place of torment for the wicked when they die. It is not the will of a loving God that man should live in fear.

Jesus came to this earth to proclaim a message of love and freedom. His message is one of joy, declaring that His people are free from the pain and burden of sin. It is not in the nature of God to bring torment to His creation. There is often some confusion in the Bible definition of fear when used in context of a relationship with God.

With the help of a concordance we learn that when the Bible gives admonishment to fear God, it does not mean that His subjects are to feel any kind of discomfort.

A proper study of God's word will show that if in harmony with God's Spirit His children will give proper honour and respect to their heavenly Father. Is it not reverence and respect that even earthly parents should expect?

To prove this point, Leviticus 19:3 and Leviticus 25:17 show how, in this context, fear has the same meaning regarding a relationship with our earthly parents and our heavenly Father, as follows:

"Ye shall fear every man his mother, and his father, and keep my sabbaths: I am the Lord your God."

"Ye shall not therefore oppress one another; but thou shalt fear thy God: for I am the Lord your God."

Regarding the experience of fear in the context of being troubled, it is a normal re-action to a dangerous situation. In this way it can be the means of a warning necessary to save life.

However, in an extreme form, in normal circumstances unfounded fear can have a debilitating effect on one's emotions.

For this reason it is one of Satan's favourite weapons in causing unease among the people.

It is for the purpose of bringing anxiety to people that Satan portrays a picture of possible terror in the natural sleep of death. Such a fear of dying kills the joy of living, bringing into the mind the pain of ten thousand deaths.

The record in 2 Timothy 1:10 is teaching that Jesus Christ has abolished death. Yet in the book of Hebrews 9:27 we are told *that "it is appointed unto men once to die"*. (One exception to this rule will be the hundred and forty four thousand who are to be alive on the earth at the Second Coming of Jesus).

The death of Jesus on Calvary is not intended to save from the first death but will save from the second death, all who choose to believe and accept salvation.

Although the Bible speaks of the first death as sleep, it is recorded in Romans 6:10 that Jesus *"died unto sin once"*. This means that although Jesus died the first death He suffered the anguish of the second death. Thus His followers are saved from the second death.

Had Jesus died the second death there would have been no resurrection, and the sinner would be lost. There is no pain in actual death. Any anguish endured occurs in the time that leads to death. It was as Jesus was dying that He experienced the eternal separation from His Father. As recorded in Hebrews 2:9, in this way Jesus *"tasted death for all men."*

In order to be a true propitiation for the sins of a fallen race, Jesus needed to die the second death. However, had Jesus died the second death this defeat would have heralded in a victory of sin over life. In these circumstances, in dying, Jesus needed a way to accomplish victory over death and sin.

Jesus demonstrated a perfect sacrifice and satisfied the demands of a broken law by experiencing the pain of eternal separation from His Father in the anguish of the second death. Thus on Calvary Jesus reconciled the demands of the law with victory for the saints.

Chapter 4
Comma from Calvary

As Jesus hung on the Cross with death approaching He felt only compassion and understanding for the weakness of the human race and cried out as recorded thus in Luke 23:34:

"Then said Jesus, Father, forgive them; for they know not what they do."

When praying to the Father to forgive them, Jesus was not just referring to those who now in awe stood before the Cross of shame that had been erected by so many consenting minds.

Included in Jesus' prayer were the devil-possessed Jewish leaders who had been instrumental in the illegal trial that had sentenced Jesus to death. The weak Roman Governor was also a subject of this prayer that was a revelation of incredible love.

The prayer was even more comprehensive than a reference to those involved directly in the death of Jesus on the day of crucifixion.

The eternal eyes of divinity focussed on Adam and Eve at the dawn of creation and extended far into the future to include the whole of mankind. Jesus prayed and died for all men.

The offer of salvation is open to all, but the choice of response must belong to each individual. Salvation is a personal exercise that is to be experienced by those who make a positive response to the pleadings of God's Spirit.

Retracing our steps a little, there is the record of two others who were sentenced to die on the same day as Jesus. In Luke 23:32, 33 it reads:

"32 And there were also two other, malefactors, led with him to be put to death. 33 And when they were come to the place, which is called Calvary, there they crucified him, and the malefactors, one on the right hand, and the other on the left."

Each one of these malefactors represented the two classes of people that divide the world's population. In the world there are believers and non-believers. The one malefactor mocked Jesus and said, as recorded in verse 37,*"If thou be the king of the Jews, save thyself."*

The other malefactor recognised himself as a sinner in need of salvation. Even though he was dying and also knew that Jesus was about to die, by the power of God's Spirit, he was able to discern a measure of truth and mystery in the drama that was unfolding before his eyes.

A work of reformation had already begun in the mind of this repentant sinner. With the eyes enlightened by the Spirit, the man had a revelation that he was in the presence of divinity, and was moved to speak the following words taken from Luke 23:40-43:

"But the other answering rebuked him, saying, Dost not thou fear God, seeing thou art in the same condemnation? 23:41 And we indeed justly; for we receive the due reward of our deeds: but this man hath done nothing amiss. 23:42 And he said unto Jesus, Lord, remember me when thou comest into thy kingdom."

In answer to the man, Jesus is on record as saying: *"Verily I say unto thee, To-day shalt thou be with me in paradise."*

Our previous study has proved the unconscious state of the dead. In these circumstances, the above declaration concerning paradise presents us with what appears to be a dilemma.

All of the dead stay dead and in an unconscious state until their day of resurrection. If we accept this as true, then we are confronted with the question as to how could Jesus make a promise that was contrary to Scripture when saying that He would be in paradise that day?

To further confuse the situation there is the following record taken from John 20:17.

Jesus said unto Mary: *"Touch me not; for I am not yet ascended to my Father: but go to my brethren, and say unto them, I ascend unto my Father, and your Father; and [to] my God, and your God."*

The above quotation is plain evidence that Jesus did not ascend to heaven on the day of His death.

To obtain a clearer understanding of what Jesus was really saying from the Cross it is necessary to appreciate that in the original manuscripts of holy writ there were no punctuation marks as a guide to a proper understanding of the text. These were added at a later date.

The reason for any misunderstanding concerning the promise made by Jesus lay in the insertion of a misplaced comma.

Punctuation marks were not introduced to early sacred writings. When producing the Vulgate translation of the Bible into Latin, St. Jerome and his colleagues developed an early system of punctuation circa 400 A.D.

Punctuation became standardised following the invention of printing. Because of the early insertion of a misplaced comma, later translators have followed this mistake to give a contradictory message regarding the claim that Jesus went to paradise on the day of His death on the Cross of Calvary.

From the Cross Jesus was saying: "I tell you to day, you shall be with me in paradise." The comma is intended to follow the words "to day", not the word "you".

Jesus was bringing comfort to the man by saying that in spite of the apparent hopelessness of the situation of the day, the man would still find a place one day in paradise with Jesus.

The record of Jesus' instructions is not always given the same interpretation by the four gospel writers. Men are not automatons guided only by an authority above themselves to the exclusion of their own freethinking minds. However, because human beings are allowed to express their own thoughts in relation to inspired messages, in accordance with human failings of memory, etc., is no reason to doubt the word of God. For example, in the following, there are slight differences between the record of Jesus' instructions as related by Mark and Luke.

In Mark 6:8 it says the following: *"And commanded them that they should take nothing for [their] journey, save a staff only; no scrip, no bread, no money in [their] purse."*

Whereas in Luke 9:3 it says: *"And he said unto them, Take nothing for [your] journey, neither staves, nor scrip, neither bread, neither money; neither have two coats apiece."*

In the book of Mark the instruction is to take a stick. In the book of Luke the instruction is not to take a stick. In both instances the messages received were divinely inspired. However, this does not mean that some messages do not bear the evidence of human failings where the memory is not the most accurate of a filing system.

Although it is possible to find discrepancies in the word of God because of human weakness, there will never be any discrepancies or contradictions in relation to sound doctrines or salvation.

These apparent discrepancies of Scripture are allowed to remain for the purpose of separating the chaff from the wheat. The Spirit that is responsible for God's final harvest will also reveal the truth.

Chapter 5
God's Law

The issue of God's law of Ten Commandments is so fundamental to any gospel message that their important link to almost any Bible theme cannot be ignored because of an effort to avoid repetition.

In this context there can be no mistaking the fact that it is the Ten Commandments of God that will be centre of the controversy in the final conflict between Christ and Satan.

The answer to the sin problem is not by effort to obey the law but by allowing the Holy Spirit into the life that enables one to live with a new heart in harmony with a holy law. In the converted heart is born abhorrence for sin and a love for the righteousness of God's law.

The question arises as to how to equate the importance of the law as set out by God on Mount Sinai when compared to some writings of the apostle Paul.

The reasons why some people have problems with Paul's observations are that they are not always used and studied in their proper context. When parts are used in isolation they can give a distorted account of the truth. For one example, in Romans 6:14 Paul is recorded as saying:

"For sin shall not have dominion over you: for ye are not under the law, but under grace."

To stop there would lead one to believe that the law of God was no longer of any concern. However, Paul wasted no time before adding in verse 15:

"What then? Shall we sin because we are not under the law, but of grace? God forbid."

As a result of reading the writings of Paul in their proper context, there should be no doubt left in any reasonable mind that the call of eternity requires people to live in harmony with God's law of Ten Commandments. Thus could Paul write as recorded in verse 16:

"Know ye not, that to whom ye yield yourselves servants to obey, his servants ye are to whom ye obey; whether of sin unto death, or of obedience unto righteousness?"

If we accept the sacrifice of Christ, we are no longer under the penalty of a broken law. However, being set free from the penalty of a broken law is not a licence to sin. Rather, the opposite is true if we are not to reject the gift of such amazing grace provided by Jesus at an unfathomable cost.

In the book of Hebrews 6:4-6 the writer is recorded as saying:

"For [it is] impossible for those who were once enlightened, and have tasted of the heavenly gift, and were made partakers of the Holy Ghost, 5 And have tasted the good word of God, and the powers of the world to come, 6 If they shall fall away, to renew them again unto repentance; seeing they crucify to themselves the Son of God afresh, and put [him] to an open shame."

The writer is expressing grave concern as to whether it is possible to sever a blessed relationship with Jesus and return again to repentance.

In chapter 2 of Paul's letter to the Romans the evidence is clearly set out demonstrating the importance of the law of Ten Commandments when seeking a relationship with God. As declared by the verse below this truth applies equally to the Jew and the Gentile.

In verses 11-13 it says: *"For there is no respect of persons with God. For as many as have sinned without law shall also perish without law: and as many as have sinned in the law shall be judged by the law; (For not the hearers of the law [are] just before God, but the doers of the law shall be justified."*

Concerning the Gentiles, in verses 14-16 Paul further explains that although they had not been informed of the law in the same manner as the Jews, when they became witnesses to the merit of the law written in their hearts they were acceptable to God.

In the remaining verses of chapter 2 Paul is teaching that knowledge of the law could not save the Jew. In verses 28,29 he says:

"For he is not a Jew, which is one outwardly; neither [is that] circumcision, which is outward in the flesh. But he [is] a Jew, which is one inwardly; and circumcision [is that] of the heart, in the spirit, [and] not in the letter; whose praise [is] not of men, but of God."

From verses 11-13 above it is clear that all are judged according to the law whether believers or unbelievers.

Paul is simply stating that in the observation of the law there is no power of salvation. Sin, with the knowledge of the law or without knowledge of the law, will still be sin. That there be no misunderstanding of the relevance of God's law, in Romans 3: 31 Paul says:

"Do we then make void the law through faith? God forbid: yea, we establish the law."

Having faith in God's grace, and His power to create a new heart in order to live in harmony with the law does not make void the law.

In Romans 7:6 it says:

"But now are we delivered from the law, that being dead wherein we were held; that we should serve in newness of spirit, and not in the oldness of the letter."

In order that there be no excuse for misinterpretation of his words, Paul further says in the next verse, 7:

"What shall we say then? Is the law sin? God forbid. Nay, I had not known sin, but by the law: for I had not known lust except the law said, Thou shalt not covet."

In verses 8-11 Paul explains how by means of commandments sin is brought to life. Without the law, sin is a dead thing. It is through the law that sin springs to life. Thus a commandment that is meant to bring life, by revealing the nature of sin, makes sin alive resulting in death. The only escape is by the Spirit of Jesus Christ.

In verse 12 Paul continues by saying:

"Wherefore the law is holy, and the commandments holy, just and good."

He then explains that it is not the law that causes death but sin which is transgression of the law.

Repeating Romans 2:13 there is confirmation of the significance attached to the law where these words are recorded:

"For not the hearers of the law are just before God, but the doers of the law shalt be justified."

There can be no reasonable doubt that whilst there is no power in the law to save, the law itself is good. Paul further explains in Romans 3:19:

"Now we know that what things soever the law saith, it saith to them who are under the law: that every mouth may be stopped, and all the world may become guilty before God."

Scripture is teaching that those who do not accept the offer of salvation in Christ Jesus will be guilty because of coming under the jurisdiction of the law. In verse 20 Paul points out:

"Therefore by the deeds of the law there shall no flesh be justified in God's sight for by the law is the knowledge of sin."

We are informed by the verse above that it is not possible to find salvation through our own effort at striving to live in harmony with the law. However, this truth does not make void the law.

The law has an essential role in bringing knowledge of sin leading to conviction of sin, but victory is through the power of Jesus Christ. Support for this truth is found thus in verse 21:

"But now the righteousness of God without the law is manifested, being witnessed by the law and the prophets."

On the matter of grace and law the message of Scripture is clear. Grace is afforded to the penitent sinner but it does not extend to those who, by embracing sin, reject grace.

The purpose of the law is to encourage reconciliation through the presence of the Spirit between God and His people. As set out below in Galatians 3:19-29 the law was, and still is, the schoolmaster to bring one to Christ.

"Wherefore then [serveth] the law? It was added because of transgressions, till the seed should come to whom the promise was made; [and it was] ordained by angels in the hand of a mediator. 3:20 Now a mediator is not [a mediator] of one, but God is one. 3:21 [Is] the law then against the promises of God? God forbid: for if there had been a law given which could have given life, verily righteousness should have been by the law. 3:22 But the Scripture hath concluded all under sin, that the promise by faith of Jesus Christ might be given to them that believe. 3:23 But before faith came, we were kept under the law, shut up unto the faith which should afterwards be revealed. 3:24 **Wherefore the law was our schoolmaster** *[to bring us] unto Christ, that we might be justified by faith. 3:25 But after that faith is come, we are no longer under a schoolmaster. 3:26 For ye are all the children of God by faith in Christ Jesus. 3:27 For as many of you as have been baptized into Christ have put on Christ. 3:28 There is neither Jew nor Greek, there is neither bond nor free, there is neither male nor female: for ye are all one in Christ Jesus. 3:29 And if ye [be] Christ's, then are ye Abraham's seed, and heirs according to the promise."*

Although the law of Ten Commandments was always in existence, Paul is making the point that it was added to the equation in its context of God's relationship with Israel.

There are people who believe that with the coming of the Saviour, Jesus Christ, the law is no longer of any effect. However, a careful study of Paul's observations quoted above should make it clear that there can be satisfaction for those who believe in the eternal relevance of the law and also for those who rightly see more relevance in Jesus Christ.

Thus both schools of thought contribute to the truth.

Paul explains in Romans 8:7 that *"the carnal mind is enmity against God: for it is not subject to the law of God, neither indeed can be."* In verse 1 Paul has revealed that the only way to avoid condemnation is to *"walk not after the flesh, but after the Spirit."*

In this way the mind of a Christian becomes transformed from being *"carnally minded"* to being *"spiritually minded."* (Verse 6). It is then that a propensity to sin changes to a desire to live in harmony with a holy law.

When, through the grace of God and the sacrifice of Jesus Christ, one is blessed with a new nature one is made free from the penalty of a broken law. However, this does not signify that one is to ignore the merit that is to be found by living in harmony with God's holy law. Nor should one be blinded to the protection and principles that living a righteous life in harmony with the law brings.

The immutable law of God is a transcript of His holy character and will forever live within the hearts of His people. This conversion is only made possible through the death of God's Son and the presence of the Holy Spirit.

Having read Paul's assertions that a converted Christian leads a spiritual life in harmony with the spirit of the law, rather than the letter of the law, the question might be asked as to what is the difference between the letter of the law and the spirit of the law? An obvious answer is that applying the spirit of the law is always motivated by a love for truth.

This is not always so regarding the letter of the law. For one example, an Israelite might not violate the Sabbath commandment by performing certain tasks on God's holy day, but would not necessarily object to another performing the same task on his behalf.

Another example would be a reluctance to offer help to another on the Sabbath day if it seemed to violate some rule to do with the law.

Paul had an overriding desire to inspire those who were neglectfully seeking freedom in the gospel of sacrifice or works to seek real freedom through the gospel of Christ.

Having eyes fixed on the law to the exclusion of Christ could never bring about any change in one's nature. Paul was fully aware that in order to live in harmony with the law, there first needed to be harmony between the spirit of man and the Divine.

Hanging up a list of the Ten Commandments and preaching the merit of the law will not necessarily indicate harmony with the Spirit of Jesus. However, proclaiming the Spirit of Christ is a living witness to God's law of love.

The evidence of Scripture reveals the importance of understanding the real meaning of salvation. Before the return of Jesus, God's word teaches that He will have prepared a people who, by the power of the Holy Spirit, will stand victorious with the perfect character of Jesus Christ.

For such a salvation the saints are *"given instruction in righteousness: That the man of God may be perfect, throughly furnished unto all good works." (2* Timothy 3:17).

Thus will the saints *"come in the unity of the faith, and the knowledge of the son of God, unto a perfect man, unto the measure of the stature of the fulness of Christ."* (Ephesians 4:13).

Many Christians sincerely believe that the following reference taken from Colossians 2:14 is saying that the moral law of the Decalogue has been nailed to the Cross:

"Blotting out the handwriting of ordinances that was against us, and took it out of the way, nailing it to the Cross."

Of course, as can be readily seen, it is the law of ordinances and not the moral law that has been nailed to the Cross.

Scripture does not contradict itself. In Isaiah *42:21 it says:*

"The Lord is well pleased for his righteousness sake; he will magnify the law, and make it honourable."

In Matthew 5:17 Jesus makes it very clear how much importance He attaches to the moral law when saying:

"Think not that I am come to destroy the law, or the prophets: I am not come to destroy but to fulfil."

The principles and importance of the moral law is clearly set out in Matthew 5:18-48.

In chapter 2 verses 9,10 James teaches that to offend on just one point of law is to be *"guilty of all."*

When explaining the purpose of the law in Romans chapter 7, Paul wonderfully portrays a picture that reveals its merit and weakness. He clearly shows that while there is no merit in striving unaided to live a life in harmony with the law this did not invalidate the law. He then beautifully sums up the whole matter in Romans 8:5-8 where is recorded the following:

"Those who live as their human nature tells them to, have their minds controlled by what human nature wants. Those who live as the Spirit tells them to, have their minds controlled by what the Spirit wants. To be controlled by human nature results in death; to be controlled by the Spirit results in life and peace. And so a person becomes an enemy of God when he is controlled by his human nature; for he does not obey God's law, and in fact he cannot obey it. Those who obey their human nature cannot please God." (Good News version).

The false conviction that salvation from past sins does not include salvation from future acts of sin could have adverse eternal consequences.

A pet answer from those who have no wish to be governed by God's law is that keeping His commandments is too legalistic. Of course, based upon the covenant between God and His people, it is a legal requirement for God's subjects to live according to the laws of His government. Without such a commitment God will institute the act of divorcement.

The guilty ones often make the excuse that their relationship with God is based upon a loving relationship rather than legalistic ties. They thus misunderstand the words of Jesus who, as recorded in John 14:15, says: *"If ye love me, keep my commandments."*

In verse 21 it further says: *"He that hath my commandments, and keepeth them, he it is that loveth me; and he that loveth me shall be loved of my Father, and I will love him, and manifest myself to him."*

It is not possible to understand salvation or to have a meaningful relationship with God if one is ignorant of the relevance and importance of His law of Ten Commandments.

From Scripture we learn of two covenants involved in God's relationship with His people. The first covenant was based upon the people of God living in harmony with His law of Ten Commandments.

Knowing that His people are unable to live unaided in harmony with His law God has instituted a second covenant based upon faith.

Under the terms of the second covenant, Jesus Christ lived a perfect life and died for our sins in order that people might be given the opportunity to die to sin and rise to life with the righteousness of Christ.

The validity of God's law has not changed. Under the terms of the second covenant the only change that takes place is the changed nature of God's people.

Because of dying to sin and taking on the new nature of Christ, God's people are no longer under the penalty and curse of the law. However, the gift of grace is not a licence to sin. If after choosing to partake of the nature of Christ through the act of baptism we then choose to sin, does this make Christ a minister of sin?

In Galatians 2:17 is Paul's emphatic answer where he says: *"But if, while we seek to be justified by Christ, we ourselves also are found sinners, is therefore Christ the minister of sin? God forbid."*

The clear message from Scripture teaches the immutability of God's law, and the inability of human nature to live in harmony with its precepts. However, through the death of His Son and the unbounded measure of His grace, God has made it possible for mankind to acquire the nature of Christ and live in harmony with the will of God, as did Jesus.

As recorded in Hebrews 8:6-10 the law of God is so important that by means of the second covenant He has promised to save His people from their sins and write His law in their hearts, thus: *"But now hath he obtained a more excellent ministry, by how much also he is the mediator of a better covenant, which was established upon better promises. For if that first [covenant] had been faultless, then should no place have been sought for the second. For finding fault with them, he saith, Behold, the days come, saith the Lord, when I will make a new covenant with the house of Israel and with the house of Judah: Not according to the covenant that I made with their fathers in the day when I took them by the hand to lead them out of the land of Egypt; because they continued not in my covenant, and I regarded them not, saith the Lord. For this [is] the covenant that I will make with the house of Israel after those days, saith the Lord; I will put my laws into their mind, and write them in their hearts."*

Chapter 6
Sign & Mark

In the Bible there is the record of a sign and also the record of a mark. A sign has a pleasant connotation implying something good. A mark signifies something that is bad or marred with an unpleasant connotation.

This is the general rule regarding a mark, but it must be said that there are exceptions.

For example, in Ezekiel 9:4-6 is the record where God's people are given a mark on their foreheads as a sign that they were to be protected from harm at the execution of God's judgement at that time against the wicked.

Thoughts of a sign conjure up a picture outside of shops and other retail outlets advertising their wares. A sign will signify a doctor's surgery or other helpful place of business.

By contrast, a mark often brings to mind something to be avoided. For example, if one were seeking to purchase an article of clothing one would be put off the purchase by a mark that was foreign to the article.

When Cain slew his brother Abel, he remained a child of God and was given a mark to prove that he was still under the care of God. However, there has developed a saying implying that someone was evil, with the phrase, "he has the mark of Cain". Thus a sign generally signifies something good, while a mark often signifies something bad.

A sign is displayed with the objective being for it to be seen by as many people as possible, whereas a mark is often concealed in order to deceive.

A sign is often a symbol of an achievement presenting a picture representative of a practical skill.

One of the most important signs in the Bible is the sign of God's creation, and a record of it is to be found at the heart of God's law of Ten Commandments.

The importance of the law of Ten Commandments proclaimed by the word of God from Mount Sinai cannot be overstated. Living in harmony with the divine precepts is the only standard of righteousness that is acceptable to Jehovah.

That there be no excuse for any form of rebellion against the divine precepts, God will provide His Holy Spirit to make it possible for all who are willing to live in harmony with the Divine.

In Exodus 20:3-17 is the record of the Ten Commandments that were proclaimed to the nation of literal Israel, and by logical definition were intended to apply equally to spiritual Israel (Christians).

At the very heart of the Ten Commandments is the fourth Sabbath commandment. In Exodus 20:11 is recorded the claim from God that in six days He created the heaven and earth, and every other thing, and rested on the seventh day. God then blessed the seventh day and hallowed it.

Among others, there are two doctrines that stand out where Satan has achieved great success in deluding people. The one is the state of the dead that was studied earlier and the other one is the Sabbath commandment.

In Exodus 31:13 God elaborates further on the Sabbath commandment when He says:

*"Speak thou also unto the children of Israel, saying, Verily my sabbaths ye shall keep: for it [is] a sign between me and you throughout your generations; that [ye] may know that I [am] the LORD that **doth sanctify you.**"*

The Sabbath commandment is the only one of the ten where the claim is made that the God, Jehovah created the heaven and the earth.

By revealing Himself in the fourth commandment as the Creator, God is also revealing to His people that He alone is in possession of the necessary power needed in order to sanctify the people.

Do we dare ignore the God of creation and His command that we honour His special sign, which is a revelation signifying His creative power?

In verse 17 it further states that not only is the Sabbath a sign but that it will be so *"forever".*

In Ezekiel 20:12, 20 there is also a reference to the God who sanctifies and the Sabbath being a sign and reads: *"Moreover also I gave them my sabbaths, to be a sign between me and them, that they might know that I [am] the LORD* that *sanctify them." "20:20 And hallow my sabbaths; and they shall be **a sign** between me and you, that ye may kn*ow that I [am] the LORD your God.*"*

The first three commandments speak of God but among the thousands to which this name can be applied there is no definition as to the identity of God.

The fifth commandment contains the words *"Lord and God,"* but again God is not defined. The last five commandments do not speak the name of God.

The only commandment that reveals the identity of the true God is the fourth. It says there: *"For in six days the Lord made heaven and earth, the sea, and all that in them is."*

Although many Christians use the Sunday as a day of worship, it can be seen from God's word that the sun is not the God of the Decalogue. The true God is the God who made all things including the sun.

Within the law of the Decalogue its Author has declared with His own finger the extent of His kingdom and His exclusive right to rule.

The change of day for Sabbath worship began as a result of the Sunday already being an established holiday throughout the Roman world. To begin with, Christians kept both the seventh day and the first day of the week.

An important event that tipped the scales in favour of a more exclusive observance of the first day of the week came about with the professed conversion to Christianity of the Roman Emperor Constantine. Following his conversion, Constantine issued a decree declaring the first day as one of rest on March 7, A.D. 321.

When people make the claim that the seventh day Sabbath has been changed to any other day they are also declaring that they are not living in harmony with the proclamation made by God that He created the world. This is because there is nothing in the remaining nine commandments to identify the name or authority of Jehovah. Thus can it be seen just how important to Christians is the fourth commandment.

While the fourth commandment occupies a prominent place in the minds of God's people they will also be perpetually reminded that He is their Creator and that by holding the power of creation, He also holds the power of sanctification. Both acts need the creative power only found in God.

The evidence in the word of God regarding the Ten Commandments, including the Sabbath commandment, is clear. Yet there are so many who claim to be Christians and followers of the way led by Jesus Christ, but deny the holy precepts of the Father revealed in the life of the Son.

There is a dense darkness of ignorance shrouding the great controversy that is taking place between Jesus Christ and Satan, the author of rebellion against God's law.

Satan, who is the one responsible for this darkness, has instituted a great deception in an attempt to cause a veil to be drawn over the eyes of those who would choose to follow the teachings of Jehovah.

As with all the lies that are being propagated by Satan, they are being fabricated with one aim in mind. This is to cause as much dissent and confusion as possible in order to keep people in darkness and out of the light that is shining from God's word.

By making the seventh day Sabbath appear to be of no consequence Satan has succeeded in changing the attitude of many who make a profession of being Christians. As a consequence many are deceived into not recognising the link between sanctification and salvation.

The popular view has often been expressed that Jesus changed the Sabbath to the first day of the week to honour His resurrection. Of course, this is not true. There has not been one change made to the moral law of the Decalogue at any time.

The immutable law of God can never be changed. Its beauty will never grow dim in spite of all Satan's attempts to shroud the beacon of God's authority in darkness and obscurity.

By rejecting the command of God to keep the seventh day holy it makes a mockery of the reason why God instituted a day of remembrance. It has always been God's will that His people remembered creation and their Creator. Remembering the first day of the week is remembering a day that is as far removed as possible from the day that God intended.

For those who try to make a separation between the God as is often falsely perceived in the Old Testament and the God of the New Testament there is a dilemma. This is because the message of the New Testament is built on the foundation of the Old Testament. And there is no Scriptural record of God making any change to the plan of salvation or the seventh day Sabbath portrayed in the Old Testament, which finds harmony with the message of the New Testament.

Confirmation of the unchanging nature of God is found as follows in Malachi: 3:6:

"For I am the Lord, I change not."

Showing the consistency of both Testaments, the apostle James says something similar in his letter as recorded in 1:17 thus:

"Every good gift, and every perfect gift is from above, and cometh down from the Father of lights, with whom is no variableness, neither shadow of turning."

Unlike the fickleness of man, God gives further proof of His consistency, as recorded as follows in Numbers 23:19:

"God [is] not a man, that he should lie; neither the son of man, that he should repent: hath he said, and shall he not do [it]? or hath he spoken, and shall he not make it good?"

Common sense dictates that it is not possible for man to change what God has decreed to be unchangeable.

(The restoration of behavioural harmony between God and humanity is not achieved through changes in God but by allowing God to change the nature of man).

It is impossible for a perfect God to change. The complete perfection that is found in God cannot be become more perfect or less than perfect.

(Of course, there is evidence in the Bible where God has changed His judgement. For one example, the record in the book of Jonah shows how God spared the repentant city of Nineveh).

Within Christendom there has been a lot of effort exerted in an attempt to establish that the first day of the week is the Christian Sabbath. When introduced to new light on any Bible subject it is folly to so desire the dark that Scripture is misquoted in an attempt to resist the truth.

There is nothing in either Testament of the Bible to indicate any change in connection with the Sabbath commandment. After the record of Jesus resting in the tomb on the Sabbath day the gospels record the resurrection of Jesus on the first day of the week but nothing is said to give reason for man to make a change to God's commandments.

There is a record in Acts 20:7 of the believers meeting on the Saturday evening for a fellowship meal before Paul left on his missionary journey. It is recorded that Paul spoke until midnight.

Midnight of the first day of the week would be a Saturday night. This was no more than a special meeting that took place after the Sabbath in order to take leave of Paul prior to his departure on the Sunday.

Then in verse 11 it says that Paul was speaking until sunrise before he left. However, the fact that Paul was prepared to take a journey on the first day of the week is proof that no sacred meaning was being attached to that day. Had this been a day of worship, Paul would not have journeyed on foot for about nineteen miles to Assos as described in verse 13.

In 1 Corinthians 16:2 it records that Paul made the appropriate suggestion that the accounting of the previous week be done on the first day of the week as follows:

"Upon the first [day] of the week let every one of you lay by him in store, as [God] hath prospered him, that there be no gatherings when I come."

In the above verse, Paul is merely making the request that mundane accountancy not be allowed to be an intrusion when he came.

There is another record in John 20:19 where it speaks of the disciples being assembled on the first day of the week. However, this gathering took place behind locked doors because the disciples were afraid of the Jewish authorities. This meeting could not accurately be described as one of joyful Sabbath worship.

It is a strange phenomenon when people will go to great lengths to misquote Scripture in order to project a false doctrine yet at the same time ignore plain Scriptural evidence that gives clear support in favour of sound doctrine.

For example, much emphasis is often placed on the texts that give space to the mention of the first day of the week in spite of there being no sacredness attached to the day. Yet the regard in which Jesus held the Sabbath day, as shown in the following words of Luke 4:16, are often ignored:

"And he came to Nazareth, where he had been brought up: and, as his custom was, he went into the synagogue on the Sabbath day, and stood up for to read."

There is equally clear evidence supplied by Jesus regarding the importance that He attached to all of God's law of Ten Commandments.

In John 14:15 Jesus is on record as saying, *"If ye love me, keep my commandments."*

In John 14:21 Jesus linked love for Him with keeping His commandments, also promising that those who did these things would be loved of the Father.

In Matthew 19:16 is the record of one asking Jesus *"what good thing shall I do, that I may have eternal life."*

As recorded in verses 18,19, and in harmony with all that is written in the gospel relating to God's commandments, Jesus advised the man to live in harmony with God's law of Ten Commandments. Yet rarely do we see much evidence in Christendom of any real importance being attached to God's law of love.

It is clearly set out in the word of God, and plainly discerned by those governed by God's Spirit, that during the end time there is going to be a final showdown. This is to take place between Jesus Christ and His followers, and Satan and his followers.

In normal circumstances no one would be foolish enough to choose Satan before the God of creation. The fact that a vast number will is plain evidence that they will not really be aware of what they do. This is the extent of Satan's success in deceiving so many souls. Now is the time to prepare while God's Spirit is still pleading to take the sinner home.

God is honoured when we accept His sovereignty by bestowing honour on the day that He has sanctified as a day of worship. It is by such means that the Creator becomes the focus of worship rather than a mere man-made system that is in opposition to the law of God.

Thus throughout Christendom in the last days, the seventh day Sabbath or the man-made Sunday Sabbath become the real issue of controversy.

In opposition to the seventh day Sabbath has been the instigation of Sunday as a false day of worship, and known to God's true servants as the "mark of the beast", whose number is 666.

From Revelation 13:18 we learn that 666 is the number of a man. *"Here is wisdom. Let him that hath understanding count the number of the beast: for it is the number of a man; and his number [is] Six hundred threescore [and] six."*

When describing the beast that is demanding worship, Revelation makes it very clear that it is referring to a power that is centred on man rather than God.

There are many and varied ways presented to qualify the number 666. It is widely believed that an explanation of this number is to be found in one title, which is applied, to the Pope.

This title is Vicarius Filii Dei (Vicegerent of the Son of God).

The official language of the Catholic Church is Latin. Taking the letters from the title, using this language, they read: V=5, I = 1, C = 100, I =1, U = 5, I =1, L = 50, I =1, I = 1, D = 500, I = 1. Total 666. There is no numerical value to the letters a, r, s, f, and e.

Seeking further to understand the significance of the number six in connection with worship, it helps if we consider the number seven. It is widely believed that the number seven represents a perfect number. The origin of this belief might stem from the repeated use of this number in the book of Revelation. There are seven churches, seven trumpets, seven seals, and seven spirits, etc.

There are seven days in a week. The seventh day is God's Sabbath. To remain symbolically with the sixth day by dwelling on the importance of man would mean to lose the blessing of the seventh day.

We have learned from God's word that 666 is the number of a man. Man was created on the sixth day. The day following the sixth day is one of Sabbath fellowship with the God of creation.

Although there is no actual fault to be found in the number six, when the focus of the mind becomes selfishly linked to self then this number of a man proceeds no further than self. In this way this number can be taken to symbolise the selfish fixation of man when refusing to accept the blessing associated with the seventh day Sabbath.

In Revelation 17:5 the harlot is linked with Babylon. The number six and multiples of this number were of significance to ancient Babylon.

The supreme gods of Babylon-named Anu and Marduk-were at different times, identified by the number sixty. The Babylonian priests also wore an amulet with a square configuration of strange numbers totalling 36 numbers consisting of 6x6 (36) that added up both horizontally and vertically to 666.

An added factor to this equation is that the number six is repeated three times. We can learn, as follows from Deuteronomy 19:15 and 2 Corinthians 13:1, that when something is repeated three times it takes on special significance.

"19:15 One witness shall not rise up against a man for any iniquity, or for any sin, in any sin that he sinneth: at the mouth of two witnesses, or at the mouth of three witnesses, shall the matter be established."

"13:1 This [is] the third [time] I am coming to you. In the mouth of two or three witnesses shall every word be established."

This is one reason why the number 6 used in the book of Revelation is repeated three times. It is a number that misguidedly emphasises the significance of man. Completing His work of creation with the creation of man, God rested on the seventh day. To anchor the mind on the works and activities of man is to proceed no further than self. Thus, man, man, man or self, self, self or 666.

The purpose of creation was fulfilled with the creation of man on the sixth day. This was followed by the crowning act of a specific and special blessing being bestowed on the seventh day Sabbath.

The seventh day Sabbath is God's gift of a unique length of time in order that He and His created beings might share sweet fellowship without the hindrance of daily chores associated with the other six days. Hence:

"The sabbath was made for man, and not man for the sabbath." (Mark 2:27).

It is very often claimed that there are glaring contradictions between the Old and New Testaments of the Bible, so as to give the impression that there is more than one God.

The most outrageous claim being made is that the God of the Old Testament is harsh and judgemental by comparison to the kind and loving God of the New Testament.

In order to reach a conclusion of truth on this matter, it is first necessary to establish that there is one God of both the Old and New Testaments. In support of this truth, it is recorded in John 10:3 that Jesus said: *"I and my Father are one."*

Jesus also said as recorded in John 14:9, *"he that hath seen me hath seen the Father."*

Showing the consistency of accounts in relation to the role played by Jesus in both Testaments, it says as recorded by the apostle Paul in 1 Corinthians 10:4 that during their desert wanderings the nation of Israel was being led by Christ:

"And all did drink the same spiritual drink for they drank of that spiritual Rock that followed them: and that Rock was Christ."

When seeking to establish the truth regarding the nature and character of the one God from both Testaments, this theme should be studied in conjunction with the garden of Gethsemane and Calvary.

As proved by the sacrifice of the Cross, God is love. In all of His dealings with the nation of Israel, God demonstrated His justice and His love.

Even today, most civilisations are content to follow the principles of justice that were first established by God in His relationship with the nation of Israel.

It is recorded in Ezekiel 18:30-32 of how God was and still is pleading with Israel to turn away from sin and live with a new resolve in peace and in harmony with the loving purpose of God.

In verse 32 these words are recorded: *"For I have no pleasure in the death of him that dieth, saith the Lord God: wherefore turn yourselves, and live ye."*

When as recorded in Exodus 21:24 God instructed the nation of Israel to exact *Eye for eye, tooth for tooth, hand for hand, foot for foot"*, it is not hard to believe that God did not mean that eyes should be gauged or that limbs were to be amputated.

It is inconceivable to believe that a God of love instituted His laws and judgements as a form of revenge. It is more in keeping with His character to believe that the execution of His judgements referred to above was in order to ensure a system of the fairest way to obtain a just recompense for suffered wrongs. This would then mean that as much as was possible, those who suffered as a result of another's actions were to receive compensation commensurate with the injury.

However, when reading the Exodus account of God's judgements in Leviticus 24:19,20, the impression is given that God was speaking literally when announcing the kind of judgements to be executed against the sins that are recorded above.

The only way that it is remotely possible to understand the horror of any of God's judgements is to appreciate the enormous offensiveness of sin, and that in the days when the nation of Israel was a theocracy it was necessary for the nation to learn the enormous consequences of sin.

However, the unfathomable love of God that was displayed in the garden of Gethsemane and at Calvary supplies overwhelming evidence that in the matter of executing the judgement of eye for eye and tooth for tooth, God was not executing a judgement as some sort of revenge but seeking that there would be a just compensation commensurate with the injury.

From verse 18 of Leviticus 24 we learn *"that he that killeth a beast shall make it good; beast for beast."* It would have been more in keeping with restitution and the implementation of a just recompense if the faculties of the guilty were placed in the service of the one who had been wronged rather than deprive the guilty ones of their faculties.

As recorded in Matthew 5:38, 39, Jesus taught His disciples that they were not to resist evil in a spirit of revenge, but to respond to evil in like manner to their Lord who gave His life for the unjust. The Scripture reads:

"Ye have heard that it hath been said, An eye for an eye, and a tooth for a tooth: But I say unto you, That ye resist not evil: but whosoever shall smite thee on the right cheek, turn to him the other also."

However, because the life of Christ is a demonstration of love for the saint and the sinner alike, this doest not mean that He approves of sin.

It is a legitimate and worthwhile exercise to turn the cheek in response to aggression when such actions can be the means of saving a soul.

In all circumstances, the Spirit of Jesus will maintain a revelation of God's love. However, Jesus also demonstrated that there comes a time when there is nothing to be gained in the senseless pursuance of peace with the antagonistic spirit of Satan, as proved from Matthew 10:14 where it says:

"And whosoever shall not receive you, nor hear your words, when ye depart out of that house or city, shake off the dust of your feet."

A hen that gathers her chicks under her wings will burn to death in a fire while protecting her offspring.

Using the analogy of the hen and her chicks taken from Matthew 23:37, Jesus gives this account as a demonstrative example of His incredible love for the nation of Israel.

However, because of their failure to respond to His pleading and His love, Jesus is on record in verse 38 as saying: *"Behold your house is left unto you desolate."*

It can be seen from the evidence supplied above that if true to their profession; Christians are expected to act with the wisdom and love that is made possible by the same Spirit demonstrated in the life of Jesus, the author of love.

At the beginning of this book the question was asked, is God there? Even if one should come to the conclusion that there is no God, it remains a worthwhile objective to live in peace and harmony with fellow human beings.

On this basis it is even more worthwhile to seek this same peace and harmony when we have the assurance that there is a God in control, who is seeking to make this kingdom of peace a reality for all those who are willing to be guided by His Spirit.

In order to learn the truth as to what is God's will for those who would be His disciples I have taken a prayerful journey through His word.

In answer to the question regarding the will of God for His people, there can be no clearer example than that proclaimed with such awesome power from Mount Sinai when, through Moses, He addressed the nation and placed before the people His law of Ten Commandments.

This book supplies overwhelming evidence that God's purpose for mankind is now to be fulfilled through the nation of spiritual Israel (Christians). Therefore, the proclamation made by God from Mount Sinai has as much relevance for modern Israel (Christians) as Israel of old.

Thus we are shown that the real issue of controversy between Satan and Christ is God's sovereignty, and the sign and fruit of this sovereignty that is the law of Ten Commandments.

Armed with this truth, we are now able to understand that in order to further his cause of rebellion Satan would logically attack the law of God. There is no more effective method of disclaiming the sovereignty of God than to cause apathy and contention involving the stamp of God's authority that is the Sabbath Commandment.

It is more than 40 years ago that someone said to me that the seventh day Sabbath had been changed on the authority of the Roman Catholic Church to that of the first day of the week. In my ignorance of the true facts I wrote to the Catholic Enquiry Centre seeking for clarification. The following are some answers:

From a letter of January 31, 1963:

"By and large we do not believe in the six days creation story. We believe that the bible is true only in the sense intended by the author. The author intends to teach us that all things are created by God, but he describes the creation in poetic terms.

"In the Old Testament the Saturday was observed as the day of the Lord, but since Christ rose from the dead on the Sunday this has now become the day of the Lord under the Christian dispensation."

From a letter of February 15, 1963:

"The authority of the Church is sufficient to change the day of the Lord from Saturday to Sunday. Christ said to His Church 'Whatsoever you shall bind on earth shall be bound also in Heaven'. Clearly then, Christ gave this power to make such authoritative decisions in His Name."

From a letter of April 9, 1963:

"The Church has not changed the substance of the law of God concerning the Sabbath. It was Christ Himself Who made Sunday the Lord's Day by rising from the dead and making that the day of victory and celebration for Christians. With the coming of Christ the Old Law was fulfilled and came to perfection. Just as we do not have to keep all the old Jewish customs and laws, so we do not have to worship God on Saturday but on Sundays."

I believe that the above answers sent to me were sincerely meant from one who was honest and faithful in what he believed, and I would not criticise that. But on the matter of obedience, it must surely be in harmony with God to be guided by His word rather than the teachings of men who could be under the influence of Satan, the beast.

When describing the beast that is demanding worship, Revelation makes it very clear that it is referring to an apostate church that has its power centred on man rather than God. Satan is the original beast of Revelation. In effect, to worship the beast is to give allegiance to Satan the author of rebellion.

Regarding the view taken by the Roman Catholic Church concerning the Sunday, most of Christendom follow her lead and also give preference to worship on the Sunday.

This is a fact that is also testified to by the Church of Jesus Christ of the Latter day Saints, proved as follows:

"Members of the Church of Latter day Saints recognise Sunday as the Sabbath in commemoration of the fact that Christ came forth from the grave on the Sunday, and the Apostles commenced meeting thereafter on the first day of the week." (Taken from Ensign 1996 May).

Chapter 7
The Spiritual Sabbath

As a preamble to the message of this chapter, I believe that if it were suggested to many Christians that their love for God might not be as genuine as they would like to profess, it could trigger a righteous or self-righteous response of indignation.

One of the biggest fabrications and shams of all time is practised by many professing Christians regarding making claims of feeling a great and overriding love for God.

When claiming to love God above any other being, people who make this claim are seemingly unaware of the absurdity of such a claim.

To have a clear understanding of the meaning of love within a relationship with God, it is necessary to appreciate that there are three kinds of love.

The first type of love is a love for the righteousness of God, and is always quantified by the related measure of the indwelling Spirit of God.

The second kind of love is agape. Among other obvious examples, this type of love finds expression within families.

Everyone is born with a measure of family love and, if allowed, it will develop apace with growth by the Spirit in Christ. Both of these two types of love are a gift from God, and not a reason for boasting.

The third kind is appreciative love and is a revelation of genuine worship for God. However, this third kind of love cannot reach fulfilment in a genuine expression of true worship before the other two kinds of love attain to full maturity in Christ.

This kind of love comes by entering into God's Sabbath rest. This is a holy state of mind manifesting a full measure of imparted righteousness and imparted love bringing the blessing of impartial love associated with the Spiritual Sabbath.

Obviously the seventh day Sabbath is a sign or seal, indicating loyalty of God's people to their Creator. Yet there remains more to this issue than apparent honour to a day. Just as there is a counterfeit Sabbath day, there exists another counterfeit leading to a spiritual violation of the Sabbath principle.

There can exist in some respects an apparently godlike character displaying a love that is as much a counterfeit as bestowing honour upon a false Sabbath.

In essence, having received the seal of "*the living God*", *referred* to below in Revelation 7:2 means to be imparted with the full righteousness of Christ through the indwelling Holy Spirit signified by God's servants being blessed with the fullness of imparted impartial love. These are described as follows:

Revelation 7:2-3: *"And I saw another angel ascending from the east, having the seal of the living God: and he cried with a loud voice to the four angels, to whom it was given to hurt the earth and the sea, 3Saying, Hurt not the earth, neither the sea, nor the trees, till we have sealed the servants of our God in their foreheads."*

Jesus promised that He would one day return to this earth and confer upon His people, eternal life. We can be very sure that Jesus will keep His promise. What is not so sure is that all who expect to partake of this eternal life will receive it.

There is a test to be faced by all of those who are seeking a place in God's eternal kingdom. Those who desire to share in the promised blessings of Jehovah must also cherish a holy desire to live in righteousness in harmony with His government.

In order to experience such a desire it is necessary for lives to be governed by the indwelling Holy Spirit. It is only through the influence of the Spirit that it becomes possible to love the righteousness expressed in God's law.

It follows that those whose lives are in harmony with the law of the Decalogue will be bestowing honour to the seventh day Sabbath. To love God is to love His commandments, including His Sabbath.

In this way, love for the righteousness of God will find a spiritual expression through a holy commitment of the mind to God's law.

We are informed in Romans 13:10 that *"love is the fulfilling of the law."* To fulfil the law is to execute its precepts to a conclusion of rest in God. Thus we are all judged as to how a profession of love measures when compared to the love that is manifest by a fulfilled law in Sabbath rest.

The last testing truth for all mankind will not be just a show of keeping God's commandments, including the seventh day Sabbath. It is a character of love that is the key to heaven, and not just a profession of righteousness.

Jesus said, as recorded in John 14:15, *"If you love me, keep my commandments."*

Thus we see that keeping God's commandments and the gift of love form the nucleus of a godly character in harmony with Jehovah.

A big mistake that is all too often made by many of those who express a desire to follow Jesus is the false declaration of a great love for Him. Herein lays the craftiness and subterfuge of Satan.

We learn from Scripture that love is from God. It is not within human power to generate any kind of love in connection with the righteousness of God.

The most that human beings are able to achieve without God inevitably falls short of what God desires. Yet we are admonished by Scripture to declare an overriding love for God.

Deuteronomy 6:5 gives us an indication of God's requirement from His people as can be seen below:

"And thou shalt love the LORD thy God with all thine heart, and with all thy soul, and with all thy might."

This statement seems to be unambiguous and clear enough. The gospels are equally clear. For example, there is this record from Matthew 22:37:

"Jesus said unto him, Thou shalt love the Lord thy God with all thy heart, and with all thy soul, and with all thy mind."

There can be no doubt that the above text reveals that God is issuing a specific command. It is not His intention that the will of man remains untempered.

With a Scriptural based conviction that without God we can do nothing, we are faced with a dilemma regarding the means we are to use in order to respond to these commands from God regarding our love for Him.

Are we to conclude from the foregoing Scripture references that we serve an arbitrary God, who bestows us with the capacity to love in order that we might exert effort to return it to Him? I think not! God's word proves that the Creator initiates all the spiritual effort. *"All things are of God, who hath reconciled us to himself by Jesus Christ, and hath given to us the ministry of reconciliation."* (2 Corinthians 5:18).

Also Romans 5:5 declares: *"And hope maketh not ashamed; because the love of God is shed abroad in our hearts by the Holy Ghost which is given unto us."*

Deuteronomy 30:6 has this to say: *"And the LORD thy God will circumcise thine heart, and the heart of thy seed, to love the LORD thy God with all thine heart, and with all thy soul, that thou mayest live."*

In Galatians 5:22 Paul is on record as saying: *"But the fruit of the Spirit is love, joy, peace, longsuffering, gentleness, goodness, faith."*

Consulting 1 John 4:7 we read something similar where it says: *"Beloved, let us love one another: for love is of God; and every one that loveth is born of God, and knoweth God."*

The above references reveal that we do not possess the power to acquire love without God. It is He that circumcises the hearts of men. It is His Spirit that is responsible for heart conversion that alone gives one the joy of love.

Having learned that it is not possible to love God without the aid of His Spirit means that we are faced with a puzzle as to why God should issue a command to love Him with all of our souls, and all of our might, and with all of our minds.

We are unable to fathom the hidden depths of God but it is important that we understand that we serve a heavenly King whose righteousness is equal in quality to His Majesty.

Consider the following as supportive evidence of God's righteous acts:

Judges 5:11: *"They that are delivered from the noise of archers in the places of drawing water, there shall they rehearse the righteous acts of the LORD, even the righteous acts toward the inhabitants of his villages in Israel: then shall the people of the LORD go down to the gates."*

1 Samuel 12:7: *"Now therefore stand still, that I may reason with you before the LORD of all the righteous acts of the LORD, which he did to you and to your fathers."*

Consult the following Scripture references where we learn that in name our heavenly Father is Righteousness:

Jeremiah 23:6: *"In his days Judah shall be saved, and Israel shall dwell safely: and this is his name whereby he shall be called, THE LORD OUR RIGHTEOUSNESS."*

Jeremiah 33:16: *"In those days shall Judah be saved, and Jerusalem shall dwell safely: and this is the name wherewith she shall be called, The LORD our righteousness."*

Is the above quotation not a reference to the day when spiritual Israel will have their Father's name of *"righteousness"* written in their foreheads as recorded below from Revelation 14:1?

"And I looked up, and lo, a Lamb stood on the mount Sion and with him an hundred and forty four thousand, having his Father's name written in their foreheads."

In effect, the collective Scripture references quoted above teach us that to love the Lord our God with all of our hearts and with all of our minds means to have a love for doing what is right.

A misunderstanding of Matthew 10:35-37 could give the impression that the Person of Jesus is demanding more by way of affection than one bestows on one's family. In this Scripture Jesus is recorded as saying:

"10:35 For I am come to set a man at variance against his father, and the daughter against her mother, and the daughter in law against her mother in law. 10:36 And a man's foes [shall be] they of his own household. 10:37 He that loveth father or mother more than me is not worthy of me: and he that loveth son or daughter more than me is not worthy of me."

Quoted out of context with the preceding verses, the last verse quoted above could quite easily lead to a wrong conclusion. When read in its proper context it becomes clear that Jesus is not creating competition between Him and one's family, but is referring to the battle between good and evil.

In such circumstances, should we choose to follow a path dominated by self or rebellion, we would then not be worthy of Jesus. This is equally true should we choose to be allied to anyone who is in rebellion, even if applicable to family members.

All the above references hinge upon a question of principle. God requires from His people that on principle they should love the righteousness of the Father and the Son. This principle of loving what is right is a gift from God.

We can choose either to accept or reject. To accept means supporting the cause of the just, who are right, rather than the unjust when they are wrong, regardless of how close is the relationship with those who are wrong.

A love for righteousness is to so yearn for true fellowship with the principles of Jesus that human nature becomes a transcript of His character.

To love the righteousness of God is to love the principle as declared by God's law of Ten Commandments. It is upon this principle of love that the kingdom of God is established.

When, as recorded in Matthew 22:36, the lawyer asked Jesus *"which is the great commandment in the law?"* Jesus revealed in verses 37-40 the heavenly principle of love with the following words:

"Jesus said unto him, Thou shalt love the Lord thy God with all thy heart, and with all thy soul, and with all thy mind. This is the first and great commandment. And the second [is] like unto it, Thou shalt love thy neighbour as thyself. On these two commandments hang all the law and the prophets."

In the first epistle of John 4:12 it says *"No man hath seen God at any time."* In verse 20 of the same chapter is further explained the difficulty of acquiring an ability to love an unseen God.

Therefore, when reference is made to the need for loving God, it is obviously a reference to the God that is seen.

There can be no mistaking the character and righteousness of God as portrayed in the Bible. Therefore, any admonishment from the Bible to love God is a reference to the character and righteousness of God that is seen.

God is not arbitrary. He is a God of love imparting to His people a character in harmony with His own. Sanctification brings imparted righteousness thus ensuring that in the new earth all beings will ever love their Creator, who is RIGHTEOUSNESS. However, a love for righteousness, or for doing what is right, is just one kind of love. There are other types.

A second type of love is agape. This love is also imparted. It is a gift from God. It is this impartial love, which was the subject of Jesus' prayer, recorded as follows:

John 17:20-21: *"Neither pray I for these alone, but for them also which shall believe on me through their word; 21That they all may be one; as thou, Father, art in me, and I in thee, that they also may be one in us; that the world may believe that thou hast sent me."*

This oneness that Jesus refers to includes compassion, together with real interest and concern towards each other. It is God's will that this oneness of purpose that emanates from God Himself should be fully reflected in our lives.

Hence the reason for this commandment of Jesus recorded in the gospel of John 15:12: *"This is my commandment, That ye love one another, as I have loved you."*

A reading of John chapter 15 makes clear that we cannot possibly love each other as Jesus loves us unless Jesus is allowed to come into our hearts and minds. For example, read these words of Jesus recorded in verse 4.

John 15:4: *"Abide in me, and I in you. As the branch cannot bear fruit of itself, except it abide in the vine; no more can ye, except ye abide in me."*

In John chapter 15 Jesus is speaking of a love that comes directly from God. It is agape! This agape type of love is something we are all born with as shown in the following text:

John 1:9: *"That was the true Light, which lighteth every man that cometh into the world."*

We see clearly from the above text that Jesus is the true light or love *"which lighteth every man."*

In Titus 2:4 it speaks of love for a husband, and love for children. The word *"love"* for a husband is taken from the Greek word, Philandros.

Maternal love for children is taken from the Greek word, Philoteknos. Although not listed as agape, these examples of love are just as much from God as is agape.

God's love that is present in every family is so strong that it takes a lot of effort on the part of Satan to destroy it. However, if we choose to take advantage of the good start that God has given, this precious love will develop apace with the mind.

By allowing Jesus to take possession of our minds impartial love will grow, bringing us into harmony with the prayer uttered by Jesus already referred to recorded in John 17:21.

Therefore, there are two qualities that righteousness requires and God desires from His people. Firstly, on principle, we are to love the righteousness of God with all our hearts and minds. Secondly, we should love each other as Jesus loves us.

Relative to Christian growth both of these blessings are imparted by Christ. It would be foolish to claim any credit for either of these gifts. Even a **desire** to love is not possible without God.

The danger for Christians today is much the same as existed in the days prior to the first advent of Jesus. Many of God's professed people of that time were claiming a love and loyalty for God that Jesus revealed to be false.

They were claiming that they honoured God and His commandments, including the Sabbath commandment. Yet their actions were often completely at variance with the God they claimed to serve.

In many respects little has changed since the days when Jesus was among men. The following comments on love refer to agape.

In all churches it is quite common for people to claim feelings for Jesus that they cannot possibly experience.

Such declarations are turned into a mockery when there is little evidence of a sincere commitment to fellow man.

With the wondrous love that begins with God it is not possible to love the Person of Jesus more than we love each other. Neither is it the will of God that we should.

Claiming a love for Jesus above the love that we should have for each other is attributing to self a power we do not possess, and is not in harmony with Scripture or the will of God.

As we have already read from John 15:12 we are commanded to love each other as Jesus loves us. Common sense dictates that we cannot love more than Jesus does. If we love each other as Jesus loves us how can we possibly love more?

It is certainly possible to love Jesus as much as we love each other but if we then make unsubstantiated claims to love Jesus more than each other, we are in violation of the Spiritual Sabbath principle by claiming to hold the power of creation.

With the love that Scripture proves comes from God, it is absurd to make the erroneous claim of loving Jesus more than fellow man. Such claims of creative power are a mockery to God.

Love is of God. It is by the evidence if this imparted and impartial love that the true beauty of Jesus shines through humanity.

Assimilating this truth enables our minds to forsake Satan's veneer of subterfuge and allows the Spirit of Christ to impart sweet Sabbath rest.

The incredible sacrifice made by Jesus on behalf of sinners inspires holy and immeasurable appreciation from the saints. However, this feeling of appreciation should not be confused with the compassionate expression of agape love that is a gift from God.

Satan uses the sacrifice of Jesus to deceive a person into believing that with the love of heaven God is expecting His servants to demonstrate a power equalling that revealed at creation in a demonstration of love for Jesus above all others.

In this way, honest appreciation of Jesus relative to holiness can be replaced by dishonest declarations of unsubstantiated love. Thus often in a misguided attempt at projecting the virtue of holiness in a false declaration of love, there can be more a projection of self.

Jesus is honoured when His servants are so filled with God's Spirit as to display the impartial love of heaven to each other. Such a witness of love is the measure of love held for Jesus.

Any claim to a power that exceeds that of Jesus is equal to attributing the power of creation to self. If we attain to such a lofty ideal as to love each other as Jesus loves us, it will be because of the sanctifying power of God, which cannot be exceeded by man.

Of course, through the sanctifying power of the Spirit, it is possible for us to love each other as Jesus loves us. However, we should not presume that we possess such creative power that would be needed to substantiate such claims of love above that imparted by our Creator. Such false claims bring dishonour upon Jesus, who died in humility that in life we might be humble. True commitment to Jesus is measured by how much love we show each other.

To insist on maintaining a false position regarding love for Jesus, we arrive at one of two conclusions. The first conclusion would be that we serve an arbitrary God as automatons or, secondly, in a subtle way, it is a claim to hold the power of creation to an extent, which equals God.

Making the claim of loving God more than fellow man, under satanic influence, is a subtle attempt to elevate self above God. This claim is false as seen in the verse below:

"The disciple is not above his Master: but every one that is perfect should be as his Master." (Luke 6:40).

With the love of agape that is a gift from God, it is possible to obey the command of Jesus, and love each other as He loves us. This is an entering into God's Sabbath rest.

When challenged on their reasons for not specifically honouring the seventh day Sabbath, people often answer by saying: *"Every day is the Sabbath"*. Although these people are right, they are not always aware that this answer is profound. It is true that once having entered into God's Sabbath rest, every day is lived in honour to God. However, this truth does not make the seventh day Sabbath a lie. One truth does not destroy the other.

Although the seventh day Sabbath is important, it is the Spiritual Sabbath that is now being referred to.

To love each other as Jesus loves us is a living Sabbath. Relative to light, our love for Jesus is measured by how much love we have for fellow man.

Making claims of a greater love for God than we display towards each other is a deviation from the command of Jesus and a violation of the Spiritual Sabbath principle. This is just as much a mark of the beast as any dishonour to the physical seventh day Sabbath.

When God's people enter into God's rest, the hearts of His people will beat in unison with each other and in complete harmony with the spiritual message portrayed by the fourth, and heart, of God's Ten Commandments.

Recognition of the principle of the spiritual Sabbath truth has the effect of revealing the sham of false claims regarding love for Jesus. It has the power to enlighten the mind and dispel any beguiling veneer of false charm.

An acknowledgement of God's power and an acceptance of His Spirit are of more merit in the eyes of God than false declarations of love, or mere acquiescence to a specific day. Not realising this truth was a mistake that many made, including some Jewish leaders, in the days of Jesus.

As can be seen from the following Scripture reference the apostle John makes an important point on the matter of love.

1 John 4:20: *"If a man says, I love God, and hateth his brother, he is a liar: for he that loveth not his brother whom he hath seen, how can he love God whom he hath not seen?"*

In the above quotation, the two extreme examples of love and hate are brought to view. However, it does not matter what degree of relativity is made, the truth remains the same. To paraphrase, it could be said with equal truth: Evidence of how much we love Jesus is mirrored by how much we love each other.

The Spiritual Sabbath comes alive in God's people when they live harmoniously in relation to God's law of liberty. As recorded in 1:25 the apostle James states:

"But whoso looketh into the perfect law of liberty, and continueth therein, he being not a forgetful hearer, but a doer of the work, this man shall be blessed in his deed."

Adding two verses, it is worth repeating the reference to God's people entering into His rest, enabling man to fulfil the claims of the law.

Hebrews 4:8-11: *"For if Jesus had given them rest, then would he not afterward have spoken of another day 9There remaineth therefore a rest to the people of God. 10For he that is entered into his rest, he also hath ceased from his own works, as God did from his. 11Let us labour therefore to enter into that rest, lest any man fall after the same example of unbelief."*

The following message from 1 John chapter four is a confirmation in truth of the previous study on love.

"7 Beloved, let us love one another: for love is of God; and every one that loveth is born of God, and knoweth God. 8 He that loveth not knoweth not God; for God is love. 9 In this was manifested the love of God toward us, because that God sent his only begotten Son into the world, that we might live through him. 10 Herein is love, not that we loved God, but that he loved us, and sent his Son [to be] the propitiation for our sins. 11 Beloved, if God so loved us, we ought also to love one another. 12 No man hath seen God at any time. If we love one another, God dwelleth in us, and his love is perfected in us."

Knowing that love must be the nucleus of any character of those claiming to be followers of Jesus, Scripture is teaching that the love that opens the door to eternity is measured by how much love we show to each other.

Neither a degenerate nor an unconverted mind is capable of fully appreciating the wondrous majesty of a God of unsurpassable love. This is one reason for misunderstanding the command of God that tells us we are to love Him with all of our minds and hearts.

People can be confused into believing error by not recognising that in His relationship with humanity, God desires His servants to love the righteousness of God before there can be established a proper relationship with the Person of God.

Unaware of the difference between the righteousness of God and the Person of God, many make false claims regarding love, with misguided or dishonest motives in the belief that they are pleasing God.

There is more than one dimension in the make-up of man. For this reason it is possible to experience an affinity for a person, to later become disillusioned with a faulty character.

In this respect each individual consists of personality and character. In His word, God has revealed His righteousness. It is the Holy righteousness of God that we are admonished to love with all our minds and all our hearts. It is perfectly proper to exercise supreme loyalty to the principles of God. However, loyalty should not be confused with love.

God has blessed the vast majority of His created beings with the five senses of sight, hearing, touch, smell and taste. Yet under normal circumstances, on a personal level, it is not possible to experience the presence of God with any of these senses.

However, by the presence of God's Spirit it is possible to experience and to love the righteous character of God that is made evident within the beauty of all creation bringing joy to all five senses, and comfort to the soul.

Many happy relationships have been ruined by new converts to Christ when they have made the arrogant and presumptuous claim that their supreme love has been switched from a devoted partner to become centred upon God.

The sad fact is that these claims are not even true, nor are they made in harmony with the will and purpose of God. It requires maturity of the Spirit to even begin to appreciate the majestic wondrous love of God.

The biggest enemy for the Christian is that of self. It is the projection of self, and a reluctance to dismiss self from the equation in any relationship with God that often erects a barrier to spiritual growth.

There are many gifts from God that are made available to man, but the greatest gift of all is the gift of God himself. God is glorified by the expression of His love that finds fulfilment within human relationships.

To love with the love of God is not to glorify self but to bring glory to God. In order for Jesus Christ to dwell in human flesh and initiate an experience of God's Spirit of love it is first necessary for the Christian to die to self. In Romans 6:3,4 it is put this way:

"Know ye not, that so many of us as were baptized into Jesus Christ were baptized into his death? Therefore we are buried with him by baptism into death: that like as Christ was raised up from the dead by the glory of the Father, even so we also should walk in newness of life."

It is through the death of self that it becomes possible for God to make a habitation with His people.

Recognising that the new life for a Christian is made possible through the presence of God's Spirit motivated Paul to say, as recorded in 1 Corinthians 3:16: *"Know ye not that ye are the temple of God, and [that] the Spirit of God dwelleth in you?"*

To become the temple of God's Spirit is for the character of self to be transformed into the very nature of Christ. It is then that the temple of God is not just projecting human love, but the wondrous impartial love of God.

In John 7:37, 38 Jesus likened this Spirit of heavenly love as rivers of living waters thus:

"In the last day, that great [day] of the feast, Jesus stood and cried, saying, If any man thirst, let him come unto me, and drink. He that believeth on me, as the scripture hath said, out of his belly shall flow rivers of living water."

With the knowledge that Christian love is a witness to Christ, there should also develop the conviction that impartial love for each other and love for the righteousness of God are gifts from God.

People believing that God and their peers expect them to feel a supreme love for the Person of God above all other loves can be the reason for false claims that are made regarding God's gift of love.

Attaching more priority to the principles expressed in loving the character of God that is a gift from God, should not be confused with agape that is also a gift from God. Neither should these types of love be confused with the appreciative loving worship of God that cannot develop before the first types of love have matured in Christ.

Motivated by a selfish spirit in a desire for salvation, many professing Christians expend a lot of effort in projecting themselves as loving a God they cannot see, while at the same time showing little or no care for the body of Christ that they can see.

Selfishly seeking salvation in isolation from a spirit of care is to be garbed in the dress of unrighteousness that brings isolation from Christ.

We learn from Jesus, as recorded in Matthew 22-14, that many are invited to the marriage between Christ and His people, *"both bad and good"* but without the *"wedding garment"* of Christ's righteousness we remain unclean to be cast *"into outer darkness"*. *"For many are called, but few are chosen."*

On the day of judgement those who now portray an uncaring attitude to the body of Christ will incur the same penalty as those who do not care for the Person of Christ or the righteousness of Christ.

A sure sign that a Christian is the temple of God is seen by evidence of the living Christ. To love Christ is to love the body of Christ. When there is no real evidence of love for the body of Christ then this provides a clear witness to the spirit of anti-Christ.

As regards to the very important subject of love, when viewed in conjunction with a caring compassionate kind of love, a Christian would have more reason to show sympathy and concern for a soul that is in dire need than for an all powerful self-sufficient God.

In 1 John 3:14 we are shown that love for the brethren is a sure sign of salvation. It says:

"We know that we have passed from death unto life, because we love the brethren. He that loveth not his brother abideth in death."

In 1 John 4:1-4 is plain evidence of the double meaning attached to the confession that *"Jesus Christ is come in the flesh"*. It is not enough to just confess that Jesus came to earth to die for the sins of the world. The potential of man is fulfilled when there is clear evidence of the Spirit of Jesus working out the will of God in human flesh, as follows.

*"Beloved, believe not every spirit, but try the spirits whether they are of God: because many false prophets are gone out into the world. Hereby know ye the Spirit of God: **Every spirit that confesseth that Jesus Christ is come in the flesh is of God: And every spirit that confesseth not that Jesus Christ is come in the flesh is not of God: and this is that [spirit] of antichrist,** whereof ye have heard that it should come; and even now already is it in the world. Ye are of God, little children, and have*

overcome them: because greater is he that is in you, than he that is in the world."

To confess that Jesus has come in the flesh is to reveal the Spirit of Christ in the life.

Proof that the above interpretation is correct is found in verse 2 where it says that *"every spirit that confesseth that Jesus Christ is come in the flesh is of God."*

There has been taken so much care to cover every angle on the subject of love because without allowing God to initiate an experience and expression of His love it is a waste of time and effort to seek an eternal relationship with God.

In 1 Corinthians 15:32 Paul declares that without the resurrection it is futile to be a disciple of Jesus.

Although there is to be a resurrection it is equally futile to claim to be a disciple of Jesus if there is a failure to follow Him in truth, making the following words of Paul equally relevant to the slothful disciple.

If there be no resurrection to life *"let us eat and drink; for to-morrow we die."*

It must surely be apparent to the reader that it would be futile for God to issue a command for His subjects to initiate an expression of love based upon their own effort when Scripture clearly states:

*"I am the vine, ye [are] the branches: He that abideth in me, and I in him, the same bringeth forth much fruit: for **without me ye can do nothing**."* (John 15:5).

As recorded in Matthew 22:37-40 we are admonished by Jesus to love the Lord our God with all our hearts, souls and minds. Yet the verse above tells us that without God we can do nothing.

Thus it can be seen that by misunderstanding and misinterpreting God's message of love, God would be portrayed as blessing us with the power to love in order to return it directly to Himself. This is an absurd situation that shows no true understanding of the wondrous love of God.

Servants of God cannot give to Him the honour that is His due until, in perfect love for the brethren, they have entered into God's rest. It is at this stage of holy perfection that it is possible to express true worship to a God from whom all spiritual blessings flow.

The word love in connection with God can be summed up in the following manner: To be of any worth, love must be built upon the foundation of the righteousness and principles of God.

This is the reason why the Bible gives a revelation of these qualities that are an attribute to God.

To love God with all of our hearts and minds is to love the righteousness of God as revealed in the Bible. Our love for the Person of God is measured by the love that we share with each other. This means that it is not possible to have a personal relationship with God to the detriment of others. There is no relationship with God that can be the cause of hurt in others.

The message of this chapter regarding God's love is in harmony with 2 John 1:6 where is found the actual definition of what is love. It says: *"And this is love, that we walk after his commandments."*

Satan is such a crafty adversary in the battle for souls as to be successful in extending his kingdom even within a professed Christian Church.

Adherence to good doctrine and supposed Christian rules and values is not always a sure safeguard against the wiles of Satan.

The Bible gives evidence of history being littered with people who make a profession of following the teachings of Jehovah but are outside of God's grace.

There is only one sure defence against the enemy of souls, and that is the love of God. It is love and not just a profession of sound doctrine that will initiate the Christian revival that is to envelop the world before the return of Jesus.

Scripture also teaches that there will be two classes of **God's people** on the earth before the advent of Jesus. All are then living in harmony with God as portrayed by the honour bestowed on His law.

However, at the return of Jesus, those of God's people who have not had sufficient time to acquire the full standard of imparted righteousness of Christ will have died under the promise associated with the third angel's message as recorded in Revelation 14:6-10. Verse 13 of the same chapter contains the promise that these people are blessed as follows:

"And I heard a voice from heaven saying unto me, Write, Blessed are the dead which die in the Lord from henceforth: Yea, saith the Spirit, that they may rest from their labours; and their works do follow them."

The other class of God's people are those who have reached full spiritual maturity and are full of Christ's imparted righteousness. These are identified thus in Revelation 14:1:

"And I looked, and, lo, a Lamb stood on the mount Sion, and with him an hundred forty and four thousand, having his Father's name written in their foreheads."

SPIRITUAL SABBATH.
BAKING OF LOAVES.

Verse 4 adds that this special class of people *"were redeemed from among men, being the first fruits unto God and to the Lamb."*

The book of Revelation is teaching that both sections of God's people will have been subjected to different tests but of equal dimension, relative to their growth in Christ.

The first class will have been tested with the choice of following the beast and receiving his mark, or heeding the commandments of God and bestowing honour to the seventh day Sabbath.

However, Scripture is also teaching that observance of the seventh day Sabbath is not to be the only test for God's people during the end time, and especially for the hundred and forty four thousand who have been sealed, having *"the Father's name in their foreheads."* (Revelation 14:1).

This is a plain indication that they are filled with God's Holy Spirit. This must mean that they will love each other with the same impartial love daily demonstrated by God.

This is an entering into God's rest, as recorded in Hebrew 4:10 where it speaks of a time when God's people have ceased from *their* own works as they enter into God's rest.

There are two types of seals presented to God's people during the end time. The one seal is observance of the seventh day Sabbath declaring the sovereignty of God. The second seal is the stamping of God's character in His people through the presence of His Holy Spirit.

Thus we are meant to understand that at the time of the end, honour to a physical day will signify allegiance to God or man. However, it is the maturity of the Spirit displayed by the hundred and forty four thousand that signals their worthiness and ability to stand through the time known as Jacob's trouble. (See Daniel 12:1). This condition of the saints signals an entering into God's Sabbath rest revealed by evidence of God's impartial love.

There is a significant Spiritual Sabbath truth displayed in the service of the temple showbread, as recorded in Leviticus 24:5-9.

"And thou shalt take fine flour, and bake twelve cakes thereof: two tenth deals shall be in one cake. And thou shalt set them in two rows, six on a row, upon the pure table before the LORD. And thou shalt put pure frankincense upon [each] row, that it may be on the bread for a memorial, [even] an offering made by fire unto the LORD. Every sabbath he shall set it in order before the LORD continually, [being taken] from the children of Israel by an everlasting covenant. And it shall be Aaron's and his sons'; and they shall eat it in the holy place: for

it [is] most holy unto him of the offerings of the LORD made by fire by a perpetual statute."

Just as there were twelve cakes of shewbread so were there twelve tribes of Israel and twelve apostles.

The table of the shewbread was overlaid with pure gold, with a crown of gold around the top.

During the Sabbath hours the Levites made twelve loaves of unleavened bread, and laid them out in two rows of six covered with pure frankincense. The loaves lay on the table throughout the week until they were eaten by Aaron and his sons (priests) on the following Sabbath. See Leviticus 24:5, 1 Chronicles 9:32.

Although it was unlawful to make common bread on the Sabbath day, the Levites were specifically instructed to make the shewbread on that day. Thus the shewbread was baked and eaten on the Sabbath Day.

The lesson of the shewbread was a type, and teaches that man is totally dependant upon God for both temporal and spiritual food.

In harmony with other types in the sanctuary service, this type reached fulfilment in Christ.

As the true bread of life, Jesus said, as recorded in John 6:47-54:

"Verily, verily, I say unto you, He that believeth on me hath everlasting life. I am that bread of life. Your fathers did eat manna in the wilderness, and are dead. This is the bread which cometh down from heaven, that a man may eat thereof, and not die. I am the living bread which came down from heaven: if any man eat of this bread, he shall live for ever: and the bread that I will give is my flesh, which I will give for the life of the world. The Jews therefore strove among themselves, saying, How can this man give us [his] flesh to eat? Then Jesus said unto them, Verily, verily, I say unto you, Except ye eat the flesh of the Son of man, and drink his blood, ye have no life in you. Whoso eateth my flesh, and drinketh my blood, hath eternal life; and I will raise him up at the last day."

From John 1:1-5 we learn that Jesus is the Word. Thus the Word of God is the true bread of life that is come from the presence of God.

John 6:63 says that the words that Jesus speak *"they are spirit. and they are life".*

As the shewbread left the presence of God and was eaten by the priests, so did Jesus leave the courts of heaven to present the Word of God to His people.

The service of the shewbread is teaching the significance of the seventh day Sabbath. It is the day set aside for special communion with Jehovah.

Through the abundant provision of His bounty, God has made it possible for man to cease from the toil and cares associated with the first six days and reap the blessing of the seventh day.

The Sabbath day is a special day established by God, enabling man to gain a deeper insight into the will of the Divine.

When the priests ate the shewbread it was assimilated into their flesh and gave them strength for their holy tasks.

It is clear from the Scriptural lessons of the shewbread, which is representative of Christ that the priests were allowed to consume the loaves only on the Sabbath day. This is telling us of a particular Sabbath connection when partaking of the body of Christ, the bread of life.

It is significant that only the priests were allowed to eat the shewbread. Because the shewbread represents Christ, who is the bread of life, this would imply that it is only the priests who are able to partake of the nature of Christ. However, this truth does not present a problem when it is realised that all who accept Jesus as Saviour become priests of God.

In 1 Peter 2: 9,10 there is this record:

"But ye [are] a chosen generation, a royal priesthood, an holy nation, a peculiar people; that ye should show forth the praises of him who hath called you out of darkness into his marvellous light: Which in time past [were] not a people, but [are] now the people of God: which had not obtained mercy, but now have obtained mercy."

See also Revelation 1:6 and Revelation 20:6.

The record above where Peter speaks of God's people being a royal priesthood is in harmony with the covenant made by God with His people as recorded in Exodus 19:6 where God promised that Israel would be *"a kingdom of priests, and an holy nation."*

God's people become fully-fledged priests with God when they have entered into His rest. Thus it is that to partake in full measure of the bread of life is to inherit the full-imparted righteousness of Christ when entering into Sabbath rest.

This then is the particular Sabbath connection when partaking of the body of Christ, the bread of life. Christ. The church of God will partake fully of the divine nature to become *"a royal priesthood"* when filled with the imparted righteousness associated with entering God's Sabbath rest.

In this way the type represented in the eating of the shewbread reaches fulfilment of anti-type when the holy nation of spiritual Israel are filled with Christ's imparted righteousness to become fully fledged priests. This represents a holy state of mind signified by entering into sweet Sabbath rest, known as the Spiritual Sabbath.

There is perfect harmony with the type expressed in the service of the shewbread and the anti-type expressed when God's people enter into His rest.

There is yet another lesson taught by the shewbread. With an understanding that Jesus is the spiritual bread of life we can appreciate that the loaves of shewbread were an anti-type of Christ. It will be noticed that the shewbread stayed in the sanctuary throughout the week until *it was consumed by* the priests. Thus we are taught that it takes time for human beings to more fully appreciate the wondrous majesty of Christ.

When in the newness of discovery Jesus first impresses the mind it is not possible to immediately understand, or assimilate, His beauty. Just as a measure of time needed to elapse before the priests could fully appreciate the shewbread, so is it in the fullness of time that Jesus will be more fully appreciated.

The delay before the priests consumed the shewbread is also teaching that the acquisition of light in understanding spiritual truth is relative to time. For *"the path of the just is as a shining light, that shineth more and more unto the perfect day.* (Proverbs 4:18).

However, one of the most important aspects related in the priests eating of the shewbread is that it was eaten on the Sabbath. It is a statement that the nature and character of Christ is not fully assimilated into human flesh until there is an entering into full Sabbath rest indicated by holy lives in harmony with the Spiritual Sabbath.

This is when spiritual Israel becomes a royal priesthood.

Some of the most significant and encouraging references to type and anti-type in Scripture are those directly connected to the life and death of Christ.

In Exodus 12:3-6 is the record of the Passover lamb being selected some days before it was slain.

As a true anti-type, Jesus was condemned to death some days before the crucifixion. See John 11:47-53.

The Passover lamb, as recorded in Exodus 12:6, was slain on the fourteenth day of Abib or Nisan. Jesus was crucified on the day that the

Jews were preparing to eat the Passover, the fourteenth day of the month of Abib or Nisan. See John 18:28: 19:14.

In Exodus 12:6 it says that the Passover lamb was slain at evening; (in the margin) between the two evenings. In Mark 15:34 the time of Jesus' death is said to be the ninth hour.

This time is the same as that recorded for the typical sacrifice in Exodus, between the two evenings. By our reckoning that would be three o'clock in the afternoon.

The day that the Saviour of the world was crucified was the preparation for the Jewish Passover. This was the same day that the typical sacrificial lamb was slain.

In the year of the crucifixion the death of the typical sacrificial lamb coincided with the death of the anti-typical Lamb. They both occurred on the same day, giving conclusive evidence of divine involvement.

The day following the crucifixion was the seventh day Sabbath. The fourteenth day of the month Abib or Nisan was the day that the sacrificial lamb was slain.

The day following, the fifteenth of the month was decreed by God to be a ceremonial Sabbath.

Christ was sacrificed on the Friday, the fourteenth day of the month Abib. This means that the day following the death of Christ was a double Sabbath, to include the ceremonial Sabbath and the seventh day Sabbath and called by the Jews a high day. See John 19:31.

What an incredible story is the sacrifice of Jesus. Not only in its display of divine love, but that Divinity ensured perfect timing for type to meet anti-type, as prophesied, on Calvary.

Jesus was prepared for the sacrifice in the exact way and at the exact time as the type had been for centuries.

In fulfilling His role as the anti-type, in harmony with prophecy, not a bone of the Saviour was broken. See Exodus 12:46 and John 19:33-36.

From the time of the first temple God's presence was with His people. However, when Jesus died on Calvary type had met anti-type and the need for an earthly sanctuary and its service no longer applied.

At the time of Jesus' death it was with a great noise that the glorious veil that separated the holy apartment from the most holy was rent from top to bottom as the Lord departed from the temple.

Yet, amazingly, the Jews still continued to use the temple in the same manner as before the death of the Lamb of God, Jesus Christ.

The trumpet is signalling loud and clear from the heavenly city of Zion to those tuned in to listen for the sound.

God's last call is being delivered with great power as the earth is lightened with the glory of the message. For the people of God, by the power of the Holy Spirit, now is a time of great light through the imparting of Scriptural knowledge.

Those who are seeking to live in harmony with God will become increasingly aware of the great light that reveals the truth of His word. While those that are allied to Satan in apathy or sinful pursuance of worldly pleasures will ignorantly be shrouded in a deep darkness.

In Revelation 18:2 it says that Babylon has fallen. If this proclaimed fall is viewed from a spiritual perspective, the world of Babylon has either been in a state of apostasy or rebellion against righteousness throughout history, and therefore unable to fall.

Regarding the confused condition of world religions, which is representative of Babylon, the above reference in verse 2 to Babylon being fallen, could be more specifically directed to the protestant daughters who left their harlot mother in an effort at reformation.

In Revelation 17:5 Babylon is described thus: *"And upon her forehead [was] a name written, MYSTERY, BABYLON THE GREAT, THE MOTHER OF HARLOTS AND ABOMINATIONS OF THE EARTH."*

In Revelation 18:2 the daughters of Babylon are depicted in a fallen state because they have broken their relationship with Christ to retain the abominable name of their harlot mother, Babylon.

The fact that they are in a fallen state shows that they were once working in harmony with God.

With the passage of time these fallen churches have become more assimilated with the mother church to display the same spirit of rebellion.

However, if the fall is a description of Babylon's relative position in the world's hierarchy, then the Papacy (Babylon) experienced a catastrophic fall in the year 1798 when the French General Berthier took the Pope prisoner.

Because the spirit that guides both a fallen church and a rebellious world are the same, the call of the messenger to Babylon applies equally to God's people in whatever part of spiritual Babylon they reside.

It is a mistake to believe that any one church or organisation is wholly representative of Babylon. Babylon represents a spirit of confusion, and can apply to any situation in opposition to the law of God.

In the context used in Revelation, it is possible to be in open rebellion displaying an allegiance to the doctrines of Babylon by being a spiritual resident of that city.

It is equally possible to be living in apparent harmony with the law of Ten Commandments, but be a spiritual visitor to the same city.

In a spiritual context, residing in Babylon is more a state of mind than a geographical location. It is possible to be a member of a pure church but be a contented visitor to spiritual Babylon.

Whether a resident or a visitor to Babylon, such disloyalty will cut off a way of escaping the judgement of her plagues.

There are to be just two classes of people on the earth at the close of time. There are those who have favourably responded to God's call and have their names written in the Lamb's book of life, and also in the book of remembrance. The other class are thus described in Revelation 13:8 as worshippers of the beast:

"And all that dwell upon the earth shall worship him, whose names are not written in the book of life of the Lamb slain from the foundation of the world."

Although the beast demanding worship is portrayed as an apostate religious system, just like the dragon, it refers primarily to Satan. Of course, it will not be seen as such by those who have rejected God's Holy Spirit, which alone can reveal the truth that will be so plain to the people of God.

The purpose of Scripture is to facilitate harmony between heaven and earth. Through the agency of His Spirit, God is pleading with the whole of mankind that they accept His Holy Spirit in order to establish eternal reconciliation with His kingdom of love.

For the world of Babylon, and all those who are spiritually immature, the final evidence of their allegiance will find expression in their response to God's final call to honour His law of commandments, including the seventh day Sabbath.

Those Christians who are spiritually immature just before the return of Jesus will be laid to rest before the final battle. For those more spiritually mature the final test is one of imparted and impartial love signified by entering into God's Sabbath rest.

There is a Sabbath test for all. One is the seventh day Sabbath. The other test also includes the spiritual Sabbath.

Thus for two classes of people, there are to be two different tests relative to their spiritual growth in Christ but of equal dimension. One test brings recognition of God's sovereignty, the other testifies to God's creative power of sanctification.

Chapter 8
Perfection

To glean the truth from the word of God it is necessary to follow the Bible instructions in the matter of study. In this respect Isaiah 28:9,10 teaches that in order to fully appreciate the true significance of Scripture the method of study must include all relevant texts of a particular subject as follows:

"Whom shall he teach knowledge? and whom shall he make to understand doctrine? [them that are] weaned from the milk, [and] drawn from the breasts.

For precept [must be] upon precept, precept upon precept; line upon line, line upon line; here a little, [and] there a little:"

Using this method of study we can come to a satisfactory conclusion as regards the make-up of God's remnant at the close of probation. For example, speaking of the end time, Jesus says the following, as recorded in Matthew 7:13,14:

"Enter ye in at the strait gate: for wide [is] the gate, and broad [is] the way, that leadeth to destruction, and many there be which go in thereat: Because strait [is] the gate, and narrow [is] the way, which leadeth unto life, and few there be that find it."

With the understanding that prophecies made to the Israel of old can have equal relevance to spiritual Israel, Old Testament support for the truth above can be found in Isaiah 17:6. This also teaches that there will be comparatively few in number worthy to stand at the end of time and reads as follows:

"Yet gleaning grapes shall be left in it, as the shaking of an olive tree, two [or] three berries in the top of the uppermost bough, four [or] five in the outmost fruitful branches thereof, saith the LORD God of Israel."

The reference above teaches that at a time approaching the end of probation there is to be first a time of shaking before the emergence of a people able to stand through the final conflict involving Satan and his angels. The way the berries are dispersed throughout the tree is an indication that the people of God will also be scattered in small groups at the return of Jesus.

It is because the remnant of saints left alive at the close of probation must be perfect in character that there is such a delay in the return of Jesus. This is also the reason why God's elect at that time are so few in number when compared to the rest of mankind.

In harmony with the rest of Scripture on this subject the teaching of Jesus is that the aim of a Christian should be character perfection, as can be seen from Matthew 5:48 where it says: *"Be ye therefore perfect, even as your Father which is in heaven is perfect."*

Confirmation that God's final remnant is to be perfect is found in Revelation 22:11 where it is written: *"He that is unjust, let him be unjust still: and he which is filthy, let him be filthy still: and he that is righteous, let him be righteous still: and he that is holy, let him be holy still."*

During the history of the church there has always been an element of controversy among believers as to what constitutes an acceptable standard of behaviour in the eyes of God. Some have ventured the opinion that it is not possible for human beings to live a perfect life in harmony with the law of God.

The thought has often been expressed that God's people will be sinning until Jesus comes. To believe this error is to cast doubt on the power of God, and His ability to sanctify the sinner. This belief is also a violation of the Sabbath principle.

Observance of the seventh day Sabbath in honour of a Creator God means nothing if one is in denial regarding God's ability to sanctify the sinner.

It is a contradiction to claim that in the beginning God created the earth and man, but is now unable to sanctify and re-create man in His image.

Thus is displayed a lack of true conviction in false witness of *"Having a form of godliness, but denying the power thereof."* (2 Timothy 3:5). This being a violation of the Spiritual Sabbath principle constitutes 'the mark of the beast'.

The stark truth is that anyone who is sinning when Jesus returns is lost. Nothing but perfection has always been the standard that God has required from His people.

The righteousness of Christ is imputed to all genuine born-again Christians. Over a period of time, through the sanctifying power of the Spirit, this imputed righteousness is replaced with the imparted righteousness of Christ.

At the time that probation closes all of God's people are filled with the imparted righteousness of Christ.

Those of God's people who have not reached this stage of imparted righteousness will be sleeping in Christ. It is in holiness that the saints will see the Lord. For in Hebrews 12:14 it is written: *"Follow peace with all men, and holiness, without which no man shall see the Lord."*

Using a concordance to interpret the word perfect relevant to this study, in the Old Testament it is said to mean integrity, truth without blemish and undefiled.

In the New Testament it is interpreted as completeness of growth in mental and moral character.

The following are some further examples of the word perfect taken from both Testaments:

"When Abram was ninety years old and nine, the Lord appeared to Abram, and said unto him, I am the almighty God; walk before me, and be thou perfect." (Genesis 17:1).

"As for God, his way is perfect." (2 Samuel 22:31 and Psalm 18:30).

"The disciple is not above his Master: but every one that is perfect should be as his Master." (Luke 6:40).

The above evidence taken from the Bible is conclusive that these accounts of perfection are likened unto the perfection of God the Father and the Son Jesus Christ.

In our own strength perfection of character is an impossible goal.

If it were that we had to rely on our own power we would be full of doubt. Yet relative to light, in Jesus is the power of creation to change all that are willing whether it is now or on the resurrection day. To be in doubt in this respect would mean doubting the power of God to re-create man in His image.

The condition of imparted righteousness evolves because of an engagement of minds between the human will and the Divine. It is on earth, and on this basis, that this unique relationship must develop before it is confirmed and consummated in heaven at the marriage supper of the Lamb as stated below:

Revelation 19:9: *"And he saith unto me, Write, Blessed are they which are called unto the marriage supper of the Lamb. And he saith unto me, These are the true sayings of God."*

The important subjects of righteousness and perfection can be summed up this way: In a Christian context there are two types of righteousness and two types of perfection.

At the time a person makes a decision to follow Jesus, he or she receives the gift of the imputed righteousness of Christ, and by virtue of joining the body of Christ is credited with Christian perfection.

In the fullness of time as a Christian, one becomes blessed with the sinless perfection of imparted righteousness symbolised by the pure wedding garment and participation in the marriage supper of the Lamb.

The relative Christian perfection of imputed righteousness and the absolute sinless perfection of imparted righteousness find expression in a spiritual love one to another.

In contrast, the imperfection of self-righteousness displayed by the scribes and Pharisees gives evidence of love for self, as seen from the following rebuke of Jesus taken from Matthew 5:20:

"For I say unto you That except your righteousness shall exceed the righteousness of the scribes and Pharisees, ye shall in no case enter the kingdom of heaven."

Thus, sinless perfection of a perfect character is measured by the perfection of imparted and impartial love that is reflected by fulfilling the law of Ten Commandments.

In Matthew 19:16 is told the story of a rich man who asked Jesus: *"what good thing shall I do, that I may have eternal life?"* The following answer that Jesus gave, as recorded in verses 17-19, makes it clear that eternal life is the reward promised to those who live in harmony with God's law of Ten Commandments.

"And he said unto him, Why callest thou me good? [there is] none good but one, [that is], God: but if thou wilt enter into life, keep the commandments. He saith unto him, Which? Jesus said, Thou shalt do no murder, Thou shalt not commit adultery, Thou shalt not steal, Thou shalt not bear false witness, Honour thy father and [thy] mother: and, Thou shalt love thy neighbour as thyself."

There is a tacit acknowledgement that professing Christians should portray a high standard of moral behaviour. Yet there is evidence of a marked reluctance to stipulate any standard of guidance in this regard.

Those who have no desire to live in harmony with the law of God as set out in His Ten Commandments sometimes seek for excuses such as the assertion that *"it is not possible for man to keep the commandments."*

The question as to whether it is possible to live in harmony with God's law of Ten Commandments is the reason for the great controversy between Christ and Satan.

To defend the integrity of the law and to demonstrate that it is possible for humanity to live in harmony with its precepts is the reason why Jesus came to earth and allowed Himself to go to the Cross of Calvary.

The false claim that it is not possible for anyone to adhere to the law of Ten Commandments is the doctrine of Satan. This is the argument that is used by Satan in order to find a reason for attacking God, His character and His law.

Fear of giving the appearance of projecting self, results in a natural reluctance to claim character perfection. Yet within human relationships there are many examples of incredible love.

In this context, some parents would claim to have perfect offspring.

Sons and daughters would similarly claim to have perfect parents. A spouse could claim to have a perfect partner. Such blessed relationships declare and testify to the glory of God. Equally, Christian perfection and sinless perfection glorify God.

In an attempted display of reverence, and unconscious of the truth, it is not uncommon for Christians to dwell so much upon the wondrous love of God to the exclusion of the majesty to be found in the nature and the character of God.

Without some understanding of the heinous and abhorrent nature of sin that causes so much offence to a holy God, it is not possible to comprehend the reason or the cost of redemption. To make it possible for man to gain eternal life God had to suffer the pain of eternal death.

Even though the love of God is beyond measure, it is vacuously shallow to claim that it is just because of love that God forgives us our trespasses against His precepts.

In order to restore harmony to His creation, God had to suffer the pain of Gethsemane and Golgotha. Love alone could not suffice. It is by the rendering of His heart brought about by the agonising death of Christ, that God is enabled to forgive violation of His law.

Without the Cross the forgiveness of sin is a direct contradiction to the holy nature of God.

The only basis for forgiveness is declared on Calvary. That the nature of God might remain true to itself and also forgive sin, God chose the path of the Cross.

It is because of the incredible tragedy of the Cross that God is able to forgive and reinstate us to His favour. To make the blasphemous claim that God could forgive the sinner without paying the penalty for sin is to position the strength of God's sense of justice no higher than that of man. It is equally blasphemous to make the absurd claim of being saved, and escape the justice demanded by a broken law, when there is no evidence of the Christian birth revealed in a fulfilling of the law of Ten Commandments.

Our salvation is made easy by the agony of Calvary. This is the miracle of grace.

It is no longer natural for the converted heart to retain a desire for any act of sin when such action brings further pain to the God that paid so high a price for the fallen race on the Cross of Calvary.

To belittle and underestimate the effect that sin had, and still has, on God and His Son is the doctrine of the devil, and the heartache that this doctrine and practice now brings to the Godhead and God's servants, will on the day of judgement be returned to the author of rebellion and his disciples in the final death of sin.

Claiming that it is not possible for man to live without sinning is supporting the cause of Satan, and is a violation of the witness displayed by the life of Christ. It is the law of God that is the centre of the great controversy between Christ and Satan.

God cannot tolerate any attitude that does not recognise the enormous tragedy of sin and the awesome significance of His law.

It is foolish to believe the contrary with the added risk of being exposed to the same condemnation of Psalms 14:1 where it says: *"The fool hath said in his heart, There is no God. They are corrupt, they have done abominable works, there is none that doeth good."*

As recorded in Philippians 4:13, Paul has written the following words of encouragement to those who are in doubt regarding the ability to live in harmony with the law of God: *"I can do all things through Christ which strengtheneth me."*

Love is the fulfilment of God's law. Evidence as to what constitutes a fulfilment of God's law is found in Galatians 6:2 where Paul is on record as saying: *"Bear ye one another's burdens, and so fulfil the law of Christ."*

A careless lack of love results in the debris of a broken law forming an insurmountable stumbling block on the pathway to the character and beauty of Jesus Christ revealed in the majesty of God's law.

The false conviction that salvation from past sins does not include salvation from future acts of sin could have adverse eternal consequences.

It states plainly in Romans 6:6-12 that a born-again Christian is free from the acts of sin, as follows:

"Knowing this, that our old man is crucified with [him], that the body of sin might be destroyed, that **henceforth we should not serve sin***. For he that is dead is freed from sin. Now if we be dead with Christ, we believe that we shall also live with him: Knowing that Christ being raised from the dead dieth no more; death hath no more dominion over him. For in that he died, he died unto sin once: but in that he liveth, he*

liveth unto God. Likewise reckon ye also yourselves to be dead indeed unto sin, but alive unto God through Jesus Christ our Lord. **Let not sin therefore reign in your mortal body***, that ye should obey it in the lusts thereof."*

In the book of Acts 26:20 is further evidence to show that in order to gain salvation from sin it is not enough just to be forgiven our sins. In this verse it is recorded that Paul said that God's people must not only repent of their sins but also *"turn to God and do the things that would show they had repented."* (Good News version).

Jesus did not condemn the woman that was caught in the act of adultery as recorded in John chapter 8, but this was not a licence to sin because in verse 11 Jesus is on record as saying: *"go, and sin no more."*

The majority of the Ten Commandments require no more than a passive response. Such passivity is not difficult when compared to the difficulties encountered with tasks requiring a positive and active approach.

Also any false assertions concerning man's ability to obey God's commandments are casting aspersions on God's divine power as our Creator. Regarding our limitations in connection with the law of God, our failings become God's enabling.

Each commandment of God requires either a negative or positive (passive or active) response, or sometimes both, with the aim of resulting in a positive conclusion.

For example:

1: *"Thou shalt have no other Gods before me."* In answer to this commandment we need do nothing other than passively respond.

2: *"Thou shalt not make unto thee any graven image."* Again, we need do nothing other than give a passive response.

3: *"Thou shalt not take the name of thy God in vain."* Once again, only a passive response is required.

4: *"Remember the Sabbath day to keep it holy."* By bestowing honour on the seventh day Sabbath we have both a positive and passive part to play.

5: *"Honour thy father and thy mother."* An expression of honour requires a positive or active response.

6: *"Thou shalt not kill."* No more than a passive response is again required.

7: *"Thou shalt not commit adultery."* Again, this commandment is seeking no more than a passive response.

8: *"Thou shalt not steal."* Another passive response required.

9: *"Thou shalt not bear false witness."* Only a passive response required.

10: *"Thou shalt not covet."* The sin of coveting can only be counteracted by a positive expression of care that eliminates all desire to covet.

It can be clearly seen that in the majority of instances it does not require a great deal of effort on the part of man to live in harmony with God's commandments. In the situations where God requires a more positive response He will supply His Spirit to make it possible.

To prevent the moral bankruptcy of His people the God of creation instituted the law of Ten Commandments. With the support of the Holy Spirit their purpose is to perform a hedge of protection against the unhappiness brought about in a conscience seared by sin.

To those who so choose, the Lord has promised that He will make it possible for them to live in harmony with His law.

When making the covenant with His people, the Lord promised as recorded in Deuteronomy 30:6:

"And the Lord thy God will circumcise thine heart, and the heart of thy seed, to love the Lord thy God with all thine heart, and with all thy soul, that thou mayest live."

As proof concerning an ability to live according to His law of Ten Commandments, it says in Deuteronomy 30:11-14:

"The command that I am giving you today is not too difficult or beyond your reach. It is not up in the sky. You do not have to ask, Who will go up and bring it down for us, so that we can hear it and obey it? Nor is it on the other side of the ocean. You do not have to ask, Who will cross thee ocean and bring it to us, so that we may hear it? No, it is here with you. You know it and can quote it, so now obey it." (Good News version).

There should be no doubt in anyone's mind that with the help of God it is possible to live according to His commandments. This is further proved in Hebrews 10:16 where it says:

"This [is] the covenant that I will make with them after those days, saith the Lord, I will put my laws into their hearts, and in their minds will I write them."

To claim that it is impossible to live in harmony with God's law of Ten Commandments is not casting doubt on man's ability to conquer sin but is doubting the power and promises of God. Reverting to the King James Version, this is further proved by the following quotation taken from 1 Corinthians 10:13.

"There hath no temptation taken you but such as is common to man: but God is faithful, who will not suffer you to be tempted above that ye are able; but will with the temptation also make a way to escape, that ye be able to bear it."

God is preparing a specific number of people for the final conflict that is to take place between Christ and Satan, as can be seen below from Revelation 7:2-4:

"And after these things I saw four angels standing on the four corners of the earth, holding the four winds of the earth, that the wind should not blow on the earth, nor on the sea, nor on any tree. 7:2 And I saw another angel ascending from the east, having the seal of the living God: and he cried with a loud voice to the four angels, to whom it was given to hurt the earth and the sea, 7:3 Saying, Hurt not the earth, neither the sea, nor the trees, till we have sealed the servants of our God in their foreheads. 7:4 And I heard the number of them which were sealed: [and there were] sealed an hundred [and] forty [and] four thousand of all the tribes of the children of Israel."

In the above reference we have the evidence of God preparing a special number of saints to be sealed for their coming conflict with the forces of evil, and in the reference below, from Revelation 14:1, is the reference to this same number being sealed as follows:

"And I looked, and lo, a Lamb stood on the mount Sion, and with him an hundred forty and four thousand, having his Father's name written in their foreheads."

To have the Father's name in the forehead is to be filled with God's imparted righteousness.

Jesus is waiting and longing to return to earth and take His people home. Before this awe inspiring event can take place it must be proven to the whole Universe that it is possible for all types that make up humanity to live free from sin.

As He prepares His people it is a simple response that God is seeking from His professed disciples. God has so constructed the mind that it has the potential for an almost insatiable desire to know and to act in order to realise any given target.

For example, in search of monetary gain a gambler quite often becomes addicted to his habit. In a search for sporting perfection a golfer can become addicted to his sport, etc.

God is expecting from His people the same kind of dedication as Satan receives from his disciples in rebellion.

In spite of Bible evidence to the contrary Satan will still try to persuade people that it is not possible to follow Jesus and be free from sin. Yet strictly speaking this is not true. Within the mind, specially constructed by God, it is eminently possible for humanity to become holy.

When faced with choices or prompted in any way we need only to ask ourselves what would Jesus do? We should then act accordingly. With such a positive approach the mind can be trained in such a way that God is enabled to develop a character in harmony with His.

In addition to this power of the mind, under the influence of God, there is also the power of God's Holy Spirit that Jesus has promised to those who seek. In Luke 11:10 it says:

"For every one that asketh receiveth; and he that seeketh findeth; and to him that knocketh it shall be opened.

The record from Scripture gives the number of saints as a hundred and forty four thousand that are able to stand through the final tribulation. However, these are not the only ones to find salvation at the end time.

There will be those of God's people who at the time when God withdraws His Spirit from the earth will have not reached a full state of imparted righteousness and therefore not spiritually strong enough to stand at the end of time.

This number who will join those who have been laid to rest under the promise made by the *"voice from heaven"* as recorded thus in Revelation 14:13: *"And I heard a voice from heaven saying unto me, Write, Blessed are the dead which die in the Lord from henceforth: Yea, saith the Spirit, that they many rest from their labours; and their works do follow them."*

The above reference is a promise that all the saints who die during the three angels' messages of Revelation chapter 14 will take part in the special resurrection carried out by God the Father from His throne in heaven at the close of the seven last plagues. (See Revelation 17:17,18). The general resurrection to follow is carried out by Jesus.

The messages of the three angels came into effect when they became generally understood from the beginning of the time of the end in 1798.

There are some facts and figures available to us in connection with the return of Jesus. Firstly, we know that there will be a need for a worldwide spiritual revival before this momentous event. Also, because it is necessary for the last standing church to be perfect the vast majority of the end church will sleep in Christ before His return. Scripture teaches that those remaining will be the number hundred and forty four thousand as described in Revelation 14:1.

The present day church is responsible for the continued delay before the return of Jesus. Jesus cannot return a failure to a defeated church.

The situation within the great controversy that is taking place between Christ and Satan can be likened in some respects to the drama of a judgement hall where evidence is presented in support of the claims of two adversaries.

The eventual just decision is pronounced in favour of one side or the other based upon the evidence of truthful witnesses.

In the drama now taking place between Christ and Satan, even though Jesus has gained the victory, the final evidence that sets the seal upon the victory of Christ, and ensures Satan's final and complete defeat, is the evidence displayed by the 144,000 witnesses who stand perfect at the end of time filled with the imparted righteousness of Christ.

These witnesses testify to the truth that by the Spirit of God it is possible for humanity to acquire the desire and the ability to live in harmony with God's law of Ten Commandments.

This is the time referred to by Paul as recorded in 1 Corinthians 15:51-54 when corruptible bodies will put on incorruption and the mortal puts on immortality.

The corruption spoken of above is not in relation to the characters of the standing saints at that time because they have the *"Father's name written in their foreheads"* and are shown to be holy as seen from Revelation 14:1 and Revelation 22:11.

If this were not true, they would be linked with the wicked, who remain sinners, who shall be consumed with the brightness of the Lord's coming.

The Bible message of salvation clearly teaches that to cling to any act of sin will bring condemnation when God destroys all sin with an all consuming fire.

There is no sin so big that cannot be blotted out by the saving blood of Christ. Equally, any kind of sin nurtured within the heart will bring separation between man and God.

The lamb that was slain in the earthly sanctuary service performed by literal Israel was a type that represented the death of Christ. The blood of this type of sacrifice was then presented before the Lord.

However, there are important lessons to be learned from the sanctuary service. Just the presentation of blood was not in itself sufficient to make the sinner clean.

After slaying the animal, the sinner with his own hands would remove the fat from the organs of the animal that had been offered as a sin offering. He would then give the fat to the priest, who burned it upon the brazen altar.

The fat of the animal represented sin, and had to be consumed. See Leviticus 7:30,31.

All that remained of the fat was ashes, which is a demonstration of what is the judgement of God for anyone who clings to sin. In Malachi 4:3 it says that those who are consumed will become ashes under the feet of the saints.

Thus is told the final end of all who will not separate from sin. To cling to sin is to be burned with it. It can be seen just how impossible it is for Jesus to return to earth while there remains any kind of sin in His people.

Chapter 9
Circumcision and two Covenants

Fundamental to God's plan for reconciliation with mankind is the co-operation of man in order to proclaim the good news of salvation to the entire world.

With limited success, Noah was initially chosen to carry out this task. Then the Patriarch Abram was chosen by God to continue this mission. Through his son Isaac, and then through his grandson Jacob, the heavenly mission was carried forward.

When the time was fulfilled, Jacob blessed and christened his twelve sons who were to make up the beginning of Israel as a nation. This was the birth of the nation of literal Israel.

It was the God given mission of Israel to respond to the Spirit by revealing to the nations around them God's plan for saving souls.

In Genesis chapter 17 verses 5 and 15 is the record of God changing the names of Abram and Sarai to that of Abraham and Sarah. Hence the reason why different names are used in relation to time.

In pursuing reconciliation with humanity, God spoke to His servant Abraham as recorded thus in Genesis 17:7-12:

"And I will establish my covenant between me and thee and thy seed after thee in their generations for an everlasting covenant, to be a God unto thee, and to thy seed after thee. 17:8 And I will give unto thee, and to thy seed after thee, the land wherein thou art a stranger, all the land of Canaan, for an everlasting possession; and I will be their God. 17:9 And God said unto Abraham, Thou shalt keep my covenant therefore, thou, and thy seed after thee in their generations. 17:10 This [is] my covenant, which ye shall keep, between me and you and thy seed after thee; Every man child among you shall be circumcised. 17:11 And ye shall circumcise the flesh of your foreskin; and it shall be a token of the covenant betwixt me and you. 17:12 And he that is eight days old shall be circumcised among you, every man child in your generations, he that is born in the house, or bought with money of any stranger, which is not of thy seed."

By conforming to the instruction in the matter of flesh circumcision given by God, Abraham was making a public and visible declaration that he accepted the need for humanity to be restored to its original beauty of righteousness.

Because of sin the human race had fallen away from harmony with the divine will. As a consequence, the debris of a broken law had shattered the peace of heaven, which had for a time also reigned on earth.

Circumcision was intended to be the beginning of a journey in a spiritual context. For the nation of Israel, circumcision was of the flesh but the objective of God was for the nation to acquire circumcision of the spirit. This meant that it was necessary for sin to be cut away from the nature of man.

Man cannot find salvation from sin other than allowing the sword of the Spirit to cut away the sin from the heart of the problem.

The knife used by Abraham for circumcision and to cut the flesh of animal sacrifices was a substitute for the sword of the Spirit, which in the hand of God would bring about the change needed to restore the original harmony that had first existed between the Creator and those whom He had created. Thus there are two types of circumcision. The circumcision of flesh and the spiritual circumcision of the heart and mind.

At the heart of the Jewish sacrificial system of rites and ordinances was the need to teach the people of Israel that they needed to be saved from their sins.

It was through the blood of their promised Saviour, Jesus Christ that like all humanity Israel was to find salvation. Jesus was the Lamb slain through promise from the foundation of the world.

Just as there are two types of circumcision so are there two types of covenants. The first covenant can be understood by appreciating the agreement made between God and Israel through Moses.

Although already in existence, from God on Mount Sinai came the awesome public introduction of His moral law of Ten Commandments as a measure of the high standard required from Israel to bring restoration of harmony between heaven and earth.

Before God had changed Abraham's name and that of his wife, using the old name in this covenant between God and Abram, Abram was to accept God's plan of salvation, which taught the sacrificial system that was to be ratified by Jesus Christ.

Thus the first covenant was an agreement between God and His people, but the second covenant was God's promised saving power made possible by the sacrifice of Jesus Christ.

In Genesis the 15th chapter, verse 2 is the record of Abram's concern that He was without a child to be his heir.

Then God promised, *"out of thine own bowels shall be thine heir."* (Verse 4).

When his wife gave no sign of giving birth to the promised heir, Abram was constrained by his wife Sarai, to seek a continuance of his seed through the servant of his wife Hagar. However, the one to be born of this union, Ishmael, was not the child of promise that God had declared to Abram. God had made the promise through the seed of Abram and his wife, Sarai.

It says in Genesis 17:1,2 that Abram *"was ninety years old and nine"* when God made a covenant with Abram, and promised in verse 4 that he would be the *"father of many nations"*.

Set out below is a record that Abram's wife was to be the mother of the promised seed.

After changing the name of Abram to Abraham, God said as recorded in Genesis chapter 17:

"17:15 And God said unto Abraham, As for Sarai thy wife, thou shalt not call her name Sarai, but Sarah [shall] her name [be].17:16 And I will bless her, and give thee a son also of her: yea, I will bless her, and she shall be [a mother] of nations; kings of people shall be of her.17:17 Then Abraham fell upon his face, and laughed, and said in his heart, Shall [a child] be born unto him that is an hundred years old? and shall Sarah, that is ninety years old, bear? 17:18 And Abraham said unto God, O that Ishmael might live before thee! 17:19 And God said, Sarah thy wife shall bear thee a son indeed; and thou shalt call his name Isaac: and I will establish my covenant with him for an everlasting covenant, [and] with his seed after him. 17:20 And as for Ishmael, I have heard thee: Behold, I have blessed him, and will make him fruitful, and will multiply him exceedingly; twelve princes shall he beget, and I will make him a great nation. 17:21 But my covenant will I establish with Isaac, which Sarah shall bear unto thee at this set time in the next year.17:22 And he left off talking with him, and God went up from Abraham."

As recorded in Genesis 21:1-3 Sarah gave birth to the promised son and he was named Isaac.

It seems that the people of Israel never did grasp the fact that the law of Ten Commandments were intended to reveal the character of the Divine that they might learn to experience the Spirit of grace and peace. It is through heart circumcision that lives return to a beauty of holiness.

The nation of Israel attached more importance to their own efforts in relation to God's law rather than their need for God's Spirit.

The Galatians seemed to be plagued with the same problem as Israel because in chapter 4 verse 10 is the record of Paul reprimanding the Galatians for clinging to the old laws of ordinances saying: *"Ye observe days, and months, and times, and years".*

This is an obvious reference to the law of ordinances. However, in this chapter more than the law of ordinances were involved. The Galatians also had a distorted view of the law of the Decalogue, believing that by striving to live in harmony with its precepts to the exclusion of Christ, it would be according to the will of God.

The key difference brought to light by Paul is that neither Jew nor Gentile was any longer under the jurisdiction of the law because of the sacrifice of Christ. They were free from its penalty, and because of the promised Holy Spirit free from the slavery to sin, as Paul pointed out by saying in verse 6:

"And because ye are sons, God hath sent forth the Spirit of his Son into your hearts, crying Abba, Father."

Regarding the promised Saviour, prophecy had been fulfilled on the Cross, and Jesus Christ had ratified the covenant of salvation.

Conscious of the significance of this truth in connection with both the law of the Decalogue and the laws of ordinances, and aware that the gospel mission had been transferred from literal Israel to spiritual Israel, meaning Christians, Paul could write:

"For he is not a Jew, which is one outwardly in the flesh: But he is a Jew, which is one inwardly; and circumcision is that of the heart, in the spirit, and not in the letter; whose praise is not of men but of God." (Romans 2:29).

Because there is no saving grace in the law of the Decalogue or ordinances, in order to bring the Galatians back into an experience of conviction in the power and covenant of Christ, Paul explained to them the two covenants.

Jesus Christ had ratified the second covenant. The first covenant represented the birth of Ishmael and the second covenant through Isaac the child of promise, as set out below:

To the Galatians (4:21-31) when speaking of the two covenants, Paul likened the one unto Agar representing Mount Sinai. The other he compared to Isaac and the promise, which is made in Christ to all of His servants. Paul said as follows:

4:21 Tell me, ye that desire to be under the law, do ye not hear the law? 4:22 For it is written, that Abraham had two sons, the one by a bondmaid, the other by a freewoman. 4:23 But he [who was] of the bondwoman was born after the flesh; but he of the freewoman [was] by promise. 4:24 Which things are an allegory: for these are the two covenants; the one from the mount Sinai, which gendereth to bondage, which is Agar. 4:25 For this Agar is mount Sinai in Arabia, and answereth to Jerusalem which now is, and is in bondage with her children. 4:26 But Jerusalem which is above is free, which is the mother of us all. 4:27 For it is written, Rejoice, [thou] barren that bearest not; break forth and cry, thou that travailest not: for the desolate hath many more children than she which hath an husband. 4:28 Now we, brethren, as Isaac was, are the children of promise. 4:29 But as then he that was born after the flesh persecuted him [that was born] after the Spirit, even so [it is] now. 4:30 Nevertheless what saith the Scripture? Cast out the bondwoman and her son: for the son of the bondwoman shall not be heir with the son of the freewoman. 4:31 So then, brethren, we are not children of the bondwoman, but of the free."

Within the law there is no power that enables one to live in harmony with its precepts. Therefore, there can be no promise in the law. The promised power to live in harmony with the law comes through the Spirit of Jesus Christ.

In this way Paul is making the distinction between the birth of Ishmael representing the law without promise, and the promise made through the birth of Isaac.

The Ten Commandments were given to the nation of Israel depicting a high standard of morality, and a pleasant way of life. However, there could be no promise of joy just by a portrayal of the law, or by effort to live in harmony with the law.

As with all of God's people, sin separates man from his Creator and from harmony with the law. Therefore, the people of Israel were taught the message of salvation and the need to acquire the Spirit that would fulfil the promise that was lacking in the law.

By fulfilling the demands of the law, Jesus was the perfect guide and example to His disciples.

The promise that was initially given to the nation of Israel has an equal implication for all nations. For in Galatians 3: 14 it says:

"That the blessing of Abraham might come on the Gentiles through Jesus Christ; that we might receive the promise of the Spirit through faith."

In the same book, 3:8 it further says:

"And the Scripture, foreseeing that God would justify the heathen through faith, preached before the gospel unto Abraham, saying, In thee shall all nations be blessed."

The first covenant that God made with man was based upon man living in harmony with His law of commandments as thus revealed in Deuteronomy 7: 9:

"Know therefore that the LORD thy God, he God, the faithful God, which keepeth covenant and mercy with them that love him and keep his commandments to a thousand generations."

Knowing that in their own strength, it was not possible for literal Israel to live in harmony with His commandments, God made provision for victory through the promise of a second covenant through faith in Christ.

Evidence of this second covenant can be found in Genesis 3:15 where it says:

"And I will put enmity between thee and the woman, and between thy seed and her seed; it shall bruise thy head, and thou shalt bruise his heel."

The fact that the second covenant of grace through faith was always available is confirmed in Galatians 3:17 where it says:

"And this I say, the covenant, that was confirmed before of God in Christ, the law, which was four hundred and thirty years after, cannot disannul, that it should make the promise of none effect."

The problem with literal Israel was that *"they being ignorant of God's righteousness, and going about to establish their own righteousness, have not submitted themselves unto the righteousness of God."* (Romans 10:3)

It is a common error to believe that the law at Mount Sinai came first, and that somehow grace was added because of the inability of man to live in harmony with the law of Ten Commandments.

It never was the will of God to unconditionally substitute grace for rebellion. Yet grace was always available as proved by Galatians 3:17 above.

That there be no mistake regarding an understanding of God's ultimate plan for His people, it is written thus in Jeremiah 31:31-33:

"Behold, the days come, saith the LORD, that I will make a new covenant with the house of Israel, and with the house of Judah: 31:32 Not according to the covenant that I made with their fathers in the day [that] I took them by the hand to bring them out of the land of Egypt; which my covenant they brake, although I was an husband unto them, saith the LORD: 31:33 But this [shall be] the covenant that I will make

with the house of Israel; After those days, saith the LORD, I will put my law in their inward parts, and write it in their hearts; and will be their God, and they shall be my people."

The above quotation is clearly stating that the day will come when God will rule in the hearts of His people, spiritual Israel, by a transformation of character that places His law in their hearts.

In 2 Corinthians 3:3 it further says:

"Forasmuch as ye are] manifestly declared to be the epistle of Christ ministered by us, written not with ink, but with the Spirit of the living God; not in tables of stone, but in fleshly tables of the heart."

Chapter 10
Two Resurrections & Return of Elijah

The first death is not to be considered as a final elimination of life but a state of rest until the resurrection whether it is of the righteous or the wicked.

As confirmation that the first death is regarded as a state of sleep, Paul says in 1 Corinthians 15:20: *"But now is Christ risen from the dead, and become the firstfruits of them that slept."*

If life of the soul continued at death of the body there would be no need for a resurrection.

The record in Scripture is that there will be two main resurrections. The first resurrection is to take place at the return of Jesus as recorded in the following quotation taken from John 5:24-28:

"Verily, verily, I say unto you, He that heareth my word, and believeth on him that sent me, hath everlasting life, and shall not come into condemnation; but is passed from death unto life 5:25 Verily, verily, I say unto you, The hour is coming, and now is, when the dead shall hear the voice of the Son of God: and they that hear shall live. 5:26 For as the Father hath life in himself; so hath he given to the Son to have life in himself; 5:27 And hath given him authority to execute judgment also, because he is the Son of man. 5:28 Marvel not at this for the hour is coming, in which all that are in the graves shall hear his voice."

Again speaking of His return and the resurrection of the saints Jesus said the following, as recorded in Matthew 24:30,31:

"And then shall appear the sign of the Son of man in heaven: and then shall all the tribes of the earth mourn, and they shall see the Son of man coming in the clouds of heaven with power and great glory. 24:31 And he shall send his angels with a great sound of a trumpet, and they shall gather together his elect from the four winds, from one end of heaven to the other."

As can be seen from the following text taken from 1 Thessalonians 4:13-17, in the day of the Lord both the dead and the living saints will join in the air with Jesus and the retinue of angels:

"But I would not have you to be ignorant, brethren, concerning them which are asleep, that ye sorrow not, even as others which have no hope. 4:14 For if we believe that Jesus died and rose again, even so them also which sleep in Jesus will God bring with him. 4:15 For this we say unto you by the word of the Lord, that we which are alive [and] remain unto

the coming of the Lord shall not prevent them which are asleep. 4:16 For the Lord himself shall descend from heaven with a shout, with the voice of the archangel, and with the trump of God: and the dead in Christ shall rise first: 4:17 Then we which are alive [and] remain shall be caught up together with them in the clouds, to meet the Lord in the air: and so shall we ever be with the Lord."

At the time of the risen saints, it says in Revelation 19:21 of the living wicked at that time: *"And the remnant were slain with the sword of him that sat upon the horse, which [sword] proceeded out of his mouth: and all the fowls were filled with their flesh."*

At the time when the dead saints are raised, it also says in Revelation 20:5, of the rest of the dead: (wicked): *"But the rest of the dead lived not again until the thousand years were finished. This [is] the first resurrection."*

At this time of the first resurrection when Jesus returns in power and glory, the earth is made desolate and the wicked are destroyed by the brightness of His coming. (2 Thessalonians 2:8).

This is the time that Jeremiah spoke of as recorded thus in 4:25:

"I beheld, and, lo, there was no man, and all the birds of the heavens were fled."

The circumstances then prevailing means that Satan and his angels are symbolically chained by circumstances because there is no one left alive on the earth to be tempted. As set out below, Revelation 20:2,3 says that this state will last for 1000 years.

"And I saw an angel come down from heaven, having the key of the bottomless pit and a great chain in his hand. 20:2 And he laid hold on the dragon, that old serpent, which is the Devil, and Satan, and bound him a thousand years, 20:3 And cast him into the bottomless pit, and shut him up, and set a seal upon him, that he should deceive the nations no more, till the thousand years should be fulfilled: and after that he must be loosed a little season."

The second resurrection takes place at the end of the prophesied 1000 years.

After the first resurrection, the devil and the fallen angels are thus left with a thousand years during which time they are to reflect on the consequences of the fall.

This might appear to be such a long time for no apparent reason. However, there is a good reason why it was considered necessary for such a long time to elapse before the return of Jesus to make earth the final dwelling place for the saints.

During the thousand years when Satan and his angels are upon the desolate earth, the saints will be given the task of judging the rebel angels and the rest of the wicked.

In 1 Corinthians 6:2,3 Paul is confirming this truth by saying that the saints are to judge the wicked including fallen angels, thus:

"Do ye not know that the saints shall judge the world? And if the world shall be judged by you, are ye unworthy to judge the smallest matters? 3 Know ye not that ye shall judge angels? How much more things that pertain to this life."

Further confirmation that the saints are to sit in judgement on the wicked who are then in their graves or lying dead on the ground can be found in Revelation 20:4-6, where it says:

"And I saw thrones, and they sat upon them, and judgment was given unto them: and [I saw] the souls of them that were beheaded for the witness of Jesus, and for the word of God, and which had not worshipped the beast, neither his image, neither had received [his] mark upon their foreheads, or in their hands; and they lived and reigned with Christ a thousand years. 20:5 But the rest of the dead lived not again until the thousand years were finished. This [is] the first resurrection. 20:6 Blessed and holy [is] he that hath part in the first resurrection: on such the second death hath no power, but they shall be priests of God and of Christ, and shall reign with him a thousand years."

It says in Revelation 20:3 that at the end of the thousand years the devil and his angels will be loosed for a little season at the time of the second resurrection, which is of the wicked that are left dead upon or in the earth during the thousand years.

The resurrection of the wicked gives the devil and his angels an opportunity to again tempt and deceive before the third coming of Jesus and the resulting second and final death.

The final return of Jesus will be the time when He will create a new earth wherein will dwell righteousness and the New Jerusalem. Read the following account of this momentous event from Revelation 21:1-7:

"And I saw a new heaven and a new earth: for the first heaven and the first earth were passed away; and there was no more sea. 21:2 And I John saw the holy city, new Jerusalem, coming down from God out of heaven, prepared as a bride adorned for her husband. 21:3 And I heard a great voice out of heaven saying, Behold, the tabernacle of God [is] with men, and he will dwell with them, and they shall be his people, and God himself shall be with them, [and be] their God. 21:4 And God shall wipe away all tears from their eyes; and there shall be no more death,

neither sorrow, nor crying, neither shall there be any more pain: for the former things are passed away. 21:5 And he that sat upon the throne said, Behold, I make all things new. And he said unto me, Write: for these words are true and faithful. 21:6 And he said unto me, It is done. I am Alpha and Omega, the beginning and the end. I will give unto him that is athirst of the fountain of the water of life freely. 21:7 He that overcometh shall inherit all things; and I will be his God, and he shall be my son."

Concerning a message of Elijah in connection with His first mission on earth, Jesus revealed an important truth in connection with His Second Coming and the same message of Elijah.

Jesus told the disciples that the same preparation that had been made to herald in His first appearance on earth would be repeated before His Second Coming.

This makes the message that He discussed at that time, now more relevant for today's disciples.

It was to proclaim the heavenly message that the people of Israel needed to be saved from sin that John the Baptist was commissioned to preach in order to prepare the nation for the coming of their promised Redeemer.

The message at that time was not a complete success but it needed to be preached. There will be a repeat of history in preparation for the Second Coming of Jesus.

The message calling people to be forgiven from their sins and to bestow honour on the law of God will need to be repeated before the return of Jesus.

In Malachi 4:5 it says:

"Behold, I will send you Elijah the prophet before the coming of the great and dreadful day of the Lord."

Aware of the prophecy concerning the coming of Elijah, the disciples, using the Greek form of the word Elijah, expressed their puzzlement as recorded in Matthew 17:10-13 as follows:

"And his disciples asked him, saying, Why then say the scribes that Elias must first come? 17:11 And Jesus answered and said unto them, Elias truly shall first come, and restore all things. 17:12 But I say unto you, That Elias is come already, and they knew him not, but have done unto him whatsoever they listed. Likewise shall also the Son of man suffer of them. 17:13 Then the disciples understood that he spake unto them of John the Baptist."

From the answer given by Jesus above we are meant to understand that when making reference to the return of Elijah, Scripture is making reference to the message of Elijah. In this way John the Baptist was proclaiming the message of Elijah when calling the nation of Israel to repentance and hearken unto the call for spiritual harmony with a holy law.

An example of the mission given to Elijah can be found as follows in 1 Kings 18:21:

And Elijah came unto all the people, and said, How long halt ye between two opinions? if the LORD [be] God, follow him: but if Baal, [then] follow him. And the people answered him not a word."

We read from Malachi 4:5 that we shall hear the message of Elijah *"the prophet before the coming of the great and dreadful day of the Lord."*

It is very important to be aware of this message of Elijah. It is a call to heed the commandments of God and to recognise their significance in relation to human destiny. This message calls for a decision as to whom we give our allegiance to obey. Is it to be the God of creation or another form of Baal?

SECTION TWO
Chapter 11
Prophetic time Scale

As an indication of its importance, within Scripture there is a period or length of time that is referred to seven times. Because this period of time is not always described the same way it is necessary to understand how the different descriptions have the same meaning.

In Daniel 7:25 the period of time is counted as *"a time and times and the dividing of time"*. In Daniel 12:7 it is said to be *"a time, times, and an half."*

In Revelation 11:2 it is described as *"forty and two months"*. Revelation 11:3 describes the same length of time as *"a thousand two hundred and threescore days."* Revelation 12:6 also records this time as *a thousand two hundred and threescore days "*

In Revelation 12:14 it is called *a time, and times, and half a time."* The final record from Revelation 13:5 describes this length of time as *"forty and two months."*

In order to understand what the terminology *"time"* means it is necessary to find the answer in Scripture.

From Daniel 4:23 we learn that King Nebuchadnezzar dwelt with the beasts of the field till seven times or seven years passed over him. Thus a time is equal to one year.

When all the references in connection with this length of time are studied in their proper context it becomes obvious that the terminology, *"times"* means two years.

This makes a time, and times, and half a time of Revelation 12:14 a total of three and half years. This would also apply to Daniel 12:7. In Daniel 7:25 the half time is described as a dividing of time.

Because the time referred to is meant to be prophetic time it is necessary to apply the Bible rule of counting each day for a year. The following Scripture references of Numbers 14:34 and Ezekiel 14:6 give evidence in support of this fact:

"After the number of the days in which ye searched the land, [even] forty days, each day for a year, shall ye bear your iniquities, [even] forty years, and ye shall know my breach of promise."

And when thou hast accomplished them, lie again on thy right side, and thou shalt bear the iniquity of the house of Judah forty days: I have appointed thee each day for a year".

A Bible year is reckoned as 360 days. This means that the 1260 days (years) above consist of 1260 years of 360 days each year.

In the seven references above, Scripture describes the 1260 years as the length of time that God's saints would suffer persecution at the hand of the beast power dressed in its garb of Christianity.

Throughout the history of God's true church there has always been the opposition of Satan and the fallen angels to contend with. This opposition has taken many forms as the enemy strives in different ways to achieve the one goal of defeating the people of God as they seek to live in harmony with the decree proclaimed from Mount Sinai by their Creator.

In order to obtain an understanding of hidden truth in God's word it is necessary to be aware of some clear rules governing the acquisition of spiritual knowledge. God does not set out truth so clearly defined that saint and sinner alike understand it to the same degree.

If the truth of God's word were so easy to comprehend the controversy between Christ and Satan would exist on a level confined by the intellect of man. The need to desire and to acquire the Spirit of God would not be an issue in the controversy between good and evil.

For example, if the word of God were to clearly set out in plain language the true identity of the anti-Christ beast power that is mentioned in the book of Revelation, without any need for an acquisition of the Spirit, then the objective of preparing a Spiritual people would be defeated.

The word of God is not difficult for His people to understand, but to those who find no joy in sacred teachings they are foolishness. In 1 Corinthians 2:14 and 2 Corinthians 10:4, 5 Paul is recorded as saying:

"But the natural man receiveth not the things of the Spirit of God: for they are foolishness unto him: neither can he know them, because they are spiritually discerned."

"For the weapons of our warfare are not carnal, but mighty through God to the pulling down of strong holds Casting down imaginations, and every high thing that exalteth itself against the knowledge of God, and bringing into captivity every thought to the obedience of Christ."

The 1260 years that are mentioned seven times in relation to the persecution suffered by the people of God are linked to the fact that the persecution is always as a result of the power of the beast.

The beast of Revelation seeking worship is described in different ways, but essentially when in rebellion, the power of the beast is really Satan using whatever means he finds most effective in securing his desired end.

In its earthly form in Revelation 13:2 this beast is described as a leopard receiving power from the dragon. This is the record of Pagan Rome in the form of a dragon transferring its power to Papal Rome in the form of a leopard.

In verses 5-7 this same beast power is described as *"speaking great things and blasphemies against God"*, and recounts the 1260 years persecution of the saints

Daniel 7:25 also provides evidence of this same power speaking *"great words against the most High."* Again there is the same record of the saints being persecuted for the same 1260 years.

The leopard beast that is mentioned above from Revelation 13:2 is shown to be a symbol of Roman Christianity as this power persecutes the saints for 1260 years.

In its present form this persecuting power did not emerge until the fall of the four world kingdoms that preceded it. The prophet Daniel gives an account of these kingdoms.

In the second chapter of the book of Daniel is the record of how Daniel interpreted the vision, which came to King Nebuchadnezzar in a dream. The king dreamed of a huge figure. This figure had a head of fine gold, a breast and arms of silver, a belly and thighs of brass, and legs of iron. Its feet were part iron and part clay.

Daniel gave the king an understanding of the dream involving the four kingdoms as follows: 2:31 *Thou, O king, sawest, and behold a great image. This great image, whose brightness [was] excellent, stood before thee; and the form thereof [was] terrible. 2:32 This image's head [was] of fine gold, his breast and his arms of silver, his belly and his thighs of brass, 2:33 His legs of iron, his feet part of iron and part of clay. 2:34 Thou sawest till that a stone was cut out without hands, which smote the image upon his feet [that were] of iron and clay, and brake them to pieces. 2:35 Then was the iron, the clay, the brass, the silver, and the gold, broken to pieces together, and became like the chaff of the summer threshingfloors; and the wind carried them away, that no place was found for them: and the stone that smote the image became a great mountain, and filled the whole earth. 2:36 This [is] the dream; and we will tell the interpretation thereof before the king. 2:37 Thou, O king, [art] a king of kings: for the God of heaven hath given thee a kingdom, power, and strength, and glory. 2:38 And wheresoever the children of men dwell, the beasts of the field and the fowls of the heaven hath he given into thine hand, and hath made thee ruler over them all. Thou [art] this head of gold. 2:39 And after thee shall arise another kingdom inferior to thee, and another third kingdom of brass, which shall bear rule over all the earth. 2:40 And the fourth kingdom shall be strong as iron: forasmuch as iron breaketh in pieces and subdueth all [things]: and as iron that breaketh all these, shall it break in pieces and bruise. 2:41 And whereas thou sawest the feet and toes, part of potters' clay, and part of iron, the kingdom shall be divided; but there shall be in it of the strength of the iron, forasmuch as thou sawest the iron mixed with miry clay. 2:42 And [as] the toes of the feet [were] part of iron, and part of clay, [so] the kingdom shall be partly strong, and partly broken. 2:43* **And whereas thou sawest iron mixed with miry clay, they shall mingle themselves with the seed of men: but they shall not cleave one to another, even as iron is not mixed with clay.** *2:44 And in the days of these kings shall the God of heaven set up a kingdom, which shall never be destroyed: and the kingdom shall not be left to other people, [but] it shall break in pieces and consume all these kingdoms, and it shall stand for ever."*

The above account of history gives an incredible insight into prophecy that began way in the past and reaches fulfilment at the end of time. God told Nebuchadnezzar through the prophet Daniel that Nebuchadnezzar was the kingdom of fine gold. History relates that the kingdom of silver to follow Nebuchadnezzar's kingdom of gold represented Media-Persia. Then followed Greece symbolised as brass. The fourth kingdom was one of iron representing Pagan Rome. This kingdom broke up to leave the nations seen as part iron and part clay consisting mainly of Western Europe. The prophecy predicts that the nations that make up mainly Western Europe will never unite to become one kingdom.

Verse 43 above says that in spite of rulers attempting to unite the nations through intermarriage the nations will *"not cleave one to another, even as iron is not mixed with clay."*

There have been many attempts throughout European history to bring about unity of these nations, but the prophecy has remained intact, and the kingdoms that were formed after the fall of the Roman Empire are still divided.

It says in verse 44 above that during the time of this break-up of the western nations that there will not emerge another empire with their involvement. The Bible record of Daniel 2:44 says that at the end of time Jesus is to set up His kingdom and that it *'shall stand for ever'*.

Chapter 12
Papacy in Prophecy

In Daniel chapter 7 is the record of a vision that came to Daniel during the first year of Belshazzer's reign (553 B.C.).

In this dream Daniel was shown the history of nations as applied mainly to the Western Hemisphere and similar to Nebuchadnezzar's dream of the *"great image"* recorded in the previous chapter. The difference between the two dreams was in the way the nations were described.

To Daniel the emerging nations were described as a lion depicting the golden Babylonian Empire of Nebuchadnezzar. Then followed the bear denoting the kingdom of Medo-Persia. A leopard beast representing the kingdom of Grecia (Greece) followed this.

The fourth beast is portrayed differently to the preceding three beasts. The iron like nature of the Pagan Roman Empire is described thus in verse 7 of chapter 7:

*"After this I saw in the night visions, and behold a fourth beast, dreadful and terrible, and strong exceedingly; and it had great iron teeth: it devoured and brake in pieces, and stamped the residue with the feet of it: and it [was] diverse from all the beasts that [were] before it; and it **had ten horns**."*

Our study will show that the fourth beast of the above verse is a reference to Pagan Rome. The ten horns mentioned above are the ten kingdoms that replaced the broken Roman Empire.

History relates the startling account of the nations that fulfil exactly the predictions given by Scripture. We have today the kingdoms of mainly Western Europe, but also relate to North Africa and the Middle East that replaced the Roman Empire.

A composition of the same four beasts referred to above is described in Revelation chapter 13:1, 2.

This composition of all four beasts makes up the fifth beast or kingdom, which is representative of the apostate Babylonian Church of Papal Rome.

Speaking of this composition, it is said that at the fall of the first four kingdoms mentioned above there was to emerge ten kingdoms and the fifth kingdom of Papal Rome.

This fifth kingdom in the form of Papal Rome emerged to replace Pagan Rome dressed in the garb of Christianity. The ten kingdoms, above, of mainly Western Europe, also followed the fall of Pagan Rome.

In Daniel 7:8 is an account of the emergence of the Roman Catholic Church under the description of *"the little horn."* described as with eyes *"like the eyes of a man"*. The Roman Catholic Church has at its head the figure of a man viewed with veneration.

We know that it is an anti-Christ power because of the record in Daniel 7:11. In verse 10 we are carried forward to the judgement. Then in verse 11 it further says of Papal Rome:

7:11 *"I beheld then because of the voice of the great words which the horn spake: I beheld [even] till the beast was slain, and his body destroyed, and given to the burning flame."*

In verse 8, as follows, there is the account of four nations being described as four horns. This verse also speaks of the Roman Church under the title of *"little horn"* defeating the other three horns or nations as they are *"plucked up by the roots"* making it possible for the Roman Church to become a dominant power among the nations as it replaced Pagan Rome.

7:8 *"I considered the horns, and, behold, there came up among them another* **little horn**, *before whom there were* **three of the first horns plucked up by the roots:** *and, behold, in this horn [were] eyes like* **the eyes of man**, *and a mouth speaking great things."*

Evidence from truly Protestant thinkers express no doubts regarding the identity of the power described in verse 8 as the **"little horn"** as it emerges among the other horns. This horn is said to be different from the others.

In verse 8 above it says that before the power depicted as the little horn, the other three horns were *"plucked up by the roots."*

Because of its different nature and its record of persecution, true Protestants believe that this power of the **little horn** is a reference to the Roman Catholic Church as it emerges to become a dominant power among the nations.

Through the eyes of inspiration, in verse 20 it was seen with a *"look more stout"* or more masterful than his fellows."

In support for the accuracy of the prophecy regarding the little horn, the Catholic Emperor Zeno (474-491 A.D.) arranged a treaty with the Ostrogoths in 487 resulting in the eradication of the Heruli five years later in 493 A.D.

From among the three horns mentioned in verse 8, the first horn was thus plucked up by the roots.

The Catholic Emperor Justinian (527-565 A.D.) ruled three kinds of Christians. They were Arians, who believed that Jesus was basically human, Monophysites who believed Jesus to be divine, and Catholics who firmly believed Jesus to be both human and divine. In 533 A.D. Justinian officially declared that the Pope of Rome was the "head of all holy churches".

Through his general Belisarius, Justinian exterminated the Arian Vandals in 534 A.D. Belisarius then returned to Italy to eventually defeat the Ostrogoths in March 538 A.D. There followed some skirmishes for a number of years, but the prophecy of Daniel 7:8 was fulfilled.

In this way were the Heruli, the Vandals and the Ostrogoths *"plucked up by the roots,"* as recorded in verse 8 above.

The reason that the three horns were plucked by their roots was because of opposition to Papal dominance.

The emperor Justinian decreed the bishop of Rome to be head of all churches in A.D. 533. However, this edict could not go into effect before the defeat of Ostrogoths in A.D. 538.

Thus it was that the little horn emerged in 538 A.D. to replace Pagan Rome with Papal Rome or the Roman Catholic Church.

This church reigned supreme for 1260 years from 538 A.D. to 1798 A.D. when the French General Berthier took the Pope prisoner, stripping him of civil and ecclesiastical power, and for a time abolished the papal government. Thus is fulfilled the 1260 years prophecy of the previous chapter that is mentioned in Scripture seven times.

Pope Pius V1 died in exile in Valence, France, on August 29, 1799.

During this period of 1260 years from 538 A.D. till 1798 A.D. this religious power was in apostasy against God, and Daniel 7:25 declares that during this time it did *"wear out the saints of the most High"*.

From Revelation 13:3 we learn that this beast is described as a power which became *"wounded unto death."* This is a reference to the Pope being imprisoned in the year 1798 A.D.

It goes on to say that this power would recover as *"his deadly wound is healed: and that all the world wondered after the beast."*

Although with less power, the deadly wound began to heal with the re-establishment of the new Pope in March 14, 1800.

Complete healing cannot take place until the church in apostasy again receives the support of the state. This restoration of power will be discussed further in chapter 23.

Of the little horn power, it says in Daniel 7:21, 25:

"I beheld, and the same horn made war with the saints, and prevailed against them; 7:25 And he shall speak [great] words against the most High, and shall wear out the saints of the most High, and think to change times and laws: and they shall be given into his hand until a time and times and the dividing of time."

Another dimension is brought to view regarding the little horn beast wearing out the saints, and seeking to change times and laws. It also makes mention of the length of time allotted to the beast power.

It denotes time, times and dividing of time. In this way the above text is referring to the 1260 years that it was to persecute the saints referred to in chapter 11.

We have read from verse 25 that the power of the little horn (Papal Rome) would *"think to change times and laws."*

Reading that the little horn power can only *"think to change times and laws"* the reference to law in verse 25 must be a reference to divine law.

It would be no great achievement to change a man made law. The only ones guilty of attempting to change the law of God are among those who falsely claim to be followers of the way led by Jesus Christ.

We can learn from Scripture and history that the leading power seeking to change God's times and laws is the Roman Catholic Church. There is no secret attached to this claim as proved by the statements of admission regarding Sunday worship by this apostate church.

In this deliberate act of arrogance, described as the little horn, the Catholic Church has made changes eliminating the second commandment forbidding the worship of graven images in order to justify the use of religious relics.

To retain the number of commandments to ten the last commandment has become two. The fourth commandment has become the third and changed from the seventh day of the week to the first.

These attempted changes is the reason that Christendom as a whole bestows honour on the first day of the week, and names it the Christian Sabbath in opposition to the day instigated by God.

Chapter 13
Destiny Foretold

Less than two years after the vision of chapter 7 in 551 B.C., Daniel received another vision similar to the one in chapter 7, but with important differences.

The vision of chapter 7 involved **four** nations, including Babylon where Daniel was residing, and ends with a detailed account of the ten horns and the little horn. (The ten kingdoms of Europe and Papal Rome).

In his vision of chapter 8, Daniel is experiencing a dream that gives the history of **three** nations that excludes Babylon, but includes an important message regarding the cleansing of the sanctuary in Daniel 8:14. This important subject of cleansing the sanctuary will be studied in the next chapter.

The vision of Daniel chapter 8 begins in verse 3 and reads:

"Then I lifted up mine eyes, and saw, and, behold, there stood before the river a ram which had [two] horns: and the [two] horns [were] high; but one [was] higher than the other, and the higher came up last. 8:4 I saw the ram pushing westward, and northward, and southward; so that no beasts might stand before him, neither [was there any] that could deliver out of his hand; but he did according to his will, and became great."

Seeking an understanding of the above verses, Daniel is told in verse 20 that *"The ram (quoted above) which thou sawest having two horns are the kings of Media and Persia."*

Speaking of the two-horned ram, (Media-Persia) in verse 3 it says that both horns were high, but one was higher and came up last. The two-horned Empire here represents two nations.

Beginning as an ally of Media, Persia is symbolised as the horn that was higher and came up last, as it became leader of the alliance.

This two-horned ram representing Media-Persia is described in chapter 7, verse 5 as a bear. Whereas in chapter 8 in the verse above, one horn of the ram is said to be higher, indicating the dominance of Persia, in chapter 7, the bear raising itself up on one side denotes Persia's leading role.

It will be noted that the power of Media-Persia depicted as the ram, by defeating Babylon *"became great."*

In verses 5-8 an account of the vision continues as Daniel records:

*"And as I was considering, behold, an he goat came from the west on the face of the whole earth, and touched not the ground: and the goat [had] a notable horn between his eyes. 8:6 And he came to the ram that had [two] horns, which I had seen standing before the river, and ran unto him in the fury of his power. 8:7 And I saw him come close unto the ram, and he was moved with choler against him, and smote the ram, and brake his two horns: and there was no power in the ram to stand before him, but he cast him down to the ground, and stamped upon him: and there was none that could deliver the ram out of his hand. 8:8 Therefore the he goat **waxed very great**: and when he was strong, the great horn was broken; and for it came up **four notable ones** toward the four winds of heaven."*

(These notable horns mentioned above are not to be confused with the little horn and three horns of Daniel 7:8, where it speaks of Papal Rome).

The goat quoted above is identified in verse 21 as the *"rough goat the king of Grecia."* (Alexander the great). Thus this verse identifies the kingdom of Greece as the one that defeated the kingdom of Media-Persia as follows:

"And the rough goat [is] the king of Grecia: and the great horn that [is] between his eyes [is] the first king."

Note that the goat (Greece) excelled in power over the ram (Media-Persia) and *"waxed very great."*

He that conquers is greater than the one that is conquered. So even though the empire of Media-Persia was described as *"great"* the conqueror, Alexander the Great of Greece was described in verse 8 as ***"very great"***.

It was when the kingdom of Greece was strong and seemingly unassailable that it became weak with division after the death of its leader, Alexander the Great.

In verse 8 we learn that at the height of its strength, the power of the goat (Greece) was broken as it became replaced by four contenders for power. (*four notable ones*).

On the death of Alexander the Great, there emerged contention among those who claimed to be heirs to the kingdom. Eventually the number was reduced to the four commanders of the army. Each one of the four notable ones described in verse 8 assumed the title of Monarch.

Verse 9 relates *"out of one of them came forth a **little horn**, which waxed exceeding great, toward the south, and toward the east, and toward the pleasant land."*

As an indication of its extensive influence on so many people over a long period of time, the little horn power is described in verse 9 as *"exceedingly great"*. In relation to the little horn power the foretold history continues in verse 10:

"And it waxed great, [even] to the host of heaven; and it cast down [some] of the host and of the stars to the ground, and stamped upon them. 8:11 Yea, he magnified [himself] even to the prince of the host, and by him the daily [sacrifice] was taken away, and the place of his sanctuary was cast down. 8:12 And an host was given him against the daily sacrifice by reason of transgression, and it cast down the truth to the ground; and it practised, and prospered."

The identity of this third major power of the little horn described by Daniel is not so clearly defined, as were the previous powers of Media-Persia and Grecia. The power mentioned above has the same title as the little horn of Daniel 7:8.

The **little** horn of Daniel 7 was identified as representing the Roman Catholic Church, but at the time now under study from chapter 8 the church did not exist. Even though this is a later chapter, the date now being referred to began earlier than the appearance of the little horn of Daniel chapter 7 verse 8. Papal Rome did not emerge until after the break-up of Pagan Rome.

The next major power following the initial four commanders, who contented to rule Greece, after the death of Alexander the great, is known to be first Pagan and then much later Papal Rome.

The message is clearly stating that the little horn of verse 9 refers to both Pagan and Papal Rome.

With the exception of Pagan and Papal Rome no other major power in the Western Hemisphere followed Alexander the Great. The line of prophecy extended so far into the future that it admits to no other conclusion than that the prophecy relates to both Pagan and Papal Rome.

Although the little horn of chapter 7 spoke only of the Papacy, here in chapter 8 Pagan and Papal are nevertheless combined.

Therefore, the little horn power of chapter 8, verse 9 represents the combined powers of Pagan and Papal Rome. Pagan Rome first took the title of little horn before the Roman Catholic Church carried on the title and mantle of Rome exchanging the title of Pagan Rome for Papal Rome.

The kingdoms to emerge from the broken Roman Empire relate to the ten kingdoms (ten horns) of Europe, North Africa, and the Middle East, and finally the domination of the little horn (Papal Rome) as it entered on to the world scene.

The power of Pagan Rome brought about the death of Jesus. Daniel 9:25 identifies Jesus as *"Messiah the Prince."*

It might seem strange that those with so much influence as Pagan and Papal Rome are described diminutively as the *"little horn"*. The reason for this could be that in its religious phase Rome had an innocuous and imperceptible beginning.

Magnifying himself to the prince (Jesus) referred to above by the little horn, and casting the truth to the ground, Daniel 8 11, 12, must be a reference to Pagan Rome. The Roman Empire extended its kingdom and *"waxed exceedingly great, toward the south, and toward the east, and toward the pleasant land"* of Judea. (Verse 9).

In the Bible a beast can be a symbol of a nation or power. A beast could represent civil power alone, or sometimes both civil and ecclesiastical power.

Scripture teaches that in its recovered state, this power that began as the little horn will be in opposition to the true people of God until the resurrection of the saints and the return of Jesus as:

"KING OF KINGS, AND LORD OF LORDS." (Rev. 19:16).

In Revelation 13 1-6 there is the following account of the beast power that it is to reign in the earth during its closing stages:

*"13:1 And I stood upon the sand of the sea, and saw a beast rise up out of the sea, having seven heads and ten horns, and upon his horns ten crowns, and upon his heads the name of blasphemy. 13:2 And the beast which I saw was like unto a leopard, and his feet were as [the feet] of a bear, and his mouth as the mouth of a lion: and the dragon gave him his power, and his seat, and great authority. 13:3 And I saw one of his heads as it were wounded to death; and his deadly wound was healed: and all the world wondered after the beast. 13:4 And they worshipped the dragon which gave power unto the beast: and they worshipped the beast, saying, Who [is] like unto the beast? who is able to make war with him? 13:5 And there was given unto him a mouth speaking great things and blasphemies; and power was given unto him to continue forty [and] two months. 13:6 And he opened his mouth in blasphemy against God, to blaspheme his name, and his tabernacle, and them that dwell in heaven. 13:7 And it was given unto him to make war with the saints, and to overcome them: and power was given him over all kindreds, and tongues, and nati*ons. *13:8 And all that dwell upon the earth shall worship him, whose names are not written in the book of life of the Lamb*

slain from the foundation of the world. 13:9 If any man have an ear, let him hear."

Although sometimes taking different forms, the dragon of verse 2 is the spirit of Satan.

The leopard beast mentioned above is identical with the little horn of Daniel 7: 8, 20, 24, 25 and is a symbol of the same Roman Papal power.

Both are blasphemous. Both speak against God and make war against the saints.

The little horn (Papal Rome) arose to power as Pagan Rome came to an end. Above in verse 2 is the record of how Pagan Rome depicted as the dragon gives the leopard beast (Papal Rome) *"his power, his seat, and great authority."*

Both the little horn and the leopard beast were allowed 1260 years of persecution. All these similarities prove that they are therefore the same power. This Satanic power reaches back to the beginning of the controversy between Christ and Satan.

Through Pagan Rome, Satan put Christ to death. As an instrument in the continued conflict, Papal Rome replaced Pagan Rome. It took this new form through the introduction of a counterfeit religious organisation that is more successful in its deception because of its apparent holiness.

Scripture says that this counterfeit religion began with the introduction of the little horn of Daniel 7 and will continue as the beast of Revelation who receives worship from those whose hearts have been hardened to the truth because of the great religious deception.

In verses 15,16 of chapter 8, is the record of heavenly beings appearing to Daniel in answer to his desire for an understanding of the vision of the previous verses.

Daniel is told the meaning of the vision regarding Media-Persia and Grecia but he became overcome by the presence of the heavenly beings.

Verse 27 then registers Daniel's discomfort, resulting in him fainting and being sick for a number of days. Neither did he understand the vision.

The first two verses of chapter 9 give the record of Daniel's understanding that Israel's seventy years captivity in Babylon was coming to an end as seen below.

"In the first year of Darius the son of Ahasuerus, of the seed of the Medes, which was made king over the realm of the Chaldeans; 9:2 In the first year of his reign I Daniel understood by books the number of the years, whereof the word of the LORD came to Jeremiah the prophet, that he would accomplish seventy years in the desolations of Jerusalem."

The vision of the previous chapter was in the third year of the Belshazzar, the last ruler of Babylon in 538 B.C. As this was the first year of Darius it is most likely that less than a year has passed since the overthrow of Babylon by Darius. This heralded the fulfilment of the prophecy regarding Israel's seventy years captivity

Coupled with his understanding that the seventy years captivity was ending, Daniel is also aware of Israel's failings.

From verse 3 to verse 19 of chapter 9 comes an acknowledgement from Daniel that the nation of Israel had sinned and strayed from the path set by God.

Daniel is praying, not only in an effort to establish righteousness but he is also praying to the glory of God. An example of this prayer is found in the following verses 10,11:

"Neither have we obeyed the voice of the LORD our God, to walk in his laws, which he set before us by his servants the prophets. 9:11 Yea, all Israel have transgressed thy law, even by departing, that they might not obey thy voice; therefore the curse is poured upon us, and the oath that [is] written in the law of Moses the servant of God, because we have sinned against him."

Chapter 14
Cleansing the Sanctuary

Although Daniel understood that Israel's predicted seventy years captivity was nearing its end and also understood the prophecy relating to the emerging nations, he did not fully understand the vision of *"two thousand and three hundred days"* relating to the cleansing of the sanctuary that is recorded as follows in Daniel 8:14.

"And he said unto me, Unto two thousand and three hundred days; then shall the sanctuary be cleansed."

Daniel 9:21 speaks specifically of the angel Gabriel whom Daniel had seen *"in the vision at the beginning."*

Because Daniel understood the vision relating to the emerging nations, this giving of understanding can only be referring to the vision of Daniel chapter 8 concerning the sanctuary and as an answer to Daniel's expression in verse 27 where Daniel is recorded as saying: *"I was astonished at the vision, but none understood it."*

To understand what this cleansing referred to above means it is necessary to appreciate the significance of the earthly sanctuary in relation to the sanctuary in heaven. Reading from Exodus 25:8, 9 it says:

"And let them make me a sanctuary; that I may dwell among them. 25:9 According to all that I show thee, [after] the pattern of the tabernacle, and the pattern of all the instruments thereof, even so shall ye make [it]."

On a daily basis throughout the year the nation of Israel sacrificed a lamb without blemish, which symbolised the Lamb of God, Jesus Christ. Then once a year on the seventh day of the tenth month, named the Day of Atonement, it became imperative for the nation to take part in the ritual of cleansing the sanctuary.

This Day of Atonement was a type of judgement for the whole nation.

Upon this day all of the sins that had been confessed throughout the year were figuratively removed in a cleansing of the sanctuary.

As with many ceremonies performed by the nation of Israel they were a type of what is real. The type of service that took place in the earthly sanctuary as a means of removing the sins of Israel has its anti-type in heaven where Jesus Christ, the anti-typical High Priest, is now pleading His blood on behalf of sinners before the presence of God.

In the message concerning the cleansing of the sanctuary, Daniel is being informed of a specific time when the judgement would begin in heaven.

Leviticus 16:1-24 gives an account of the earthly type of service that typified the judgement that was to take place in heaven. There was a great significance attached to the whole sacrificial system used by the nation of Israel. It was important to learn daily that it was only through the shedding of blood that they could be purged of sin.

However, on the Day of Atonement there was an even more solemn atmosphere permeating the camp as preparation was made for this annual ceremony.

Before beginning the main service on the Day of Atonement, the high priest made an offering of a bullock for himself and his household.

This most important Day of Atonement was an occasion of great solemnity when the high priest entered the holy of holies alone.

"But into the second [went] the high priest alone once every year, not without blood, which he offered for himself, and [for] the errors of the people." (*Hebrews* 9:7).

Upon the breastplate of the high priest were inscribed the names of the twelve tribes of Israel. This typified the anti-typical High Priest, Jesus as the names of His people are presented before God the Father.

Any Israelite, who failed to honour the Day of Atonement, as he should, resulted in his sins being unconfessed over the scapegoat. He would then be cast out from among the people.

It truly was a day of judgement. To follow the same pattern of type and anti-type in like manner, the names of all who make a profession of following Jesus Christ will have the record of their lives opened to scrutiny in the investigative judgement now taking place in heaven.

This means that there are consequences of an eternal dimension at stake in understanding the meaning of the investigative judgement.

The important purpose of this solemn Day of Atonement was the selecting and offering of two goats, which were brought to the door of the sanctuary. Lots were cast for the goats.

One goat would be named Azazel, and in type represent Satan. The other goat was named the Lord's goat symbolising Jesus Christ.

The high priest slew the Lord's goat and took the blood into the most holy place within the second veil.

Carrying a golden censer filled with coals of fire from the altar, the priest placed incense upon the burning coals of fire creating a cloud of fragrant incense making a covering as the high priest came before the presence of God.

Blood was sprinkled upon the mercy seat of the ark that housed the broken law of God.

Upon leaving, passing through the first apartment, the high priest touched the horns of the golden altar, and sprinkled *"blood upon it with his finger seven times,"* and cleansed it.

In type, the priest had now confessed all of the people's sins and transferred them into the sanctuary.

In this way the priest made reconciliation between God and the people. Figuratively speaking, he then took the sins of the whole nation, and laying his hands upon the head of the scapegoat confessed them upon the head of the scapegoat. The goat was then taken into the wilderness. See verse 22 of Leviticus chapter 16.

Jesus Christ is the true sacrifice and Saviour of the world. He is also our High Priest. Regarding the judgement and reconciliation, the typical Day of Atonement was an enactment of that which was prophesied would take place in heaven.

The Lord's goat typified the death of Jesus. The scapegoat typified Satan, who is the one ultimately responsible for sin and therefore will be the one taking the ultimate blame for sin.

There are misguided people of some Christian denominations who cannot see the truth of the above-recorded service on the Day of Atonement. They believe that confessing sins over the head of the scapegoat is giving credit of salvation to Satan.

That the sins are being confessed in this manner cannot be denied. However, this is not implying credit to Satan, but simply stating that he is the one that is guilty and takes responsibility for all sin.

With their final banishment, all the sins will be properly placed upon the head of Satan where they truly belong.

From his experience of the annual Day of Atonement, Daniel understood this important aspect of the cleansing work of the earthly sanctuary. He also understood the message of the angel Gabriel as far as it dealt with the kingdoms of Media-Persia and Greece, and the little horn (Pagan and Papal Rome).

However, he did not understand this vision referring to the cleansing of the heavenly sanctuary, which extended beyond the time allotted to the nation of Israel in prophecy as it related to spiritual Israel and the Christian era.

It was while he was praying and confessing the sins of his people that Daniel was given a more comprehensive understanding of the vision concerning the 2,300 days, or prophetic years, of Daniel 8:13, 14.

In chapter 9, verses 21-27 is the following record of the angel Gabriel giving Daniel understanding of the vision that had previously eluded him.

"9:20 And whiles I [was] speaking, and praying, and confessing my sin and the sin of my people Israel, and presenting my supplication before the LORD my God for the holy mountain of my God; 9:21 Yea, whiles I [was] speaking in prayer, even the man Gabriel, whom I had seen in the vision at the beginning, being caused to fly swiftly, touched me about the time of the evening oblation. 9:22 And he informed [me], and talked with me, and said, O Daniel, I am now come forth to give thee skill and understanding. 9:23 At the beginning of thy supplications the commandment came forth, and I am come to show [thee]; for thou [art] greatly beloved: therefore understand the matter, and consider the vision. 9:24 **Seventy weeks are determined upon thy people** *and upon thy holy city, to finish the transgression, and to make an end of sins, and to make reconciliation for iniquity, and to bring in everlasting righteousness, and to seal up the vision and prophecy, and to anoint the most Holy. 9:25 Know therefore and understand, [that] from the going forth of the commandment to restore and to build Jerusalem unto the Messiah the Prince [shall be] seven weeks, and threescore and two weeks: the street shall be built again, and the wall, even in troublous times. 9:26 And after threescore and two weeks shall Messiah be cut off, but not for himself: and the people of the prince that shall come shall destroy the city and the sanctuary; and the end thereof [shall be] with a flood, and unto the end of the war desolations are determined. 9:27 And he shall confirm the covenant with many for one week: and in the midst of the week he shall cause the sacrifice and the oblation to cease, and for the overspreading of abominations he shall make [it] desolate, even until the consummation, and that determined shall be poured upon the desolate."*

Continuing our study of the 2,300 days prophecy, let us remember that there is a need to apply the principle that in prophetic time one day equals one year.

By way of an explanation to the part of the vision which troubled Daniel, we read of how Gabriel explained in chapter 9 verse 24, that: *"Seventy weeks* (490 years) *are determined"* or allotted to the nation of Israel to bring an end to their rebellion against Jehovah.

With an understanding that in prophecy one day represents one year, it means that, translated into plain English, the angel is informing Daniel that the nation of Israel was being allowed a further 490 years to test their determination to engage in the honoured commission of propagating the gospel through accepting the principles of salvation.

Verse 24 gives the length of time as 490 years that was allotted to the nation of Israel, but it is verse 25 that gives a starting point to the prophecy.

We can understand from reading verse 25 that the starting point for the 490 years would be the same as applied to the baptism of Jesus as the Messiah.

Concerning the Messiah, it says in verse 25 *"that from the going forth of the commandment to restore and to build Jerusalem unto Messiah the Prince (*Jesus' baptism*) shall be seven weeks, and threescore and two weeks."* (69 weeks or 483 years).

This means that the starting point of the 490 years allotted to the Jews and the 483 years that reached to the baptism of Jesus was the same.

In verse 25 above, we are told that the prophecy being studied had its beginning with the commandment to restore and rebuild Jerusalem.

Thus in order to gain a clear understanding of the prophecy under study, it is necessary to establish the date that the commandment went forth to rebuild the devastated Jerusalem, which came about through Israel's 70 years captivity by Babylon.

Once the starting point of the prophecy is established it will be possible to appreciate the significance of events linked with its end.

As the seventy years captivity of Israel by Babylon was drawing to its end, there is the record of three decrees being issued concerning the devastated Jerusalem. They are found in Ezra 1:1-4, Ezra 6:1-12, Ezra chapter 7.

All of these decrees played a part. However, the only decree that meets the requirement *"to restore and to build Jerusalem"*, and find fulfilment of the whole prophecy, is to be found in Ezra chapter 7, verse 7.

It was in the year 457 B.C., and the seventh year of King Artexerxes that this decree was issued. In chapter 2 of Nehemiah is also the record that 13 years later Nehemiah was granted permission by the same king to go to Jerusalem in order to assist in the re-building of the city.

This date of 457 B.C. was of great significance to the nation of Israel. From that date would begin the ticking of time unto the completion of the 490 years allotted to cease their rebellion, or bring an end to their status as a favoured nation.

Measuring 490 years from 457 B.C. reaches to A.D. 33, which was three and half years after the death of Jesus. Measuring the 69 weeks (483 years) of verse 25, we reach A.D. 30, which was the time of Jesus' baptism as Messiah the Prince, as foretold in verse 25.

In Daniel 9:27 is the record that Jesus would *"confirm the covenant with many for one week"*, or seven years." And that *"in the midst of the week"* He would cause the sacrifice to cease.

Thus it was that half way through the final seven years allotted to the Jews, Jesus was crucified.

In summary, Scripture has informed us that the nation of Israel was to be allowed 490 years for a last opportunity to fulfil their God given mission to evangelise the nations around them. These seventy weeks of verse 24 (490 years) that were allotted to Israel had its starting point *"from the going forth of the commandment to restore and build Jerusalem."*

We have learned from the seventh chapter in the book of Ezra that this re-building and restoration of Jerusalem began when the king, Artaxerxes, made a decree authorising such a programme in the year 457 B.C.

The re-building programme took 49 years, which coupled with the predicted three score and two weeks, or 434 years that are to be cut off (verse26), makes up the 483 years, or 69 weeks, which *reached "unto Messiah the Prince"* (Verse 25). Jesus became Messiah the Prince at His baptism exactly at the time prophesied.

This prophecy is so amazing that it is truly baffling to the mind that it has not been headlined news to every generation. So we have the prophecy telling us that the nation of Israel was to be allotted 490 years to change their spiritual direction.

It was foretold that seven years before the allotted time was complete, Jesus would become baptised Messiah the Prince. The following record in Luke 3:21, 22 proves the accuracy of the prophecy that became fulfilled exactly on time:

"Now when all the people were baptized, it came to pass, that Jesus also being baptized, and praying, the heaven was opened, 3:22 And the Holy Ghost descended in a bodily shape like a dove upon him, and a voice came from heaven, which said, Thou art my beloved Son; in thee I am well pleased."

Incredibly, it was foretold that in the midst of the week, or three and half years after His baptism *"he shall cause the sacrifice and the oblation to cease."* (Dan: 9:27).

It will be noticed that the nation of Israel were allotted 490 years, but Jesus their promised Messiah was put to death in the 487th year. This means that there still remained three and half years of the time allotted.

This period of time the disciples used as a fulfilment of the prophecy which ended with the stoning of Stephen recorded, as follows, in Acts 7:59:

"And they stoned Stephen, calling upon [God], and saying, Lord Jesus, receive my spirit."

Thus it was that Jesus could truly say of Israel *"Behold, your house is left unto you desolate."* (Luke 13:35).

For the purpose of clarification on this important subject, let us re-cap. Daniel 9:24 is prophesying that the nation of Israel was to be allowed a further 490 years to accomplish harmony with God.

This period of time began in the year 457 B.C. Verse 25 says that 483 years from 457 B.C. would reach to the baptism of Jesus. This has proved to be true.

Supporting the veracity of the prophecy, verse 26 says that after 434 years, plus the 49 years of the re-building of Jerusalem, that Messiah would be *"cut off"*. (Jesus was cut off; He died after the 483 years in the midst of the 70th week or final seven years of the prophesied 490 years).

Completing this section of the prophecy, and in agreement with verse 26, verse 27 says that Jesus would confirm the covenant with many for one week, and in the midst of the week would cause the sacrifice to cease.

Thus verse 26 is saying that Jesus would be sacrificed after the 69th week, and verse 27 says that Jesus would die in the middle of the 70th week.

This account finds harmony with the timing of Jesus' death on Calvary, which stated that in the midst of the seventieth week, or the final seven years of the original 490 years, that Jesus would be crucified. This has been proved to be true.

Thus, as recorded in Daniel 9:27, Jesus did *"confirm the covenant with many for one week."* (Seven years). This included the three and half years ministry of Jesus and the three and half years of the disciples until the final rejection of the gospel by the nation of Israel.

Chapter 15
Choice

God has risen up people in all churches to be beacons of light in a darkened world. In this theatre of conflict each one of us is responsible for shedding a little light, even if it is only to bless each other in our own immediate circle. In this way it is possible that light begets light to reflect beams that helps disperse darkness and lift the spirit in minds of doubt.

In the matter of salvation it is foolish to allow others to be the barometer of our commitment to Christ. Jesus warned His people not to be adversely influenced by those who will not see, even if they occupy lofty positions. He says: *"Let them alone: they be blind leaders of the blind. And if the blind lead the blind, both shall fall into the ditch."* (Matthew 15:14).

It is not wise to neglect truth because of indolence and believe another's interpretation of Scripture.

In the great controversy, the battle is not ours to win. Having defeated the foe, Jesus enables us to choose.

Regarding the matter of choice and ultimate blame for sin we can learn something from the account of the scapegoat of Leviticus chapter 16. From the same source we can also learn the cost of Satan's opposition to the perfect will of a loving God.

In exercising the will we are responsible for our own choice, yet it would be as wrong to take the ultimate blame for sin as to take the credit for victory over sin.

In the final analysis there is no reason to blame each other for any confessed faults. As indicated in the ceremony of the scapegoat and the Lord's goat, Satan is the one truly responsible for the great controversy.

Satan was highly esteemed in heaven, holding a high position but chose to follow his own will. Jesus was lowly esteemed and despised while on earth but chose to follow the will of His Father in heaven.

The lesson of the two goats as recorded in Leviticus chapter 16 is that symbolically they both had the potential for following the will of the Father or not. The moral behind the lesson of the two goats applies to all.

The scapegoat represents the consequence of following our own will. We die for our sins because of harmonising with Satan.

The Lord's goat opens up the way of salvation. We escape the punishment for our sins.

There is an equal opportunity for both kinds. The significance was not in the casting of lots. Both goats were presented before the Lord representing symbolic choice. The lesson of the two goats is meant to convey the result of choice. Initially both goats were sound. The effect of sin as a result of choice made the difference.

We all begin by inheriting partial spiritual blindness and as such we are not ultimately responsible for our rebellion. To deny this truth would place us in conflict with Jesus who said: *"Father; forgive them; for they know not what they do."* (Luke 23:34).

Satan entered into the great controversy with his eyes fully opened to the possible consequences of his action. Hence the reason for the accountability of the scapegoat in type.

This also shows how there is no sound or loving reason for a God of love to punish unnecessarily those who have chosen blindly to follow Satan in rebellion.

If we choose to blame ourselves for any rebellion, then by the same reasoning we would be claiming credit for a loving response to God's word, which brings salvation.

To neglect so great a reward of salvation brings no eternal blame, but what profit is that if we neglect such an eternal gain? What horror it will be, if we ignore God's call all because being blind we refuse to see.

Chapter 16
Judgement of the Saints

Within a long time prophecy of 2,300 years the fate of the nation of Israel was foretold. The word of God has fully explained that the nation of Israel was allotted a final period of time in which there remained the opportunity to fulfil its God-given mission to evangelise the nations around them. However, that period of time came to an end with the stoning of Stephen. This long period of 2,300 years culminated in the cleansing of the sanctuary as declared in Daniel 8:14.

"And he said unto me, Unto two thousand and three hundred days; then shall the sanctuary be cleansed."

We have learned from the book of Leviticus that the cleansing of the sanctuary was a type and time of judgement. In the Jewish dispensation this time was known as the Day of Atonement.

From this we are meant to understand that on the completion of 2,300 years from the going forth of the decree to rebuild Jerusalem would begin a kind and time of judgement.

2,300 years after the decree from when the commandment went forth to rebuild and restore Jerusalem in the year 457 B.C. would reach to the year 1844 A.D. This would consist of 490 years to the stoning of Stephen and 1810 years after.

The time allotted to the nation of Israel had come to an end, so this cleansing of the sanctuary had nothing to do with the nation of physical Israel. Therefore, it must surely be a reference to the anti-typical cleansing of the sanctuary that was to take place in heaven, and in connection with the nation of spiritual Israel.

This is a tremendous experience for the saints to know that even now, Jesus as High Priest is pleading His blood on behalf of the saints in the anti-typical service of Atonement in the heavenly sanctuary.

Literal Israel approached the type of Atonement in awesome solemnity. However, without heart conversion a solemn service is never enough. In the anti-typical service there is a final judgement that can only bring reconciliation between God and those who have experienced heart circumcision.

Our previous study of chapter 10 of this book has shown that the saints are to judge the lives of the wicked during the 1000 years millennium. Yet is there further evidence in support of the conviction that the saints are now being judged as related to the Old Testament Atonement service?

We have learned from the Day of Atonement service in the Old Testament that it was only God's people who were under investigation in that time of judgement. Like the type, this judgement must also come about for the people of God before Jesus the High Priest leaves the heavenly sanctuary and changes His priestly robes into that of a King.

To follow the same pattern means that it is spiritual Israel (those professing to being Christians) who are first to come under investigation. Should there not first be a time of judgement for the saints in order for the returning Jesus to bring His promised reward with Him? We are told in 1 Peter 4:17 that the judgement begins with the saints thus:

"4:17 For the time [is come] that judgment must begin at the house of God: and if [it] first [begin] at us, what shall the end [be] of them that obey not the gospel of God?"

So there is the answer from Scripture. The judgement begins at the house of God, or with the people of God. Of course, there would need to be a judgement of the saints before the return of Jesus. How else could Jesus bring His promised reward with Him?

Consider how beautifully the Jewish Day of Atonement fits in with the investigative judgement now taking place in the heavenly sanctuary. In the one on earth, the priest came forth to declare the people clean, only for the ritual to be repeated annually.

When Jesus, the heavenly High Priest, comes forth it will be as King to declare His people clean for eternity.

This judgement of the saints now taking place in heaven began with Adam and Eve and continues until it reaches the living. We do not know the result or time when this final judgement will be completed, but it does mean that all who have claimed to be followers of Jesus Christ will have their names entered into the Lamb's book of life and, therefore, come under the judgement now taking place in heaven.

Of course, the name in the Lamb's book does not guarantee eternal life. It is the record in the books of remembrance, which will be the deciding factor for every soul.

Scripture is teaching that in the year 1844, Jesus our High Priest became the fulfilment of the type and entered into the inner compartment of the heavenly sanctuary.

Clouds of angels will herald the next awesome event, and sitting high on the clouds will be Jesus a heavenly spectacle to every eye.

The fallacious argument has been projected that such an investigative judgement as the cleansing of the sanctuary cannot take place in heaven because there is no sin in heaven to be cleansed. It is said that sin is not allowed to contaminate the holiness of the heavenly sanctuary.

This is an absurd assertion that can obviously have no basis in truth. Such an implication is suggesting that the most holy compartment of the earthly sanctuary was not holy at all. There is no sound reasoning in the formulation of such an argument. The record of sin is neither sin nor contamination.

Just as there were confessed sins taken into the earthly sanctuary so are there confessed sins recorded in heaven. Petitions for the forgiveness of sins go daily into the sanctuary and before the Father's throne.

There is obviously a record of sins being investigated through the merit of the saving grace of Jesus Christ, the Lamb of Calvary.

Chapter 17
Rites, Jacob and the 144,000

Throughout their history as the people of God, the people of Israel were taught of the Lamb who was *"slain from the foundation of the world."* (Rev. 13:8).

For the literal nation of Israel, slaying the sacrificial lamb was a type of sacrifice that pointed the way forward to the Cross and the death of the Lamb on Calvary.

Israel's high priests who officiated in the Jewish sanctuary were also types of priests teaching of the then future work of the true Priest (Jesus) in the heavenly sanctuary. Now *"We have such an high priest who is set on the right hand of the throne of the Majesty in the heavens."* (Hebrews 8:1).

All of the holy rites performed by Israel were intended as lessons of the way God had planned to deal with the problem of sin. The sole purpose of the daily and yearly rites was to instruct the nation of God's plan of salvation.

Except for the sacrificial rites the whole system ordained of God was a type or shadow of the real service that was to take place in the sanctuary of heaven. On the yearly Day of Atonement Israel was acting out a form of judgement that shadowed the real judgement that was to take place in heaven.

In this service the sins of Israel were in figure placed upon the head of the goat, typifying Satan as it was taken into the wilderness. The one chosen to perform the final act of escorting the goat was named fit man.

Just as the earthly sanctuary was a type of that in heaven, the priest who performed the associated rites was a type representing the anti-type Jesus Christ.

Fit man was also a type representing those who would have the task of bringing about the final defeat of Satan.

Revelation 14:1-4 speaks of the hundred and forty four thousand as having the *"Father's name written in their foreheads"* and *"not defiled"*.

Because of their complete victory over sin, the hundred and forty four thousand can be linked as anti-types to fit man who was responsible for disposing of the nations' sins. They can also be linked to their spiritual ancestor Jacob who, by the blood of the Lamb, also overcame sin.

Jacob had wronged his brother Esau, and as a consequence feared meeting him. For this reason when returning to his own country, Jacob *"sent messengers before him to Esau his brother unto the land of Se-ir, the country of Edom."* (Genesis 32:3-7). Jacob was greatly afraid and distressed. In this state of anguish and guilt for the sins he had committed against his brother, Jacob felt the need to be forgiven and find peace. It was in this helpless condition that Jacob turned to God for forgiveness and help in his hour of great need.

After sending forth his wives, their servants and his eleven sons, *"Jacob was left alone; And there wrestled a man with him until the breaking of the day."* (Genesis 32:24).

The story tells of how Jacob found victory from his sins, and peace in Christ as his name was changed from Jacob to that of Israel, the one who by the power of God overcame. God said to Jacob: *"Thy name shall be called no more Jacob, but Israel: for as a prince thou hast power with God and with men, and hast prevailed."* (Genesis 32:28).

Thus it was that Jacob gained victory and peace after much anguish and tribulation. His spiritual descendants, the hundred and forty four thousand will also find eventual peace after their time of anguish from the final conflict with the beast of Revelation and Satan.

When reference is made to God's people going through the time known as Jacob's trouble, it means that they will suffer an experience similar to that endured by Jacob.

The troubled and final conflict to face God's people will be a time of great fear because of Satan's threat to their safety. This fear is compounded because the people of God visualise their previous sins being an obstacle separating them from the love, protection, and forgiveness of God. In Daniel 12:1 the time known as the time of Jacob's trouble is related this way:

"and there shall be a time of trouble, such as never was since there was a nation even to that time: and at that time thy people shall be delivered, every one that shall be found written in the book."

At the time of Jacob's trouble when these closing events involving the 144.000 take place, obviously there will be no mediation in heaven. The condition of the earthly population at the time under consideration is described as follows:

Revelation 22:11: *"He that is unjust, let him be unjust still: and he which is filthy, let him be filthy still: and he that is righteous, let him be righteous still: and he that is holy, let him be holy still."*

The above Scripture reference makes it clear that the only people left alive on earth at that time will be those who worship the beast and those who with a perfect character worship God.

Although the record in Scripture foretells victory for the people of God at the end of the controversy between Satan and Christ, such a victory cannot become established before the actual event. Satan still believes that victory for him is a possibility.

Throughout church history the hundred and forty four thousand of Revelation have often been the centre of discussion with many varied conclusions being reached in connection with what is meant by this figure.

God is preparing hundred and forty four thousand saints for the final conflict between the forces of good and evil. In these circumstances it must surely be the will of God that His people should understand the significance of the number hundred and forty four thousand in relation to the prophetic end of the controversy between Christ and Satan.

They are mentioned in connection with the end time enough to lend support for the conclusion that the hundred and forty four thousand are the saints who will have been prepared by God to take part in the final conflict. This conflict will be between Christ, the leader of the saints, and Satan, the leader of the beast and his associates.

Support for this belief is found in the following two references:

Revelation 14: 1, 4: *"And I looked, and, lo, a Lamb stood on the mount Sion, and with him an hundred forty four thousand, having his Father's name written in their foreheads. These are they which are not defiled with women; for they are virgins, These are they which follow the Lamb whithersoever he goeth. These were redeemed from among men, being the firstfruits unto God and to the Lamb."*

Revelation 14:12: *"Here is the patience of the saints: here [are] they that keep the commandments of God, and the faith of Jesus."*

To reach a clearer understanding of those who make up this number, they should be studied in conjunction with the one described as "fit man" of Leviticus 16:21.

This number has not been defiled by the false doctrines of any fallen churches and consequently is described above *"as not defiled with women; for they are virgins."*

Because the hundred and forty four thousand are so described, the claim is often then made that the figure of hundred and forty four thousand cannot be literal because this would indicate that they were all men. However, if this is not a literal number, why should so much emphasis be placed upon the beauty of their character?

It is known that an apostate church is described as something which defiles and is also described as a fallen woman.

In these circumstances it would be perfectly reasonable to describe those who by the blood of the Lamb had become spotless and undefiled, as virgins *"not defiled with women."* Being defiled refers to false doctrines of an apostate church.

Women who defile represent any kind of church opposed to God. It is in the guise of religion that Satan is most effective in his opposition to the law of God.

The battle between the hundred and forty four thousand and Satan will really be a battle between Christ and Satan because in spite of Jesus' victory leading up to and including the Cross, this battle is not yet over. In some respects there is to be a re-enactment of a battle already won. The Spirit of Jesus in His sanctified people will finally vanquish Satan.

The hundred and forty four thousand will stand or fall together. It will not be possible for even a small section to fail the test and for Jesus to claim a victory. If just one of the saints is defeated, Satan will claim to be the victor.

We know that before the close of probation all of God's people will have been sealed. This of course would include any children then left alive. In their case it is possible that they might be afforded special protection.

Satan is a defeated enemy. Of this there is no doubt. However, this fact would not prevent Satan casting doubt on the manner of Christ's victory. His accusation would be that Christ used divine power in His battle against evil, claiming that victory would not have been possible any other way.

Such a controversial accusation will be forever silenced with the victory of humanity in the form of the hundred and forty four thousand who will be known to possess no supernatural powers.

They will be relying on the same limited power that was available to Christ in His battle against evil. Jesus had only His inherited fallen human nature and His being born of the Spirit to rely upon during the ordeal of Gethsemane and Golgotha. He used no more power than is available to human beings.

Regarding man's historical position at this time, we now stand near the very end of the sixth seal. In Scripture, we are positioned between the following 13th and 14th verses of Revelation, chapter 6.

"And the stars of heaven fell unto the earth, even as a fig tree casteth her untimely figs, when she is shaken of a mighty wind. 14. And the heaven departed as a scroll when it is rolled together; and every mountain and island were moved out of their places."

The next awesome event to take place in heaven is the opening of the seventh seal and the close of probation.

In Revelation 7:1-3 we are informed that there are four angels holding in check the winds of strife that are waiting to be unleashed upon the earth.

We are told that these angels will maintain this position until a special number of God's elect are sealed.

Most Christians are familiar with the number hundred and forty four thousand but there remain four questions, which need to be answered in connection with this number.

1: Are these people members of a particular nation, such as literal Israel?

2: Is the number of one hundred and forty four thousand a specific number or symbolic?

3: What is meant by the description used of God's people being sealed as portrayed in Revelation?

4: Why is the numbered hundred and forty four thousand listed so as to represent the following twelve tribes?

Revelation 7:5-8: *"Of the tribe of Juda were sealed twelve thousand. Of the tribe of Reuben were sealed twelve thousand. Of the tribe of Gad were sealed twelve thousand. 6, Of the tribe of Aser were sealed twelve thousand. Of the tribe of Nepthalim were sealed twelve thousand. Of the tribe of Manasses were sealed twelve thousand. 7, Of the tribe of Simeon were sealed twelve thousand. Of the tribe of Levi were sealed twelve thousand. Of the tribe of Issachar were sealed twelve thousand. 8, Of the tribe of Zabulon were sealed twelve thousand. Of the tribe of Joseph were sealed twelve thousand. Of the tribe of Benjamin were sealed twelve thousand."*

Addressing these questions in the same order, let us first consider who makes up this number being referred to.

From the verses above we learn that the twelve tribes of Israel are to be sealed. The obvious question now arises as to whether this passage of Scripture is referring to literal Israel. A review of the following text indicates the answer to be emphatically no.

Speaking of the Jewish nation in Matthew 23:38 Jesus is on record as saying: *"Behold, your house is left unto you desolate."* Expressed in a different manner Jesus was saying that, as a nation Israel was no longer to be considered a favoured people chosen to evangelise the world. As a nation, they had failed miserably in their appointed mission to spread the message of salvation to the Gentiles, and had finally rejected the Saviour.

Further to this, in Romans 2:28 29 Paul declares:

"For he is not a Jew, which is one outwardly; neither is that circumcision, which is outward in the flesh: 29But he is a Jew, which is one inwardly; and circumcision is that of the heart, in the spirit, and not in the letter; whose praise is not of men, but of God."

In Ephesians 2:12, Paul again defines a true Israelite this way:

"That at that time ye were without Christ, being aliens from the commonwealth of Israel, and strangers from the covenants of promise, having no hope, and without God in the world:"

We learn from Galatians 3:29:

"And if ye be Christ's, then are ye Abraham's seed, and heirs according to the promise."

Continuing with the evidence that the people of literal Israel no longer hold a special place in God's plan for the world, it says of Christ in John 1:10, 11:

"He was in the world, and the world was made by him, and the world knew him not. 1:11 He came unto his own, and his own received him not."

In Matthew 21:33-40 there is the record of Jesus telling a parable that not only reveals Israel's rejection of the Saviour, but there is also the record in verse 41 of their leaders' admission to their failure.

Unaware of the extent of their own failings, Matthew 21:41 records that the leaders in Israel condemned themselves before they realised that Jesus was referring to them.

Thus it was that Jesus could say of Israel as previously quoted: *"Behold, your house is left unto you desolate."*

Finally, to prove that the reference in Revelation chapter 7 to the tribes of Israel does not mean literal Israel, the record in Revelation speaks of the tribes being sealed. A nation that has been rejected by Jesus could hardly be sealed by God's Spirit.

It can be clearly seen that in answer to the first question, that any promise made to literal Israel now applies to spiritual Israel, meaning Christians.

The answer to the second question is both yes and no.

The number being referred to in connection with the hundred and forty four thousand is a specific number. However, there is a need to first understand the way used for a certain kind of reckoning in the Bible, where only the **males**, and sometimes just mature men, are subject to the count.

A man and his wife are counted as one. This oneness can also include other members of the same family such as children. Evidence of this fact is found in the book of Numbers 3:22, Matthew, and John as follows:

*"Those that were number of them, according to the number of all the **males**, from a month old and upward, [even] those that were numbered of them {were} seven thousand and five hundred."*

Matthew 19:5, 6: *"And said, For this cause shall a man leave father and mother, and shall cleave to his wife: and they twain shall be one flesh. Wherefore they are no more twain, but one flesh. What therefore God hath joined together, let no man put asunder."*

John 6:10: *"And Jesus said, Make the **men** sit down, Now there was much grass in the place. So the **men** sat down, in number about five thousand."*

Having acquired evidence of how the Bible numbers people, it can be seen how a reference to one man could also include his wife. A similar application could equally include the whole family, or in some circumstances a clan. With these facts in mind it can be seen that the number hundred and forty four thousand could be doubled, trebled or even quadrupled. The actual number of saints could easily range from 400,000 upwards.

In such circumstances, using this method of reckoning, the number hundred and forty four thousand special people mentioned in Revelation 7: and Revelation 14:1, would depend on a variety of scenarios.

Armed with this information, let us imagine that at the end of this dispensation and the beginning of the plagues, that there are four hundred thousand saints having the seal of God.

In a quest for a logical application of these figures let us examine the words of David, recorded in Psalm 91:7, which open up a reasonable explanation. It says here referring to the day of the Lord:

"A thousand shall fall at thy side, and ten thousand at thy right hand; but it shall not come nigh thee."

Understanding from the above text that David was referring to the day of the Lord and the time of the plagues, and that there will remain one of God's elected saints to every eleven thousand of Satan's army, we can proceed further.

Multiplying the estimated 400,000 living saints at that time by the stated 11,000 wicked to each standing saint, would indicate a world population of the wicked to be 4,400,000 at the time of the final battle between the forces of good and evil.

The American way of assessing one billion is with nine zeros. The English way is with twelve zeros. Of course, the value and ratio of the figures remain the same no matter which method of description is used.

Using the American method of assessing the number one billion, the 4,400,000,000 would represent 4.4 billion. Using the same way of reckoning the associated figures, the present world population is estimated to be approximately 6.6 billion, or 6,000,600,000,000.

Let us now consider the fact that at the time nearing the end, many Christians, lacking a full measure of imparted righteousness, will have been laid to rest. Also, it must be realised that many belonging to the cause of Satan will have died during the plagues. Neither should it be forgotten that the number of God's saints could be subject to fluctuation dependant how they are numbered using the Bible method of reckoning.

In any attempt at assessing the population of the world at the time of the end, it is necessary to realise that Jesus does not return to earth until the chaos of the plagues have ended. Then the wicked are destroyed with the brightness of His coming as recorded in 2 Thessalonians 2:8 thus:

"And when that Wicked be revealed, whom the Lord shall consume with the spirit of his mouth, and shall destroy with the brighntness of his coming."

It is impossible to estimate how many Christians will be laid to rest during end time events because of a lack of imparted righteousness. However, when calculating numbers, facts like this need to be taken into account. Although it is not possible to define actual numbers, many of the all embracing number of the saints living at that time will be saved and laid to rest because of the righteousness of Christ.

Even though lacking a full measure of imparted righteousness they will be saved by the imputed righteousness of Christ.

In relation to the projected population number at the end of time it can now be seen how reasonable a figure is the original 144,000, which could actually be 400,000 or even more.

Subtracting the estimated 4.4 billion wicked standing at the end of time from the present population of 6.6 billion leaves a figure of 2.2 billion. In addition, to be subtracted there are also those of God's people who because of not reaching a state of full-imparted righteousness will have been laid to rest.

We are left with a reasonable figure that makes up the combined number of wicked that die in the plagues and the standing saints.

The third question to be answered is what constitutes the seal of God? Obviously, the seventh day Sabbath is a sign or seal indicating loyalty of God's people to their Creator. Yet there remains more to this issue of a seal than apparent honour to a day. Just as there is a counterfeit Sabbath day, there exists another counterfeit leading to a spiritual violation of the Sabbath principle.

There can exist in some respects an apparently godlike character displaying a love that is as much a counterfeit as bestowing honour upon a false Sabbath

Having received the seal of *"the living God"* referred to below in Revelation 7:2 means to be imparted with the full righteousness of Christ through the indwelling Holy Spirit.

Revelation 7:2-3: *"And I saw another angel ascending from the east, having the seal of the living God: and he cried with a loud voice to the four angels, to whom it was given to hurt the earth and the sea, 3Saying, Hurt not the earth, neither the sea, nor the trees, till we have sealed the servants of our God in their foreheads."*

In the above reference we have the evidence of God preparing a special number of saints to be sealed for their coming conflict with the forces of evil, and in the reference below from Revelation14:1 is the reference to this same number being sealed as follows:

"And I looked, and lo, a Lamb stood on the mount Sion, and with him an hundred forty and four thousand, having his Father's name written in their foreheads."

The hundred and forty four thousand will have been sealed with the character of Christ. These are those who go through the final tribulation known as Jacob's trouble.

Looking to the future as a time to prepare to meet Jesus could be a fatal mistake. Now is the time to be ready. It is of no consequence if this readiness consists of imputed righteousness or imparted righteousness. The important thing is to be in harmony with the will of God. This means that we must be born again. See following:

John 3:5-8: *"Jesus answered and said unto him, Verily, verily, I say unto thee, Except a man be born of water and of the Spirit, he cannot enter into the kingdom of God. That which is born of the flesh is flesh; and that which is born of the Spirit is spirit. Marvel not that I said unto thee, Ye must be born again. The wind bloweth where it listeth, and thou hearest the sound thereof, but canst not tell whence it cometh, and whither it goeth: so is every one that is born of the Spirit."*

Once the sealing work of God's people has been accomplished it can surely be only a relatively short time before the opening of the seventh seal. We refer to Revelation 8:1.

"And when he had opened the seventh seal, there was silence in heaven about the space of half an hour."

To discover the answer to the fourth and final question regarding the number of tribes that make up what we now know to be spiritual Israel, it is necessary to study Genesis chapter 49.

From there can be found a record of Jacob calling together all of his sons before he died. He then proceeded to give a graphic account of the type of people they were, addressing each one individually. Jacob catalogued them in such a way as to leave no doubt in the mind that no two were alike.

This account of his sons given by Jacob gives us an insight as to why the last book of the Bible describes how at the end of time there will exist twelve tribes. It is generally accepted that mankind consists of the twelve types categorised by Jacob.

We all know how variable people can be. Some are of a calm and tranquil nature, while others can be volatile and quick tempered. The important thing to be aware of regarding these different types is that there is no need for one person to be outside of God's grace. All can be equally saved from sin and gain a victory in Christ.

Therefore, when the controversy between good and evil is ended, it will be shown that no one will be left with an excuse for being lost. Not one person will be in a position to claim that there had been no opportunity to be saved because of what type of person they were. God can save any and all.

The final battle involving the hundred and forty four thousand is the anti-type to the wilderness battle that took place every year, on the Day of Atonement, between the scapegoat and fit man. It also parallels Jesus' battle of forty days with Satan in the wilderness.

When the battle involving the hundred and forty four thousand is over, there then remains the final act of Satan being banished to the desolate earth, an uninhabited and dreary wilderness by the angel of Revelation 20:1-3. However, this banishment of Satan is only made possible because of the positive outcome of the final battle which will have already taken place between the hundred and forty thousand and Satan and his followers.

The hundred and forty four thousand will only become free of Satan when their journey of conflict comes to an end with their final deliverance. Soon after, the angel of Revelation 20:1,2 binds Satan for a thousand years.

Having been allowed an allotted time to prove his false claims regarding God's law, Satan will begin the time of Jacob's trouble.

After reaching its climax, it will be as if the angel says to Satan: "Your time is up", and removes Satan from the battle, leaving God's remnant as victors in the great controversy. The great chain in the angel's hand signifies power lacking in the hundred and forty four thousand.

There is a distinction between the hundred and forty four thousand, who are the anti-types to fit man and the angel of superior heavenly power.

It is important to understand that the hundred and forty four thousand are the victors over Satan, and not an angel. By the Spirit of God, they will vindicate the character of God and magnify His law.

For the eternal well being of the Universe it is essential that it be clearly seen that God can prepare a people that will so closely follow Christ as to be able to resist Satan's temptations in like manner to their Lord in His wilderness temptations of forty days.

In the great controversy between Christ and Satan, throughout history many of God's people have proved that they were prepared to die for Jesus. Before the final conflict is ended, the people of God will also prove that they can live for Jesus.

God has been preparing and longing for a people in whom He can reproduce His character for the final conflict. Through the limitations of mankind, this preparation could not be done quickly or easily. Why else is it taking so long?

Through the agency of His Spirit, God is pleading with the whole of mankind that they accept His Holy Spirit in order to establish eternal reconciliation with His kingdom of love. For the world of Babylon, and all those who are spiritually immature, the final evidence of their allegiance will find expression in their response to God's final call to honour His law of commandments, including the seventh day Sabbath.

When the time is right the final battle between Christ and Satan will commence and the eyes of the whole Universe will witness the event, and be anxiously awaiting the outcome; not for 360 days plagues as many people think, but for a period of not more than 15 days.

The severity of Jacob's trouble was not measured in time but intensity. So will it be for the 144000. In like manner, the anguish of the seven last plagues will not be measured in time but the resulting gulf as the wicked separate themselves from God.

The thought has been expressed that it is ridiculous to claim that God is waiting to fill the number 144,000 and cut of the rest. This has led to the question as to what God would do with those numbered above 144,000? Are we then to challenge God in His use of mathematics? In the interest of simplicity, is it so unreasonable that God would round off the figures of some tribes that were more of less than the specified 12,000?

Chapter 18
Fit man

During the time of the end the 144,000 are portrayed in Scripture to be the victors over Satan. Therefore, not only are they a kind of Jacob but this victory helps to confirm that they are also the anti-types to fit man of Leviticus as follows:

Leviticus 16:21-22: *"And Aaron shall lay both his hands upon the head of the live goat, and confess over him all the iniquities of the children of Israel, and all their transgressions in all their sins, putting them upon the head of the goat, and shall send him away by the hand of a fit man into the wilderness: 22And the goat shall bear upon him all their iniquities unto a land not inhabited; and shall let go the goat in the wilderness."*

The goat referred to in the above text is a type intended to represent Satan. *"Fit man"* referred to in the same text is also a type and where there is this type we should find more evidence to support the conclusion that the 144,000 are the anti-types.

The Hebrew description of this figure, *"fit man"* is not clear. Modern versions translate this person in several ways, *"suitable man"* (NKJV], *"a man appointed"* (GNB) etc.

Whichever description is used it is fairly obvious that this man was set apart for the task of escorting the goat into the wilderness and, because he represents a type that was responsible for casting out sin, it must therefore be of some importance to establish the anti-type.

It is assumed that the reader is familiar with Scripture's references to the physical and spiritual nature in respect to certain matters. For example, in the past, God spoke to physical Israel. Today, He has plans for spiritual Israel. (Christians).

The physical river Euphrates of old served the physical city of Babylon. In Revelation 16:12 we find evidence of a spiritual connotation in connection with the same named river. People depicted as the river Euphrates are upholding present day apostasy by supplying a river of life to sustain spiritual Babylon.

The reader will most probably be aware, that the book of Revelation makes reference to spiritual Babylon as the spiritual enemy of God's people. In the Old Testament emphasis was placed upon the male members of Israel being physically circumcised. We now understand that spiritual circumcision of the heart is much more important. These are some examples of spiritual lessons from a physical base. In like manner we have type and anti-type.

There are those who hold to the conviction that the anti-type to fit man is an angel. Let us move for a moment to the identity of the angel of Revelation 20:1, 2, who is mentioned in this connection.

"And I saw an angel come down from heaven, having the key of the bottomless pit and a great chain in his hand, 2And he laid hold on the dragon, that old serpent, which is the Devil, and Satan, and bound him a thousand years."

There are reasons why this view of an angel as an anti-type to fit man cannot sensibly be substantiated:

1: Being of the human race and a sinner it would not be appropriate for fit man to be cast as a type of an unfallen angel. There is no sound basis to reason that *a sinless* angel could be an anti-type to a sinner.

2: By means of a potentially tenuous rope, fit man led the scapegoat "into the wilderness unto a land not inhabited" where he was let go. (See Lev. 16:22).

The angel of Revelation 20, 1,2 binds Satan with "a great chain" in his hand. No struggle is involved or implied.

3: In the fullness of time the hundred and forty four thousand will also lead their opponent Satan into the wilderness.

It is because the hundred and forty four thousand do not succumb to the temptations of Satan that he too must inevitably go into a land not inhabited, where the angel of Revelation 20:1-2 symbolically binds him for a thousand years.

4: Symbolically there was a clash of wills between fit man and the scapegoat. There can be no corresponding clash of wills or struggle between an angel of superior power and Satan.

The scapegoat could have escaped from fit man. Satan will not be able to escape the angel of Revelation 20:1,2.

The goat, being a type of Satan, indicates a reluctance to be escorted into the wilderness. It was for this reason that a fit man was chosen for this symbolically awesome task.

So much was symbolically at stake in this battle between the man and the scapegoat that every conceivable precaution needed had been taken in order for the scapegoat to be defeated. Hence the reason for choosing a "suitable man", "a man appointed", etc. An angel of God has no need to battle with Satan.

5: Angels are not directly in conflict with Satan. The outcome of their battle in this respect was decided many years ago in heaven. This was when Satan and his fallen angels were cast down to earth. For this reason alone it would be absurd to conclude that an unfallen angel could possibly be an anti-type to fit man.

Let us consider this issue from another angle. We can quite easily visualise Jesus our heavenly Priest being superior to a type of earthly priest. The real priest is better than the type.

Fit man was a sinner, symbolically attempting to dispose of sins being carried by the goat. It would be silly to suggest that an angel is a better sinner or superior type of man than fit man, more able to defeat sin in a similar manner to the type, and therefore representing the anti-type.

This conclusion, if true, would also be identifying an angel as one directly involved in humanity's war against sin.

Just as fit man symbolically wrestled with the goat, which represented Satan, so will the hundred and forty four thousand wrestle with the fury and power of Satan in the final conflict. As fit man led the scapegoat into a land not inhabited so will the hundred and forty four thousand defeat Satan resulting in him being cast into a land not inhabited.

By implication there can be little doubt that fit man was especially chosen for the task that lay before him. It seems that no ordinary member of Israel would have been equal to the ordeal.

The same criterion must be equally applicable today. The hundred and forty four thousand of God's saints would also need a special preparation for the contest that lies before them. Fit man was physically prepared for his battle because he was a type.

The hundred and forty four thousand will need to be spiritually prepared by the Holy Spirit because they are the anti-types. I am not suggesting that the hundred and forty four thousand will be physically unfit.

When the time comes for the hundred and forty four thousand to do battle with Satan, the heavenly sanctuary will have been cleansed from sin. Through the blood of Christ there will have been a complete and perfect atonement.

In Leviticus we are studying a type of atonement. However, this type did not represent a perfect delineation of God's plan. The sanctuary of the old dispensation could have only remained clean after the cleansing providing that the fit man succeeded in his appointed task.

Had the scapegoat escaped and returned to the camp then all the priestly work that had taken place would have been to no avail.

In this respect the type of method used in disposing of the nation's sins was premature and provisional. It was possible for fit man to fail. Then the priestly work would have meant nothing.

Such will not be the case regarding the battle between the hundred and forty four thousand and Satan. It is when Satan has been defeated that the sins will be placed upon Satan.

Chapter 19
Anti-type differs from Type

With reference to fit man of Leviticus 16:21, comparing the type with the anti-type, it can be seen that they are different in one important respect. In the type the sins were placed upon the head of the scapegoat before fit man went into a type of Jacob's trouble.

This is an indication that the conflict between fit man and the goat (Satan) was in relation to the disposal of the nation's sins. However, victory for the nation could not be claimed before the defeat of the scapegoat.

In the anti-type the sins are placed upon the head of Satan after victory of the hundred and forty four thousand. However, both instances testify to the battle against Satan.

In type fit man was responsible for the defeat of the scapegoat and the disposal of the nation's sins. In anti-type the 144,000 will by the power of Jesus be responsible for the defeat of Satan followed by Jesus placing the sins on the head of Satan the instigator of all sin.

The tussle between fit man and the scapegoat typifies the struggle that is to take place between the hundred and forty four thousand and Satan at the end of time. However, the sins could not truly be disposed of in type until defeat of the scapegoat by fit man. It will be the same in anti-type. The sins cannot be disposed of until Satan has finally been defeated by the hundred and forty four thousand.

In the anti-type it is after the defeat of Satan by the 144,000 anti-types to fit man that Jesus places the sins upon the head of Satan where they belong.

In search for an understanding of the account of fit man in relation to the final conflict let us consider verses 20,21, of chapter 16 in Leviticus:

"And when he hath made an end of reconciling the holy place, and the tabernacle of the congregation, and the altar, he shall bring the live goat. And Aaron shall lay both his hands upon the head of the live goat, and confess over him all the iniquities of the children of Israel, and all their transgressions in all their sins, putting them upon the head of the goat, and shall send him away by the hand of a fit man into the wilderness."

The above quotation that gives an account of the type involved in the cleansing of the sanctuary does not strictly harmonise with the anti-type cleansing of the sanctuary.

The type makes no allowance for the seven last plagues. It would not have been reasonable to inflict upon the Israelites the seven plagues of Revelation every year on The Day of Atonement. It is also different in another important aspect. In the type we have observed that the priest comes out and lays his hands upon the scapegoat immediately after the cleansing operation.

In the anti-type the time known as Jacob's trouble intervenes before the sins are placed upon the head of Satan. However, although the sins are placed on the head of the scapegoat before fit man's tussle with the goat, in type the struggle typifies the time known as Jacob's trouble when God's people engage with Satan in the final battle.

In the respect of sequential timing, the type could not accurately represent the anti-type. To attempt reconciliation between the type and anti-type regarding fit man is to make a wrong approach in dealing with this subject.

On the matter of timing it was not possible for the type to exactly represent the anti-type. In the typical service the sins were visibly placed upon the head of the goat **before** the projected struggle, and before they were disposed of in the wilderness.

In anti-type the same struggle is depicted, but the sins are placed upon Satan **after** the time known as Jacob's trouble. However, in both instances the sins are not disposed of until the bearer of sins is defeated.

To further prove the differences between type and anti-type, verses 23, 24 reveal how Aaron re-entered the tabernacle after the sins have been disposed of as recorded in verse 22, and changed his garments and cleanse his body before making atonement for them all. (Verse 24).

As will be readily observed this ceremony is at variance with the anti-type.

When Jesus puts the sins upon the head of Satan, He will have completely finished the cleansing and changed His garments. It will be as King that He places the sins upon the head of Satan. Neither is anything said about Jesus re-entering the sanctuary once He has finished His work if intercession and mediation described in Daniel 12:1. Leviticus 16:26 further states:

"And he that let go the goat for the scapegoat shall wash his clothes, and bathe his flesh in water, and afterward come into the camp."

Once again it can be seen how difficult it is to sustain a conviction that a clean angel is an anti-type to fit man.

Or that fit man, who needed cleansing before returning to the camp, could be a type of angel. It could be a vain attempt to sustain a pet conviction when one attempts to harmonise the theory that fit man is a type to the angel of Rev. 20:1, 2. Using any criterion the theory completely falls apart.

Approaching the issue from any angle it is not Scripturally accurate to say that fit man is a type of angel.

One should not expect the type to exactly replicate the anti-type nor should one seek to distort Scripture in order to make it appear so. To attempt this brings greater distortion.

Would anyone suggest that the angel who symbolically binds Satan would need to wash his clothes and bathe his flesh before coming into a camp he did not vacate in the first place?

For Aaron to perform such an act of placing the sins on the head of the goat after the wilderness experience would have been inappropriate and would not represent a true type involving the 144,000 and the final battle involving God's law.

Also, had Aaron been truly portraying a message of victory for the 144,000 when placing the sins before the wilderness experience, this would also have been untrue to anti-type.

This act would have been supplying Satan with ammunition. Satan would be able to suggest pre-determination of the anti-typical outcome - that in some way the battle between Satan and the 144,000 would be rigged through unfair divine intervention.

He could then make the legitimate claim that conveying a message that the goat was defeated before the battle would by implication be predetermining victory for the hundred and forty four thousand.

In type Aaron would have been prematurely proclaiming the result of the conflict that is to take place in anti-type.

It could be argued that the result of Jesus' sacrifice as the anti-type was foretold, so why not the outcome of the future battle between the 144,000 and Satan? However, the circumstances are different. Jesus was promised by a divine Creator as our substitute from the foundation of the world.

Regarding the last day saints they make no such promise. Nor can they. It becomes an issue as to whether it is possible for humanity to acquire a Godlike character, and defeat Satan by no other means than is available to all. Just as rebellious humanity will be left with no excuses for their action, equally, Satan will be left with no excuse for his rebellion.

In type and anti-type Jesus leaves Satan without excuse of any kind for any reason. What an excuse Satan would be dealt if the power of an angel of God were needed in order to bring about his defeat. This would be the implication if an angel were the anti-type to fit man. The big question as to whether or not mankind can keep the commandments of God would still remain unanswered.

Surely, the Universe would be left wondering that if such an action would suffice then why not allow an angel to defeat Satan a lot earlier? An angel anti-type to fit man would make a mockery of the last battle involving God's people.

The problem with the theory that the angel of Revelation 20:1,2 depicts an anti-type to fit man is that not only does it make no allowance for the time of Jacob's trouble, it eliminates the necessity for such a battle. Also, the angel of Revelation 20:1,2 is portrayed as the victor.

The type of atonement is a replica of the anti-type, but it does not exactly replicate the anti-type. In type Aaron placed the sins upon the head of the scapegoat when he vacated the sanctuary directly after the symbolic cleansing.

In the anti-type Jesus places the sins upon Satan after the plagues and the wilderness experience of Jacob's trouble. They cannot be placed where they belong until Satan has suffered his final defeat, followed by banishment to the desolate dreary wilderness by the angel of Revelation 20:1,2.

In the type Aaron re-enters the temple after disposing of the nation's sins on the head of the scapegoat. We learn this from the following quotation, taken from Leviticus 16:23, 24.

"And Aaron shall come into the tabernacle of the congregation, and shall put off the linen garments, which he put on when he went into the holy place, and shall leave them there. And he shall wash his flesh with water in the holy place, and put on his garments, and come forth, and offer his burnt offering, and the burnt offering of the people, and make an atonement for himself, and for the people."

In the anti-type Jesus changes from His Priestly garments into the robes of a King, and does not re-enter the sanctuary. In type Aaron appears to his people who remain sinners. In anti-type Jesus appears to a victorious church in the form of the hundred and forty four thousand, who have defeated sin, together with the risen saints.

In type fit man needed cleansing before returning to a camp of sin. In anti-type God's remnant people are already cleansed after the final battle with Satan and, together with the risen saints, are translated to heaven.

Please note that the scapegoat takes the *"iniquities unto a land not inhabited"* where fit man *"shall let go the goat in the wilderness"* (Lev.

16: 22). This differs greatly from the action to be taken by the angel of Revelation 20:1,2. He binds Satan with a *"great chain."*

On the issue of substantiation as to who represents the anti-type to fit man the evidence is overwhelmingly in favour of supporting the hundred and forty four thousand.

Regarding this question of type and anti-type, surely it must be folly to try and equate the old system of atonement with the one now taking place in heaven? Israel of old never did attain to the intended standard. It was a type, lacking much compared to anti-type.

In summary, the struggle of fit man that is recorded in Leviticus typifies the time known as Jacob's trouble involving the hundred and forty four thousand. This also represents the time of the seven last plagues.

However, because in type it was neither possible nor practicable to portray a type of plagues, the sins were placed upon the head of the scapegoat before the typified struggle. In the anti-type Jesus puts the sins upon the head of Satan after the anti-typical battle and after the seven last plagues.

Chapter 20
The Plagues

The theory has been projected that the one-hour judgement plagues recorded in Revelation chapter 18 are not the general seven last plagues of chapter 16, but are specific to the nucleus of apostate Babylon. This assumption makes allowance for the existence of other powers that are not subjected to this one-hour of judgement. (The one-hour in prophetic time represents fifteen days actual time.).

If God is differentiating between several different powers at the end of time we would then have to give some serious consideration to the following Scripture references taken from Revelation 18:2-4.

In these Scripture references God's attention is centred upon one power named Babylon. Does this mean that God is referring to one specific power within the whole world? Or is it more sensibly a reference to apostasy as a whole?

Revelation 18: *"2 And he cried mightily with a strong voice, saying, Babylon the great is fallen, is fallen, and is become the habitation of devils, and the hold of every foul spirit, and a cage of every unclean and hateful bird. 3 For or all nations have drunk of the wine of the wrath of her fornication, and the kings of the earth have committed fornication with her, and the merchants of the earth are waxed rich through the abundance of her delicacies. 4 And I heard another voice from heaven, saying, Come out of her, my people, that ye be not partakers of her sins, and that ye receive not of her plagues."*

It can be seen from the above quotation that God's people are being called out of Babylon; that they *"be not partakers of her sins, and that they receive not of her plagues."*

Would this signify that God is not interested in His people who are not closely associated with this one specific power?

By implication this theory that the plagues of Revelation chapter 18 are restricted to one power makes provision for another significant power in addition to Babylon, which remains isolated from her plagues.

If it were true that these plagues are specific to one power it would create a dilemma as to what is God's message to those who are not part of this Babylonian empire?

Just because God makes reference to *"her plagues"* does not mean that other rebellious powers are not subjected to the same judgmental plagues. Satan uses many agencies or powers in his war against righteousness but there is just one spirit of rebellion. God is calling His people out from all of Satan's agencies. Strictly speaking Babylon is a coalition of *"three unclean spirits"*. (Revelation 16:13).

The other political powers include *"The kings of the earth"* Rev. 18:9. The reference in Revelation 16:19, to *"the great city and the cities of the nations"* also indicate that more than one power is in opposition to God.

Satan has used, and is using different methods of sophistry to appeal to a variety of minds. Even so this should not lead us to become confused into trying to make sense out of a theory, which promotes the idea of two end time judgements involving several different rebellious powers.

The general seven last plagues of Revelation chapter 16, and the one-hour of judgement of Revelation chapter 18 reserved for Babylon mean the same thing.

There is just one rebellion and one judgement at this time being referred to. Regarding the many different organisations in operation against God near the end of time we should not make too much effort in making a distinction that does not exist in Scripture. Scripture teaches us that all the wicked possess the same character of rebellion against God.

All who receive the mark of the beast, *"The same shall drink of the wine of the wrath of God...."* (Revelation 14:10).

The question of a message to a separate, isolated power (Babylon) does not arise. Just as the saints cannot be separated from God, rebels become part of the whole world of Babylon.

If we believe that chapter 18 of Revelation is singling out a particularly nasty number this would indicate that God is calling His people out from there but ignoring His people elsewhere.

The references to her plagues coming in one day and the hour of her judgement are inextricably linked.

The plagues of Revelation chapter 16 end with the final battle between the forces of good and evil before the return of Jesus. The judgement and plagues of chapter 18 also indicate a similar end. It is inconceivable that we are being given two separate accounts of the end of this dispensation.

It is true to say that an argument could be made for a special 15 day judgement reserved for original Babylon, and no one would doubt that there will be varying degrees of suffering. However, a separate 15-day judgement will not find sensible harmony in periods of time or eventual action with the rest of the judgement.

As the seat of Satan's power modern day Babylon is no more deserving of a special judgement (fifteen days of plagues) than any previous kingdom used by Satan for his same rebellious purpose, including Pagan Rome, who killed the Son of God and an untold number of His servants.

The evidence of Revelation chapter 16 in connection with the plagues, and the judgement of Revelation 18 verse 8, and the judgement of verses 10, 17, and 19 refers to the same Babylonian Empire is conclusive and should prove beyond any doubt that all the above mentioned plagues are a reference to the one Babylonian power involving one world-wide rebellion against God.

It is plainly stated in Revelation 18:9, as follows, that those who are associated with Babylon are equally guilty, and therefore equally deserving of her punishment.

"And the kings of the earth, who have committed fornication and lived deliciously with her, shall be-wail her, and lament for her, when they shall see the smoke of her burning."

Verse 10 then indicates that these are *"Standing afar off for the fear of her torment...."* Babylon being a world power it would not be possible for one to be far away from her influence and power. Therefore, this reference to distance must be in the heart's desire rather than geographical.

Chapter 21
Time of the end

To be aware of events that will take place at the close of earth's history it is necessary to study five portions of Scripture. They are as follows:

1- Revelation 18: 8: *"Therefore shall her plagues come in one day, death and mourning, and famine; and she shall be utterly burned with fire: for strong is the Lord God who judgeth her."*

Here is described how the plagues shall come in one day. Can this really be true?

2- Revelation 8:1: *"And when he had opened the seventh seal, there was silence in heaven about the space of half hour."*

Obviously this refers to the opening of the seventh seal and a period of silence in heaven lasting about half an hour, but what is the hidden truth to be revealed in this text?

3- Revelation 15:8: *"And the temple was filled with smoke from the glory of God, and from his power; and no man was able to enter into the temple, till the seven plagues of the seven angels were fulfilled."*

This gives a vivid description of the heavenly temple at the commencement of the plagues.

4- Daniel 12:1: *"And at that time shall Michael stand up, the great prince which standeth for the children of thy people: and there shall be a time of trouble, such as never was since there was a nation even to that same time: and at that time thy people shall be delivered, every one that shall be found written in the book."*

Daniel speaks of a time when Michael [Jesus] stands up to take His kingdom. This is an indication that the work of mediation will be at an end.

5- Revelation 22: 11: *"He that is unjust, let him be unjust still: and he which is filthy, let him be filthy still: and he that is righteous, let him be righteous still: and he that is holy let him be holy still."*

Here we find a description of the human race at the close of probation. Because they occur at the end of probation all of the above Scriptural references seem to be alluding to a specific and identical time period.

What makes the subject under consideration difficult to unravel is the fact that the relevant Scripture references are interrelated. Not one of them will bear fruitful results when studied alone.

Before these end time events take place there remains a time of decision for the human race. Set before every living soul will be presented a choice. There will be just two options. The one is to follow God by a display of harmony with His Sabbath sign of creation. The other is to follow Satan, and receive the mark of the beast. The sad thing about the situation that is to prevail is that many will decide their destiny in ignorance of the significance of their choice.

Serious students of Scripture will know that the beast and his followers will be subjected to the judgement of God during the seven last plagues.

In time and significance the reference in Daniel 12:1 to Michael standing up can be linked with Revelation 8:1 which describes the opening of the seventh seal.

We will begin this section of study by consulting our first reference, Revelation 18:8. Here it is repeated:

*"Therefore shall her plagues come **in** one day, death, and mourning, and famine; and she shall be utterly burned with fire for strong is the Lord God who judgeth her."*

The popularly held view is that the word *"in"* is used as a preposition linked to the word *"one"* as a noun that would indicate one day of plagues.

In prophetic time this would mean that the duration of the plagues would be 360 days that equals one Bible year. However, by holding to this view we are left with too many imponderables.

Firstly, the phrase being studied does not make grammatical sense if it is meant to convey duration of time. It would be more reasonable if it read that her plagues should last for whatever period of time was intended. In these circumstances the word *"for"* would be a more suitable preposition than *"in"*.

Secondly, when probation closes, why would a God of love desire to punish for a whole year a generation that by logical definition, though having rejected Christ, would not necessarily be as wicked as each other? Put another way, common sense suggests that some people will be more evil than others will.

Thirdly, it would mean that the wicked so unfortunate as to be then alive would be subjected to an additional punishment that similar people who had lived previously had escaped.

Fourthly, bearing in mind that for thousands of years God has been longing to see an end to the controversy between good and evil, why would He choose to extend this misery for a further year, knowing that it was too late for any other being to be saved? This would be an agony that heavenly beings would also be obliged to witness.

The question takes on added significance when one considers that the heavenly beings at that time will be anticipating the greatest party that will ever have been seen, the marriage supper of the Lamb, as shown in the following text:

Revelation 19:7-9: *"Let us be glad and rejoice, and give honour to him: for the marriage of the Lamb is come, and his wife hath made herself ready. 8And to her was granted that she should be arrayed in fine linen, clean and white: for the fine linen is the righteousness of saints. 9And he saith unto me, Write, Blessed are they, which are called unto the marriage supper of the Lamb. And he saith unto me, These are the true sayings of God."*

The fifth reason is that the hundred and forty four thousand of God's saints, who will be sealed for the final conflict against Satan, would be suffering for the most part of a year under his temptations. This period, which includes the time of trouble for the saints, would be much more than the forty days of Jesus' temptation in the wilderness.

In consideration of evidence to follow, the sixth and perhaps the most important reason for casting doubt on the commonly held view that the plagues will last for one year, is that it could be without Scriptural foundation. There are also peripheral reasons why it is unlikely that the plagues will last for one year.

Speaking of His return in connection with the end time recorded as follows in Revelation, Jesus used the phrase: *"I come quickly"* three times.

Revelation 22:7 *"Behold, I come quickly: blessed is he that keepeth the sayings of the prophecy of this book."*

Revelation22: 12: *"And behold I come quickly and my reward is with me, to give every man according as his work shall be."*

Revelation 22:20: *"He which testifieth these things saith, Surely I come quickly. Amen. Even so, come, Lord Jesus."*

Revelation 22 verse 12 makes reference to Jesus bringing His reward with Him. After identifying the end time with His proposed actions when speaking with John it does not seem reasonable that Jesus would wait 360 days before bringing His promised reward.

Although it was 1900 years ago when Jesus spoke to John, Jesus was speaking in connection with the close of probation as can be seen from the following reference taken from verse 11:

"He that is unjust, let him be unjust still: and he which is filthy, let him be filthy still: and he that is righteous, let him be righteous still: and he that is holy, let him be holy still."

This would indicate the close of probation as the starting point of Jesus' discourse with John in relation to His quick return and the condition of the world at that time. If this is true, Jesus' return could indeed be quick. In the light of supporting facts to follow, it might be proven to be just a matter of days after the close of probation.

Whatever period Jesus intended, the time span is not a critical point to the truth of this message. If the duration of the plagues is one year, it would certainly be a contradiction in terms for Him to say that He would come quickly, and then wait for the most part of a year before His return.

It is equally certain that the hundred and forty four thousand would find this time period of a long duration. This being the time that includes their agony as they battle with the beast power who will not allow them to buy or sell because they refuse to receive the mark of the beast. (Rev. 13:17).

Let us now approach the text under review from a different angle. Instead of assuming that the word *"in"* of Revelation 18:8 is a preposition linked to the word *"one"* in the form of a noun, let us change tack. Consider the word *"in"* to be an adverb followed by a comma, linked to another adverb, the word *"one"*. We now have an entirely different meaning delivered by the same part of Scripture.

Instead of reading: *"Therefore shall her plagues come in one day"* the words now read: *"Her plagues shall come in, one day."* The insertion of a comma has made a difference. Because punctuation was not included in the original text, this change to the text is permitted.

In effect, all that this Scripture is saying is that a day will come when probation will close, and that the plagues will begin. This would be similar to saying: My ship will come in, one day, or decimalization will come in, one day, or hanging as a punishment will come in, one day.

We are now presented with a vastly different scenario from the same text regarding the plagues. However, no time span for the plagues is given in this section of God's word. To ascertain the truth as to their duration, we need to consult with other parts of Scripture. The answer for this is to be found in the following quotation taken from Revelation 18:10, 17 and 19.

Revelation 18:10: *"Standing afar off for the fear of her torment, saying, Alas, alas, that great city Babylon, that mighty city! For in* **"one hour"** *is thy judgement come."*

Revelation 18:17: *"For in* **"one hour"** *so great riches is come to nought. And every shipmaster, and all the company in ships, and sailors, and as many as trade by sea, stood afar off,"*

Revelation 18:19: *"And they cast dust on their heads, and cried, weeping and wailing, saying, Alas, alas, that great city, wherein were made rich all that had ships in the sea by reason of her costliness! for in **"one hour"** is she made desolate."*

Verse 10 refers to *"one hour" of judgement."* Verse 17 gives evidence of *"**in one hour"** great riches are brought to nought."* Verse 19 reveals that in *"one hour, Babylon is to be made desolate"*.

In this one chapter the duration of the plagues is repeated three times, and stated to last for a period of **"one hour"**. In Scripture the rule is that when something is repeated three times, such an emphasis indicates an established and important truth. See Deuteronomy 19:15 and 2 Corinthians 13:1.

Deuteronomy 19:15: *"One witness shall not rise up against a man for any iniquity, or for any sin, in any sin that he sinneth: at the mouth of two witnesses, or at the mouth of three witnesses, shall the matter be established."*

2 Corinthians 13:1: *"This is the third time I am coming to you. In the mouth of two or three witnesses shall every word be established."*

With the understanding that the hour of Revelation chapter 18 represents prophetic time it can reasonably be concluded that the plagues will last for fifteen days.

The logic is straightforward: -

1 prophetic day = 1 literal year = 360 literal days.

1 prophetic hour = 360 divided by 24 = fifteen days.

The day / year prophetic principle is being applied with regard the *"hour"* referred to above because a length of time is indicated. Whereas in connection with the event and supposed duration of the plagues the verb *"come"* indicates location in time. (*"Come"* Rev. 18:8).

Regarding the duration of the seven last plagues there are those who have difficulty in reconciling a 15 day time span with the famine that is recorded in Revelation 18:8.

However, the dictionary defines a famine more as a condition than length of time. Such terminology as *"extreme scarcity of food"* and *"extreme hunger"* being an example.

It would not necessarily need a great duration of time to achieve such a state of being. There is also the troubled times leading up to the plagues and beyond to consider. In addition to the 15 days of plagues there will also be a period of time involving a number of days extending beyond the plagues.

It would be difficult to imagine that this great controversy between Christ and Satan would end in a whimper, or a whisk of time that would have so little impact to fit the end of thousands of years of turmoil. The duration of the plagues and the manner of the climactic end implied would seem to harmonise with the glory and justice of a loving God.

Our second listed text records the silence in heaven:

Revelation 8:1: *"And when he had opened the seventh seal, there was silence in heaven about the space of half an hour."*

The half an hour being referred to is recognised as being prophetic time. This would mean that this period of half an hour represents seven and half days in actual time. Regarding this time period, it is generally believed that the reason for this silence is that heaven will be empty of its inhabitants at the return of Jesus.

The supposition is that Jesus will be returning with His Father and all the angels of heaven. It is true that Jesus could return and leave heaven empty at the conclusion of the seven last plagues. However, a theory of an empty heaven at any time during the plagues is not borne out by Scripture. Revelation 16:5 records that the angel of the waters is speaking to God during the 3rd plague as follows:

Revelation 16:5: *"And I heard the angel of the waters say, Thou art righteous, O Lord, which art, and wast, and shalt be, because thou hast judged thus."*

In verse 7 another being from heaven is recorded as saying:

"And I heard another out of the altar say, Even so, Lord God Almighty, true and righteous are thy judgements."

In verse 17 God Himself is on record as speaking from the throne, saying, *"it is done!"*

Revelation 16:17: *"And the seventh angel poured out his vial into the air; and there came a great voice out of the temple of heaven, from the throne, saying, It is done."*

Thus heaven is proved not to be empty during the time of the plagues. One can imagine the relief in God's voice when He said *"It is done"*. Showing the same kind of reaction to a time of extreme trauma there was a similar expression of relief uttered by Jesus from the Cross, given as follows:

John 19:30: *"When Jesus therefore had received the vinegar, he said, It is finished: and he bowed his head, and gave up the ghost."*

It has now been proved by our recent study that heaven is not empty during the plagues. Further proof of this can be found in one of our other listed verses, Revelation 15:8, where reference is made of the temple being filled with the glory of God at the time of the plagues.

Revelation 15:8: *"And the temple was filled with smoke from the glory of God, and from his power; and no man was able to enter into the temple, till the seven plagues of the seven angels were fulfilled."*

Also, the word silence does not equate to the word empty. If a place is empty there is no one there to whom the word silence can apply.

Even though Jesus' return could leave heaven empty this is an unlikely scenario. This could have a disquieting effect on some because we can read from Matthew 25:31 that the *"Son of man shall come in his glory, and all the holy angels with him...."*

The above text could imply that heaven is empty at that time. However, there is no evidence of contradiction. Out of all the gospel references to Jesus' return, this is the only one that uses the embracing word "all". It could mean no more than what it says: All the angels that are coming with Jesus will be with Him.

We have had proof from God's word that heaven is not empty during the plagues. However, this truth doest not deny the possibility of heaven being empty at the end of the plagues. Yet it is more reasonable to believe that the Father and many others will be in heaven to greet the victorious Jesus and those angels who accompanied Him to earth as they return in triumph to heaven.

We have learned from Scripture that heaven is not emptied at the opening of the seventh seal. So there must be another reason why heaven is described as being silent. This reason will soon become clear. Let us explore one valid clue. We know that sometimes there can arise circumstances, when because of critical situations, an aura of silence prevails.

By using an analogy we are able to establish a reasonable explanation for such a silence. Imagine a crowd watching a race on the athletic field when the silence would occur and be broken at different stages of the race.

This would be because different sections of the crowd were coming to various conclusions at different stages of the race.

To use the same analogy, at the time of the silence in heaven, the occupants there will also be watching a type of contest.

It would be reasonable to presume that the temple in heaven, in the form of a court, is a vast place where angels and beings from the far reaches of a populated Universe are taking an intense interest in the investigative judgement now taking place.

Those beings that are in heaven will anxiously be witnessing the final conflict between Satan and the people of God. Although it is unlikely that those involved will be aware of Satan's involvement and the significance of their actions, it is the beast power as servant to Satan who is persecuting the people of God in the end time. The issues at stake will be of such magnitude as to cause silence as the watching millions in heaven await the outcome of the contest that is being waged on earth.

When referring to the silence in heaven, Revelation 8:1 makes the point that the period under observation is *"about half an hour."*

Revelation 8:1: *"And when he had opened the seventh seal, there was silence in heaven about the space of half an hour."*

The use of the above word *"about"* is significant. It means that the time scale used above is not specific. The time factor could not be specific because not all the occupants of heaven at that time will be thinking and acting alike. Hence the reason why a precise and specific God uses an unspecific word. Regarding the silence in heaven, as we shall now learn, there is a good reason for this.

In the events surrounding Gethsemane, in His humanity, Jesus took unto Himself the full burden of sin. In this battle against the evil accusations of Satan, the destiny of the whole human race hung in the balance.

Had Jesus lost this battle, the fate of humanity would have been sealed, and humanity would have been forever lost. This was no ordinary battle.

In the Garden of Gethsemane Jesus was under tremendous pressure. We can learn something of His ordeal by reading from Mark 14:34, where it says:

"And saith unto them, My soul is exceeding sorrowful unto death: tarry ye here, and watch."

As can be seen, this could not just be described as a heavy burden under the weight of sin. This was a sorrow *"unto death."* Put another way, the Saviour was dying. Jesus was suffering the strain and mental agony of a nervous breakdown.

That Jesus might be a perfect Saviour for everyone; He needed to feel the pain and suffering of everyone. Not one person will have suffered more than Jesus as proved by the words of Hebrews 4:15 where it says:

"For we have not an high priest which cannot be touched with the feeling of our infirmities; but was in all points tempted like as [we are, yet] without sin."

In the Garden of Gethsemane and on the Cross, Jesus was full of despair and without hope. His suffering went beyond anything that man could possibly suffer and live. Jesus would have given anything, other than abandon His principles in order to ease the agony. He pleaded three times with the Father that the cup of suffering might be removed from His lips. See Matthew 26:38-44. Yet each time the thought remained uppermost in His mind that He should carry out the will of His Father in heaven.

The agony that Jesus endured in the garden of Gethsemane was wholly mental. At this time He had suffered no physical pain. This ordeal lay before Him. Even so He would have died there and then had not an angel been sent to strengthen and comfort Him.

It is reasonable to believe that there was silence in heaven as its occupants witnessed the drama of Gethsemane.

Knowing now what was at stake it is not difficult to understand the reason for this silence. Indeed it would be a great wonder had there been anything but silence at that critical time.

As the destiny of humanity was under attack and in the balance so will history be repeated at the close of probation. Will it be any wonder that there will again be silence in heaven as Satan engages God's people (the hundred and forty four thousand) in the final conflict of the ages?

The question now arises as to why this silence will last about seven and half days. It will readily be seen that seven and a half days represent half of the fifteen days, which will be the duration of the plagues.

Understanding that the plagues will last fifteen days, the occupants of heaven will be in a position to appreciate that after a period short of fifteen days, one way or another, the result of the battle will have reached a critical point of decision.

If in a race on the athletic field someone were well in the lead at an advanced stage of the race, there would be reason for rejoicing from his supporters. So will it be at the time when the hundred and forty four thousand are engaged in an allegorical race that is really a battle upon which the destiny of the human race depends.

If after seven and half days the people of God remain relatively strong, having survived every ordeal that Satan through the beast power has imposed, there is every reason for heavenly occupants to visualise victory. Hence the reason for the broken silence after the space of **about** seven and half days.

The silence will not be broken at the same time by all the onlookers because different ones at varying times will reach different conclusions thus the reason for the reference to the time span being *"for about the space of half hour"* (about seven and half days). This could be just a matter of days short of the appearance of Jesus sitting in *"the clouds of heaven."*

Let us finally test the theory that at the end of the present dispensation there will be an empty heaven for a period of seven and half days, and the misconception that there will be the beginning of 360 days of plagues.

Please note that if Jesus were to leave heaven empty for the space of seven and half days once the seventh seal had been opened, we would be faced with a dilemma in our reckoning. He would need to proceed very slowly during supposedly 360 days of plagues in order to time His appearance during this time. This makes nonsense of the seven and half days empty heaven theory, which is supposed to coincide with His return to earth.

Another alternative to be considered is that Jesus would be waiting in heaven until the supposed year of plagues are finished, and then begin His return journey to earth leaving heaven empty.

This assumption would also be untenable because this means that Jesus would stand waiting in His kingly robes for a year. Considering all the implications in the seven and half days when Jesus is supposed to be returning, the whole theory becomes absurd.

Although the period will not be 360 days, it is unlikely that Jesus will return to earth before the seven last plagues have done their work. It is at that time that every eye then living will witness His return. This will include those who pierced Jesus as set out below:

Revelation 1:7: *"Behold, he cometh with clouds; and every eye shall see him and they also, which pierced him: and all kindreds of the earth shall wail because of him. Even so, Amen."*

The prophecy regarding every eye seeing Jesus will not reach complete fulfilment until the resurrection of the wicked in the second resurrection.

It would be wrong to assume that the silence, which is to take place in heaven, will be a total silence.

The awesome silence at that time does not necessarily mean that there will be no communication among the angels of heaven at the time of comparative silence.

Even so, it can safely be concluded that the events occurring on earth will ensure an anxious type of silence as those in heaven witness the drama unfolding on earth between Satan and the hundred and forty four thousand which will decide the destiny of humanity.

It should now be quite apparent that it is impossible to make a sound argument for the theory that there will be 360 days of plagues coinciding with seven and half days of an empty heaven. In addition, as previously stated, if the plagues are intended to last for a period of 360 days, an unsuitable preposition has been used.

Prior to the introduction of the plagues, Babylon is depicted as an apostate and wicked organisation deserving of punishment. If the duration of the plagues is intended to reflect length of time as the nature of the punishment, surely the preposition used should have been "for", not "in"?

If we wished to indicate the extent of rainfall, we would use such terminology as "it rained four inches in one day". On the other hand, if we wished to convey the duration of something unpleasant to be emphasised, we would not say, "it came in one day". We would be more inclined to say it lasted "for a whole year". In prophetic time this would be for "one day."

To summarise, we need to consult the following Scripture references.

1 Daniel 12:1: *"And at that time shall Michael stand up, the great prince which standeth for the children of thy people: and there shall be a time of trouble, such as never was since there was a nation even to that same time: and at that time my people shall be delivered, every one that shall be found written in the book."*

Revelation 8:1: *"And when he had opened the seventh seal, there was silence in heaven about the space of half an hour."* [Seven and half days]

Revelation 15:5-8: *"And after that I looked, and, behold, the temple of the tabernacle of the testimony in heaven was opened: And the seven angels came out of the temple, having the seven plagues, clothed in pure white linen, and having their breasts girded with golden girdles. And one of the four beasts gave unto the seven angels seven golden vials full of the wrath of God, who liveth forever and ever. And the temple was filled with smoke from the glory of God, and from his power; and no man was able to enter into the temple, till the seven plagues was fulfilled."*

Revelation 15:5 shows that the temple is opened, indicating a similar state of a finished work of mediation in harmony with Revelation 8:1, and the silence in heaven. It can be seen that there is perfect harmony between Daniel 12:1, Revelation 8:1, and Revelation 15:5-8, and the conclusions of this study.

It is quite impossible to reconcile the above Scriptural references in order to accommodate the following convictions:

Seven and half days of silence in heaven because of Jesus' return to earth to raise the saints leaving heaven empty and 360 days of plagues.

There is another interesting fact to be considered in relation to the return to earth of Jesus. When the high priest challenged Jesus before the cross, the priest asked: *"Art thou the Christ, the Son of the blessed? Jesus said, I am: and ye shall see the Son of man sitting on the right hand of power, and coming in the clouds of heaven."* (Mark 14: 61,62).

As further proof that some of those who were responsible for His death will witness the return of Jesus, Revelation 1: 7 speaks of those *"which pierced him"* will witness His return to earth.

This special resurrection involving those who pierced Jesus will most probably be as a result of God's voice speaking from the throne, saying *"it is done"* as recorded in Revelation 16:17, 18.

We have been provided with Scriptural proof that the seven last plagues are not to last for 360 days but 15 days. It is for sure that God would not specially resurrect the high priest together with selected wicked and the selected saints during the chaos of the plagues.

It is in harmony with common sense to believe that the special resurrection for the selected saints and the selected wicked takes place at the end of the 15 days plagues in response to the voice of God spoken from the throne of heaven as recorded in verse 17.

The main resurrection of the dead saints takes place at the command of Jesus followed by the great gathering as the saints are caught up in the air with Jesus and the accompanying angels.

It does not matter how the events and times are jiggled in relation to the Second Coming of Jesus; they just cannot be made to harmonise with the false assumptions that have been made.

Based on the evidence we can conclude that the plagues will last for a period of fifteen days. The duration of the saints' trouble in its most bitter form is some days less than this.

The seven and half days silence in heaven is because of the eternally tremendous significance of the battle then taking place on earth. Although the ordeal of the hundred and forty four thousand cannot remotely be compared to the suffering of Jesus it will be a similar situation to that which prevailed in the garden of Gethsemane when the whole population of heaven were in silence witnessing the drama of the ages.

The silence is not broken until signs of victory are witnessed in the hundred and forty four thousand; not long before the appearance of Jesus.

At some time God's people (the hundred and forty four thousand) will enter into a black tunnel of despair, as did Jacob in type. Like the type, the hundred and forty four thousand will have been prepared for the ordeal. Like the type, the anti-types will have been trained in the school of Christ.

After some days, the hundred and forty four thousand will remember the promises of God and hope will give birth to a glimmer of light. Then the heavens will herald the way to the beginning of glory when their Teacher, and Saviour, Jesus Christ is seen sitting *"in the clouds of heaven."*

Chapter 22
One Hour & the Ten Kings

The Bible teaches that it is not in God's plan that the saints should be ignorant of the issues involving the controversy between good and evil. Thus could the prophet Amos under inspiration say: *"Surely the Lord God will do nothing, but that he revealeth his secret unto his servants the prophets."* (Amos 3:7).

The fulfilment of prophecies will do nothing for those who do not believe or understand what is written in the Bible. *"Prophesying serveth not for them that believe not, but for them which believe."* (1 Corinthians 14:22).

The prophecies of the Bible are there for the purpose of bringing enlightenment to the minds of God's people. In the closing stages of earth's history there is little that is more important to the saints than knowledge of Bible prophecies.

According to Scripture, probation for the human race cannot come to an end before there has been established a new world-order made up of ten regions that in Revelation 17:12 is described as ten kings thus:

*"And the ten horns which thou sawest are **ten kings**, which have received no kingdom as yet; but receive power as kings "**one hour**" with the beast."*

It is prophesied that this new order will be in opposition to God and His people. We know that this new world-order is to be against God because it is going to work in harmony with the beast.

Action against the saints will be perpetrated by a pseudo religious system in spiritual ignorance of the folly of its actions

The verse above is referring to a time close to the end of probation for the human race, and indicates that this new world-order is not intended to last for more than **"one hour"**.

This is such a short length of time as to be of no apparent significance. In these circumstances there must be a more sensible explanation to the use of the word *"hour"* in the context now being studied from Revelation.

Before considering the repeated use made of the above words *"one hour"* it is first necessary to establish that when used in prophetic time, this 'one-hour' represents fifteen days in actual time. We learn this from Numbers 14:34, and Ezekiel 4:6. In both places reference is made to the interpretation of *"each day for a year."*

Broken down, and applying this rule, this would mean that one hour in prophetic time = 15 days in actual time.

By way of an introduction to the *"one hour"* mentioned above, I believe it would also be of benefit to first consider the references to the words *"one hour"* in their proper context, as recorded several times in Revelation, with their relevance to end time events and the people of God.

For example, when considered in their context, the following Scripture references are plainly indicating that a period or point in time is being conveyed:

Revelation 3:3: *"Remember therefore how thou hast received and heard, and hold fast, and repent. If therefore thou shalt not watch, I will come on thee as a thief, and thou shalt not know what **"hour"** I will come upon thee."*

John 2:4: *"Jesus saith unto her, Woman, what have I to do with thee? mine **"hour"** is not yet come."*

Luke 12:12: *"For the Holy Ghost shall teach you in the same **hour** what ye ought to say."*

Luke 12:40: *"Be ye therefore ready also: for the Son of man cometh at an **"hour"** when ye think not."*

While the above quotations are obviously a reference to a point in time, by contrast, the following quotations, taken from Matthew 20:12 and Luke 22:59, are obvious examples where the *"hour"* described adjectively indicates length of time.

Matthew 20:12: *"Saying, These last have wrought [but]"* **one hour"**, *and thou hast made them equal unto us, which have borne the burden and heat of the day."*

Luke 22:59: *"And about the space of "**one hour**" after another confidently affirmed, saying, Of a truth this [fellow] also was with him: for he is a Galilaean."*

The quotations to follow from Revelation are also examples where the words *"one hour"* are being described adjectively to indicate a length of time. The difference between the two examples is that the references to follow from Revelation are, I believe, in connection with prophetic time whereas in Luke and Matthew above, normal time is obviously being referred to.

It is reasonable to believe that the use of the noun word *"hour"* in the following quotations from Revelation is being described adjectively. Why else would the word *"one"* be used as an adjective to qualify the noun *"hour"*?

Thus it is sensible to conclude that each of the following quotations from Revelation chapter 18 speak of a literal hour in prophetic time, which is equal to 15 days actual time.

Verse 10: *"Standing afar off for the fear of her torment, saying, Alas, alas that great city Babylon, that mighty city! for in '**one hour**' is thy judgment come."*

Verse:17: *"For in "**one hour**" so great riches is come to nought. And every shipmaster, and all the company in ships, and sailors, and as many as trade by sea, stood afar off,"*

Verse:19: *" And they cast dust on their heads, and cried, weeping and wailing, saying, Alas, alas, that great city, wherein were made rich all that had ships in the sea by reason of her costliness! for in "**one hour**" is she made desolate."*

Just as the above references are examples where *"***one hour***"* in prophetic time equals fifteen days in actual time, the same rule logically applies equally to our opening reference of Revelation 17:12 concerning the world-wide order of ten kings that are to reign for fifteen days with the beast.

From the book of Revelation we have read a detailed account of two periods of fifteen days, making a total of thirty days that are to lead up the final days of earth's history and the return of Jesus.

The first fifteen days are taken up when the world in rebellion unite making a worldwide order of ten kings. (Revelation 17:12). There is then to follow a further fifteen days of plagues before the return of Jesus. See references from Revelation chapter 18 above.

The ten horns or ten kings quoted above from Revelation 17:12 are not the same ten horns or ten kings of Daniel chapter 7 and Revelation chapters 12, 13.

It has long been accepted that the kings of Daniel chapter 7 and Revelation chapters 12, 13 are referring to countries and historical leaders heading Western Europe. Whereas the ten horns or ten kings of Revelation 17:12 will be leaders encompassing the whole world.

This world kingdom comprising of the ten kings will emerge with the restoration of power to the beast. Revelation 17:8 refers to it as the beast that *"was"* until the year 1798. (Apostate church and state united) At that time it became the beast that *"is not"* but is yet to ascend before it finally goes *"into perdition."*

From previous study we are acquainted with the dream of King Nebuchadnezzar recorded in Daniel chapter 2. The king had a dream where he saw a head of gold (Babylon). Arms of silver (Media-Persia).

Thighs of brass (Greece). Legs of iron (Rome). And the feet of part iron and part clay. (Mainly Western Europe).

As previously noted these same kingdoms are also recorded in Daniel chapter 7.

In Daniel 7:1-7 the emerging nations are described as a lion, a bear, and as a leopard. The forth beast, Rome is portrayed as a beast, *"dreadful and terrible."*

From this beast was to emerge the ten kingdoms of Western Europe. A composition of the four beasts is described in Revelation chapter 13:1, 2.

This composition of all four beasts makes up the fifth beast or kingdom that is the apostate Babylonian Church of Papal Rome.

In its opposition to God, the fifth kingdom retains a composition of the same pagan characteristics as the previous four kingdoms. Therefore, it is numbered with them, as recorded in Revelation 13:1,2.

Showing a consistency of apostasy in verse 6 it says of this beast power: *"And he opened his mouth in blasphemy against God, to blaspheme his name, and his tabernacle, and them that dwell in heaven."*

Revelation 17: 10 says *"there are seven kings: five are fallen, and one is, and the other is not yet come; and when he cometh, he must continue a short space."*

In vision John of the Revelation speaks of a time when five kings are fallen. (Babylon, Media-Persia, Greece, Pagan Rome, Papal Rome)

This indicates a time when all five kingdoms have lost their power.

This point in time is focussed on the year 1798 at the fall of the Babylonian fifth kingdom of apostasy; signified by the *"deadly wound"* suffered at the removal of state power from the apostate church. See Revelation 13:3.

This is also the time when the United States of America came to ascendancy, to become the sixth king and became the one that *"is"* of Revelation 17, verse 10. Verse 10 also speaks of another kingdom that *"is not yet come."*

This kingdom, which also involves the U.S.A., will come into being when the U.S.A. joins with the apostate church in order to enforce the mark of the beast. This will be the seventh king of verse 10. *"He must continue a short space"*

The original fifth beast of apostasy is the beast that *was*, before 1798. (Verse 8, when the Pope was imprisoned). He then becomes the beast that is not after 1798.

After its restoration to power, this beast will link with the U.S.A. (The sixth king) thus is making the seventh king.

With its power of enforcement this king becomes the eighth king of worldly power, and is of the seventh. (Verse 11).

Revelation 17:12 reveals that this power of the eighth king has *"received no kingdom as yet; but receive power as kings "**one hour**" (*fifteen days*) with the beast."*

This eighth kingdom, which can be said to have derived from the seven or is of the seventh, involves the whole world. When motivated by the beast power, the U.S.A. leads the world to bestow honour on Papal Rome, which is a church in apostasy.

In connection with the coming kingdom of the ten kings (new world order) and their *"one hour"* reign, it has already been established that this one-hour is in prophetic time, which is equal to fifteen days of actual time.

Thus at the end of time, overall there seems to be a total of a *"short space"* of time referred to in verse 10 when the U.S.A. links with Papal Rome to make the seventh king.

With the end of this unspecified period of a short time there then follows another period of fifteen days when there emerges a worldwide kingdom comprising of ten kings, which make the eighth king.

These two periods are followed by fifteen days of plagues. Before the return of Jesus there is yet a further period of time, which extends beyond the plagues.

Chapter 23
U.S.A. and the World Order

There is often some confusion regarding the identity of the beast and the dragon of Revelation.

Regarding the dragon, there can be no denying that primarily the dragon symbolises Satan. Secondly, it is a symbol of the Pagan Roman Empire.

Revelation 12:7 relates the war that took place in heaven between the angels of God and Satan, the original beast and his fallen angels. In this verse Satan is described as the *"dragon."* In verse 9 Satan is described as *"that old serpent, called the Devil, and Satan."*

In its secondary role as the dragon representing Pagan Rome, in Revelation 12:1-6 there is evidence of this power trying to prevent the mission of Jesus when He was just a baby. This attempt to kill the baby Jesus was made through the governor, Herod. It was from Rome that Herod derived his power.

In Revelation 13:1,2 there is a record of the dragon and the beast. The beast is described as a leopard rising up *"out of the sea"* (from among peoples). We learn from verse 2 that the dragon gave the leopard beast *"his power, and seat, and great authority."*

This is a record of Pagan Rome, in the form of a dragon, passing on its power to Papal Rome in the form of a leopard. This is an indication of the changing nature in its religion as Rome moved from its Pagan form of worship to a declared commitment to Christianity.

In the Bible a beast can symbolise a nation or power. For an example showing both working in conjunction with one another there is need to go to Revelation 17:1-4, where it says:

"And there came one of the seven angels which had the seven vials, and talked with me, saying unto me. Come hither; I will shew thee the judgment of the great whore that sitteth upon many waters: With whom the kings of the earth have committed fornication, and the inhabitants of the earth have been made drunk with the wine of her fornication. So he carried me away in the spirit into the wilderness: and I saw a woman sit upon a scarlet coloured beast, full of names of blasphemy, having seven heads and ten horns. And the woman was arrayed in purple and scarlet colour, and decked with gold and precious stones and pearls, having a golden cup in her hand full of abominations and filthiness of her fornication."

Here is shown how the civil power (beast) of the state is supporting the ecclesiastical power of the woman. In this instance the woman is in a fallen state of apostasy.

The colours of purple and scarlet aptly describe the robes worn by popes and cardinals of the Papal Church. The golden cup in the woman's hand is said to be *"full of abominations and filthiness of her fornication"* instead of purity and truth that is the symbol of a doctrinally pure church.

It will be noticed that although the strength of the beast is needed to support the woman, it is the woman (Apostate church) astride the beast that is the intelligence that does the steering.

Before the return of Jesus, God's people are to suffer persecution at the hand of the beast power. This persecution cannot begin until the beast as made a complete recovery from the deadly wound inflicted in the year 1798.

The deadly wound is an indication that supportive power of the state has been removed from the apostate church. The deadly wound cannot be completely healed before there is a return of lost power. The power can only be restored when the church receives the support of a powerful state.

As the power was removed from the Roman Catholic Church in 1798, Scripture gives evidence of another significant power emerging. In Revelation 13:11, it is thus described:

13:11 *"And I beheld another beast coming up out of the earth; and he had two horns like a lamb, and he spake as a dragon."* (U.S.A.).

This is a cryptic account giving the history of the United States of America as it emerges as the sixth king of Rev. 17:10. At the time located by John it is identified as the one that *"is"* that replaced the fallen kingdoms of Babylon, Medo-Persia, Greece, Pagan Rome and Papal Rome.

Every nation in history connected in any way with God's people is mentioned in Bible prophecy.

In this connection it is noted that in Scripture, Babylon and Medo-Persia incorporates the civilised part of Asia. Greece covered Eastern Europe. Pagan Rome, Papal Rome and the ten kingdoms of Daniel 7 cover mainly Western Europe but also relate to parts of North Africa and the Middle East.

The dragon of Revelation 12, together with the ten horns, also covers Western Europe. So do the leopard beast and ten horns recorded in Revelation 13. In this respect, it makes perfect sense that such an important power as the U.S.A. with its Protestant pedigree would occupy a place in Bible prophecy representing the New World.

In specifying the lamb like character of a beast, John was denoting the emerging power of the U.S.A. as being innocent and youthful.

There is no record of a young nation arriving on the world scene at the time indicated by John other than the U.S.A. This is the nation that began quietly then became a power of world prominence. It then matured to become the beast that Revelation 13:13 says is to perform *"great wonders."*

The two horned beast (U.S.A.) recorded by John cannot be a reference to a new symbol of any existing or previously mentioned power because it is described as *"another beast"*.

Further evidence proving the identity of the two-horned beast is the manner of its emergence. New nations are generally formed when replacing other nations that have been overthrown.

Regarding the United States, it is said to have emerged by *"coming out of the earth."* (Rev. 13:11).

This is a description of a new nation emerging in a different manner than is normal. The emergence of a new nation is normally said to take place among people.

It would not be reasonable to suppose that the United States would not be mentioned in Bible prophecy. Any nation that holds a prominent position in world history and is connected with the people of God cannot fail to be mentioned in prophecy.

Any reasonable check will reveal that the only young nation that came into existence as the Papal dominion declined is the U.S.A.

It is recorded in Scripture that the U.S.A. will bring about a restoration of the power to enforce doctrines of the Roman Catholic Church.

The Scripture references to follow give a vivid account of the role to be played by America in the closing stages of earth's history. As the sixth king of prophecy proclaiming its association with king seven and eight, Scripture references to follow details the part to be played by America before God drops the final curtain on the great controversy.

Revelation 13:11: *"And I beheld another beast coming up out of the earth; and he had two horns like a lamb, and he spake as a dragon."* (U.S.A.).

13:12 "And he exerciseth all the power of the first beast before him, and causeth the earth and them which dwell therein to worship the first beast, whose deadly wound was healed."

13:14 *"And deceiveth them that dwell on the earth by [the means of] those miracles which he had power to do in the sight of the beast; saying to them that dwell on the earth, that they should make an image to the beast, which had the wound by a sword, and did live."*

The act of persecution by the U.S.A. described above will ignorantly be done in the name of God.

The kind of persecution recorded above is also recorded in John 16:2 where it says: *"that whosoever killeth you will think that he doeth God service."*

Although the wound suffered by the beast power is partly healed with the reinstatement of the Pope on March 14, 1800, it is only the U.S.A. who has the authority to bring about a complete healing of the deadly wound suffered by the beast power which was also described as the fifth king.

The U.S.A. is the only nation which because of its moral stand and great world domination is able to bring about an image to the beast referred to above in Revelation 13:14.

Restoring the power of the state to the apostate church brings about this healing to make an image of the beast.

There are various views as to what constitutes an image to the beast. Some believe that when Protestantism joins with the state in persecution of God's people there is formed an image of the beast that persecuted God's people for 1260 years. However, in consideration that the original beast is Satan, any organised form of rebellion is a reflection of action from the beast.

Because of its publicly declared views on Christianity it can be clearly seen how plausible it is for such a nation as the U.S.A. to take a moral stand in what is believed to be a return to old fashion standards of Christianity.

As quoted in verse 13 above it says of the U.S.A.: *"And he doeth great wonders, so that he maketh fire come down from heaven on the earth in the sight of men."*

A concordance rendition of the word *"fire"* above is the same as that used in Acts 2:3 where it says that on the day of Pentecost there appeared to God's servants *"cloven tongues like as of fire"*.

The *"fire"* referred to in connection with the U.S.A. might well be a devilish counterfeit of that recorded in Acts.

Evidence of an unhealthy upsurge in religious fervour from the U.S.A. would indicate a fulfilment of the above prophecy.

Events now taking place are plain evidence as to the truth and accuracy of the above predictions regarding the authority of the U.S.A. Again referring to the U.S.A. we learn from the text below of its ability to restore power to the beast:

Revelation 13:15: *"And he had power to give life unto the image of the beast, that the image of the beast should both speak, and cause that, as many as would not worship the image of the beast should be killed."*

This religious fervour is to be translated into a message of deception as shown in the verse recorded above.

Satan has engineered a counterfeit of every important Bible truth including the seventh day Sabbath and the state of the dead. He has also introduced a false type of love.

Therefore, there is reason to believe that he would also counterfeit the blessings described on the day of Pentecost as recorded in the second chapter of Acts. Thus would the deception continue as recorded above.

As noted in the previous chapter, Revelation 17:12 informs us that this coalition of evil which will involve the U.S.A. and the apostate church will, under the title of *"ten kings"*, create a new world-order opposed to God and His people. Verse 11 tells us this new-world order, under the title of the eighth king, will go *"into perdition."*

The new world-order, which is close at hand, has not yet been fully established. When it does inherit this all-embracing power, persecution of God's elect will begin in earnest.

We are told that this power of oppression against religious liberty will reign for one prophetic hour (15 days).

In the light of circumstances now prevailing in the world it is not so strange to visualise the truth made so obvious in Scripture and in political dialogue. Talk of a new world-order has been in existence for a number of years.

Regarding the ten kings that are to reign over one kingdom as a team with one purpose in mind, there has already been talk of a worldwide division of ten economic regions.

That there is unity of purpose in this respect involving the whole world is apparent from the following quotation taken from Revelation that indicates the measure of world support given to the beast power:

Revelation 17:15: *"And he saith unto me, The waters, which thou sawest, where the whore sitteth, are peoples, and multitudes, and nations, and tongues."*

The following quotation taken from Revelation 7:13 also testifies to this unity of purpose:

"These have one mind, and shall give their power and strength unto the beast."

Then finally we learn from Revelation 17:14 that:

"These shall make war with the Lamb, and the Lamb shall overcome them: for he is Lord of lords, and King of kings: and they that are with him [are] called, and chosen, and faithful."

The reference in verse 15 to the whore and *"peoples, and multitudes"* indicates that she will have international support for her persecution of God's saints. The ten kings making up the new world-order have not received their kingdom as yet.

It is God's desire that no one should come under the spell of an apparently godly power that is succeeding in deceiving much of the world. He is pleading:

Revelation 18:4: *"Come out of her, my people, that ye be not partakers of her sins, and ye receive not of her plagues."*

It should be realised that the above reference to Babylon is not a reference to any geographical location or particular division of people. Spiritual Babylon is the mind of anyone who is not in harmony with the God of creation. Therefore, to be in sin is to reside in Babylon.

Of course, this means that one could be attending a true and doctrinally pure church and still be a resident of Babylon.

Chapter 24
Come out of Her My People

In the book of Revelation there are several references to *"the mark of the beast"* in connection with the time of the end.

Revelation 13:16,17 speaks of a worldly power inflicting financial restriction upon those who refuse to display allegiance to this power by refusing its mark.

There is ample proof from the word of God that His sign of creation to His people is the seventh day Sabbath. Therefore, any opposition to this fact by bestowing honour to another day, or any other form of rebellion against the law of God is tantamount to receiving the spirit of anti-Christ and the mark of the beast.

There are many creeds that profess a belief in the relevance of God's law of Ten Commandments. However, there is evidence of the same people declaring a contemptuous disregard, for God's seventh day Sabbath.

Evidence of the final battle involving the question of allegiance can be found in Revelation 13:4 where it says:

"And they worshipped the dragon which gave power unto the beast: and they worshipped the beast, saying, Who [is] like unto the beast? who is able to make war with him?"

In Revelation 18:1-4 is an urgent message from God pleading to people to come out of Babylon in order that they may escape the punishment of her plagues. The message reads as follows:

"And after these things I saw another angel come down from heaven, having great power; and the earth was lightened with his glory. 18:2 And he cried mightily with a strong voice, saying, Babylon the great is fallen, is fallen, and is become the habitation of devils, and the hold of every foul spirit, and a cage of every unclean and hateful bird. 18:3 For all nations have drunk of the wine of the wrath of her fornication, and the kings of the earth have committed fornication with her, and the merchants of the earth are waxed rich through the abundance of her delicacies. 18:4 And I heard another voice from heaven, saying, Come out of her, my people, that ye be not partakers of her sins, and that ye receive not of her plagues."

A measure of the urgency and significance of this heavenly messenger is found in verse 1 above, which proclaims this latest call from heaven as being delivered by *"another angel"*. This is an indication that there have been other angels involved in the heavenly effort at restoring harmony between heaven and earth.

A record of the other angels can be found in Revelation 10:1-3 and Revelation 14:6-10. There is the mighty angel of chapter 10, and the three angels of chapter 14. This brings the number of angels to five.

They are all warning of the consequences for those who neglect the call of heaven, and continue to give worship to the beast.

Revelation 10:1 speaks of a **mighty** angel coming down from heaven. In Scripture, God is often referred to as "Lord God Almighty". It is unlikely that any normal angel would be described with the same title. Therefore, I believe that we can safely conclude that the mighty angel is none other than Jesus.

Revelation 10:3 describe the loud voice of the mighty angel as *"when a lion roareth"*. To further support the belief that the mighty angel is Jesus, Revelation 5:5 describes Jesus as the lion from the tribe of Judah.

The first angel of Revelation 14:6 proclaims the *"everlasting gospel"*. Verse 8 recounts, *"another angel, saying, Babylon is fallen, is fallen"*. In verses 9. 10 there is the record of a third angel and a warning to those who ignore God's call, and bestow worship to the beast.

Thus, firstly, there is the call from the mighty angel of Revelation chapter 10. This is followed by the messages from the three angels of chapter 14. There is also the angel from chapter 18:1. This makes a total of five angels. In addition, there is also the voice from heaven recorded in chapter18:4 as follows:

"And I heard another voice from heaven, saying, Come out of her, my people, that ye be not partakers of her sins, and that ye receive not of her plagues."

There is now evidence of six heavenly agencies combining with earthly messengers involved in the final call to all people, indicating the importance being applied to the messages.

The above message of Revelation reveals the urgency of the message being delivered in heaven's final endeavour to draw the world's attention to the fact that its people are approaching the climax of the world's history.

The fate of all the living, for eternity will be decided in the final conflict of the ages. Of those final remnant that have chosen to be allied to the cause of God by recognising His sovereign Majesty, it will be said as follows in Revelation 14:1-3:

"And I looked, and, lo, a Lamb stood on the mount Sion, and with him an hundred forty [and] four thousand, having his Father's name written

in their foreheads. 14:2 And I heard a voice from heaven, as the voice of many waters, and as the voice of a great thunder: and I heard the voice of harpers harping with their harps: 14:3 *And they sung as it were a new song before the throne, and before the four beasts, and the elders: and no man could learn that song but the hundred [and] forty [and] four thousand, which were redeemed from the earth.*

The contrast for the wicked could not be starker. In verses 9, 10 is the following record:

"And the third angel followed them, saying with a loud voice, If any man worship the beast and his image, and receive [his] mark in his forehead, or in his hand. The same shall drink of the wine of the wrath of God, which is poured out without mixture into the cup of his indignation; and he shall be tormented with fire and brimstone in the presence of the holy angels, and in the presence of the Lamb:"

The book of Revelation reveals that in the time of the end the beast seeking worship is an agency involved in much action in its war against God. The controversy between the beast power and the saints is not a new phenomenon. This movement was already at work in Paul's day.

In 2 Thessalonians 2:3, it also speaks of *"a man of sin."* Then verses 7-9 goes on to say of this man centred power:

"For the mystery of iniquity doth already work: only he who now letteth [will let], until he be taken out of the way. And then shall that Wicked be revealed, whom the Lord shall consume with the spirit of his mouth, and shall destroy with the brightness of his coming: [Even him], whose coming is after the working of Satan with all power and signs and lying wonders."

Referring again to the beast power that is to reign during the end time, let us be reminded of Revelation 13:16-18 where it says:

"And he causeth all, both small and great, rich and poor, free and bond, to receive a mark in their right hand, or in their foreheads: And that no man might buy or sell, save he that had the mark, or the name of the beast, or the number of his name. Here is wisdom. Let him that hath understanding count the number of the beast: for it is the number of a man; and his number [is] Six hundred threescore [and] six."

This Scripture is a sobering statement that it is to become a matter of life or death for eternity regarding which religious power is the object of service. We have just read something of the lengths that the apostate power is prepared to go in order to enforce subjection to its cause during the end time.

The real strength of its appeal is in the fact that it is a religious organisation that claims to hold the authority of the God of heaven.

Faced with the awesome might of a long established system of apparent godliness it is not difficult to visualise the level of success that is to be enjoyed by this apostate system that sets itself above God as regards law and grace.

The message of Revelation, regarding the anti-Christ is a clear prophetic account of the war between heaven and Satan, who is giving his power to the beast.

It is God's desire that no one should come under the spell of an apparently godly power which is succeeding in deceiving much of the world and is pleading: *"Come out of her, my people, that ye be not partakers of her sins, and ye receive not of her plagues."*

Chapter 25
One God in Plurality

The many different messages on the subject of the Trinity and Holy Spirit can be confusing and unconvincing. For this reason I believe that it is of some consequence to establish an explanation of the Holy Spirit that it is compatible with reason.

It may be that sensible answers to some important questions might be simpler than imagined.

There is no evidence in Scripture that in any way suggests that there is a fundamental separation between God the Father and His Holy Spirit. After a study of this subject I believe it is possible to put to rest any confusion regarding inspired writings.

Rather than cause discord it is better to be in ignorance of certain doctrinal matters. A loving harmony of purpose in Christ is more to be favoured. Yet God would not have those who are to stand through the final conflict ignorant of relevant truth, especially when the loving character of God is brought into question.

With these issues in mind the following thoughts are being expressed with the understanding that this message will only appeal to those who are inclined, by nature, to have a desire to more fully explore subjects that others might find of no consequence and not worth their study.

It is impossible to comprehensively define the Spirit of God. So any conclusions reached on the subject cannot exceed the limitation of our minds. Neither is it essential to salvation to delve unnecessarily into such a profound subject. Nevertheless, I believe that it is in harmony with God's will that we understand enough to enable us to give sensible answers when the door is opened to false doctrines.

"God is a Spirit..." (John 4:24. In the Greek *"God is Spirit"*).

Because the Holy Spirit is God in God the Father He must be immortal. Yet nowhere in Scripture is the Holy Spirit described as immortal. This is an important point because if the eternal Spirit were described as immortal it would mean that dead souls would live on in the spirit.

Opinions are divided when attempting a reasonable assessment as to the form of the Holy Spirit.

The question one most frequently encounters is whether the Spirit is a power or a Person. The answer is, He is both.

As awesome as is the power of the Spirit, there are ample Scriptural references to prove that the Spirit is more than a power.

Scripture proves that the Spirit is in possession of executive prerogatives. He has a mind of power that, though able to operate independently of the physical presence of the Father, is one with the Father because He is the Father. And herein lays the mystery.

As is generally presented, teaching on the Holy Spirit makes too much of a separation between God the Father and the Holy Spirit. The danger with this type of thinking is that the door is then opened to the false doctrine that life is indigenous to the spirit. We are made in the image of God (Genesis 1:26).

So any belief, which makes a separation between God and His Spirit, would need to also apply to man. Assuming that there exists an immortal separate being of the spirit could easily lead to the belief that the spirit lives on after death of the body.

As an added safeguard against this kind of reasoning we are told that at death that *"the spirit shall return to God who gave it."* (Ecclesiastes 12:7).

We know from Hebrews 9:14 that the Spirit is eternal but the Bible does not speak of the Holy Spirit as being immortal. Thus are we further discouraged from the error of believing in the existence of a live spirit after death.

Any doctrine that could allow a belief in the existence of a live spirit after death, finds a certain amount of harmony with Babylon. All these kind of conclusions could have the effect of projecting God in an unkind light. It is then just a step from the doctrine of purgatory and eternal torment as the wicked become separated from the presence of God.

It might be tedious to quote a lot of Scripture when studying one topic but I do not see any other way to establish the truth and bring reconciliation between Scripture and observations made by other respected sources on this subject of the Holy Spirit.

No great difficulty is experienced when making an assessment regarding God the Father and God the Son. Such as the following text supplying the answer:

John 14:9: *"...he that hath seen me hath seen the Father...."* This seems to settle most conclusions regarding the Father and the Son.

Listed below are some of the qualities, abilities and sensitivities etc. attributed to the Holy Spirit, proving His Personality. However, when this list is studied it becomes obvious that in general it could apply equally to God the Father or God the Son.

Matt. 12:31   Can be blasphemed.

Matt. 12:32	Can be sinned against.
Matt. 28:19	Has a name.
John 14:16	Comforter like Jesus.
John 14:26	Teaches.
John 15:26	Testifies.
John 16:8	Reproves.
John 16:13	Guides.
John 16:14	Glorifies Christ. Every Christian does this.
Acts 5:3	Can be lied to.
Acts 10:20	Spoke to Peter.
Acts 13:2	Spoke to Antioch brethren.
Acts 15:28	Selects.
Acts 16:6	Can forbid.
Rom. 8:26	Intercedes.
1 Cor. 2:11	Has knowledge.
1 Cor.12: 11	Divides gifts.
Eph. 4:30	Can be grieved.
Heb. 10:29	Can be insulted.
1 Pet. 1:2	Can sanctify.

It is important to understand the part played by the Holy Spirit rather than allow our eyes to be restricted by tunnel vision. Thus not realising that the Father and the Son are equally affected. It is a mistake not to equate the Father and the Son with the Holy Spirit.

God consists of substance, as we understand it, and Spirit. It is unwise attempting to separate the two. In so doing, we would be left with the question as to what would make the Father holy?

Would it be that the Holy Spirit could make God the Father redundant? The truth of the matter is, God the Father, and God the Holy Spirit are one and the same. It is the Holy Spirit that is the power that enables our heavenly Father to be Omnipresent.

By His Spirit, the Father can be present everywhere both in heaven and on earth. It is through the presence of the Holy Spirit that the Father can be two in one. In the same way Jesus and the Spirit are two in one. Being made in the image of God would suggest that therefore mankind has the potential of becoming two in one.

One should not become confused into thinking that the Spirit of the Father and the Spirit of the Son (Jesus) are different Spirits. It could then so easily lead to the conclusion that there exist four Gods, including two of the Spirit.

Just as the Spirit is in God, God is in the Spirit. Rephrased, it could be said that the Spirit is in the mind of God and the mind of God is in the Spirit.

God's mind is holy and of a much higher dimension than we can even begin to understand. The Spirit is an extension of His mind which enables Him to think and act on a scale that we find difficult to visualise, and impossible to comprehend.

It was by such power that *"Jesus perceived in his spirit that they so reasoned within themselves, he said unto them: Why reason ye these things in your hearts?"* (Mark 2:8).

Here is an example of a power that exceeded both the body and the mind.

Both the Father and the Son are one because the same harmonious Holy Spirit motivates them. This is not to say they are one Being, but one Spirit. Jesus is one with the Father. *"I and my Father are one."* (John 10:30).

In the same way the Spirit is one with the Father, and is also one with the Son. The Holy Spirit of the Father and the Son make up the third Person of the Godhead.

Thus, the Father and the Son and the Holy Spirit are accurately portrayed in Scripture as one, and a Trinity.

John and his spirit are one. Jill and her spirit are one. Should they both be in total rebellion against God they become one in spirit. This would then create a trio in opposition to God.

In the fullness of time the church in Christ will become one by the same Spirit. Hence the following prayer from Jesus, which is recorded in John, 17:20-23:

"Neither pray I for these alone, but for them also which shall believe on me through their word; That they all may be one; as thou, Father, (art) in me, and I in thee, that they also may be one in us: that the world may believe that thou hast sent me. And the glory which thou gavest me I have given them; that they may be one, even as we are one: I in them, and thou in me, that they may be made perfect in one; and that the world may know that thou hast sent me, and hast loved them, as thou hast loved me."

Jesus prayed to the Father and not the Holy Spirit. It is also important to recognise that our prayers need to go into the heavenly sanctuary in the presence of Christ and before the majesty of the Father's throne.

Only God has the power to live in the Spirit. Beings can be in possession of this gift only by the will of God.

Jesus was able to perceive by the mind of His Spirit when on earth. An inkling of this truth can be found in the following observation: John of Revelation was *"in the Spirit on the Lord's day* .(Revelation 1:10) penning the revelation of Jesus Christ. Of course, the Spirit was also in John.

In like manner, the Father and the Son are in the Spirit. Unconstrained by circumstance or matter, God is able to impart His Spirit, detach His Spirit, and still retain His Spirit in full measure.

Thus was He able to take of the spirit that was upon Moses and *"give it unto the seventy elders."* (Numbers 11:25).

Since the fall there basically exists two spirits. It is the second spirit, which mankind has acquired that needs to be changed. God gives His Spirit: John 3:34. Acts. 10:38. Jesus gives this same Spirit. John 20:22.

The second spirit comes from Satan. See 1 John 4:3. Yet surely no one would suggest that there is in existence another devil in addition to Satan? For example: A Satan of bodily substance, and a separate Satan of the spirit.

Neither should it be suggested that there is another separate God in addition to the Father and His Son.

In an effort at confirmation of previous conclusions, and in order to make sense out of apparent contradiction regarding the Holy Spirit, we need to study God's word where I am persuaded that by His Spirit there is a plurality of function in God.

There is also evidence of this same plurality in Jesus who revealed the Father. It is because man is made in the image of God that mankind also has the potential for plurality of function.

In order that we might learn this lesson is, I believe, one reason why the apostle Paul was inspired by the Spirit to write the following from: Ephesians 3:16: *"That he would grant you, according to the riches of his glory, to be strengthened with might by his Spirit in the inner man;"*

Recognising this plurality would simplify, to a large extent, some questions that now present a problem.

The above text gives added evidence that there is available to man another dimension needed to fulfil man's heavenly potential.

In Colossians 2:5, Paul further says: *"For though I be absent in the flesh, yet am I with you in the spirit, joying and beholding your order and steadfastness of your faith in Christ."*

Whatever were Paul's desires, he was limited in power. With God, there are no limitations. The above text seems to indicate support for believing in the possible plurality of man.

This would be in harmony with a necessity for man to acquire an added dimension to his being in order to be able to travel over vast spaces at phenomenal speeds at the return of Jesus.

With the new birth, a born again Christian begins to experience a fourth dimension in the life that, to an unsanctified mind, remains a mystery. In common with many who are not Christians, a Christian believes in the existence of Christ, but in addition to this, there comes a conviction of the Spirit. He or she believes with the Spirit. Hence the reason for the following observation by the apostle Paul:

1 *Corinthians 2:14: "But the natural man receiveth not the things of the God: for they are foolishness unto him: neither can he know them, because they are spiritually discerned."*

From the above quotation it can be seen that our vision of man cannot be limited to the three dimensions of mind, body and spirit. Allowance must be made for the additional dimension of the Holy Spirit. This dimension of man, under the influence of the Creator, has a potential that would leave the mind of man aghast.

Romans 8:26 gives an example of how the Spirit of God will help us even in our prayers. When we cannot fluently articulate our feelings and desires, God will accept our Spirit led groaning as is made clear by the following quotation:

"Likewise the Spirit also helpeth our infirmities: for we know not what we should pray for as we ought: but the Spirit itself maketh intercession for us with groanings which cannot be uttered."

When we are feeling so low as to be clearly unable to articulate our need, the Spirit of God will intercede to join His Spirit with our spirit sharing our groanings that cannot be uttered. Reading Romans chapter 8, verse 24 to the end of the chapter we will see that by His Spirit God will be with us through all of our tribulations. He will guide us and never leave us. These verses are in harmony with Hebrews 13:5 where we are told that God *"will never leave thee, nor forsake thee"*. It shall come to light as we progress through this study on the Spirit, that when the Spirit makes intercession, it does not mean that there is another God of the Spirit interceding with the Father.

We learn from the first chapter of the first book of the Bible an account of creation. In verse 22 God says: *"Let us make man in our image."*

Evidence given in Scripture indicates that Jesus was involved in creation. Therefore, it would seem that in the beginning there was God the Father, God the Son and God the Holy Spirit.

God, having said *"Let us make man in our image,"* means we are faced with a dilemma in trying to assess the situation from a human point of view.

How can we be made in the image of the Godhead consisting of God the Father, God the Son and God the Holy Spirit? It is obvious that we cannot be made in the image of the Spirit because in Luke 24:39 Jesus is on record as saying: *"spirit hath not flesh and bones, as ye see me have."*

However, of course, we know that flesh and bones possess a spirit. It is also evident that before appearing to the disciples on this occasion, Jesus was a spirit enabling Him to pass through a wall.

Acts 5:1-9 reveal the lies of Sapphira and Ananias, and in so doing prove that the Lord God, and the Holy Ghost [Holy Spirit] are the same God.

Chapter 26
One Spirit

Scripture gives ample evidence that the Holy Spirit, the Spirit of the Father, and the Spirit of Christ are the same in every important aspect. It is always the one and same Spirit.

Once it is appreciated that God the Father and God the Holy Spirit is one God, all relevant Scripture relating to the Godhead will fall into place and make perfect sense. For example, in Matthew 10:20, Jesus is on record as saying:

"For it is not ye that speak, but the Spirit of your Father which speaketh in you."

Below is another example linking the Father with His Spirit:

Luke 11:13: *"If ye then, being evil, know how to give good gifts unto your children: how much more shall your heavenly Father give the Holy Spirit to them that ask him?"*

There is evidence in Scripture of the throne of God and the Lamb as follows:

Psalm 47:8: *"God reigneth over the heathen: God sitteth upon the throne of his holiness."*

Isaiah 6:1: *"I saw also the Lord sitting upon a throne, high and lifted up, and his train filled the temple."*

Acts 7:49: *Heaven is my throne, and earth is my footstool: what house will ye build me? saith the Lord."*

Revelation 22:3: *"The throne of God and the Lamb shall be in it; and his servants shall serve him."*

Why no mention of the throne of the Spirit? Is the answer to be found in 1 Corinthians 3:16.17, where Paul says:

"Know ye not that ye are the temple of God, and that the Spirit of God dwelleth in you...for the temple of God is holy, which temple ye are?"

Also:

Ephesians 2:21, 22: *"In whom all the building fitly framed together unto an holy temple in the Lord: In whom ye also are builded together for an habitation of God through the Spirit."*

In Genesis 6:3 is one of the many examples where the noun *"Lord"* is used and could equally apply to the Father or the Son. It reads: *"And the Lord said, My spirit shall not always strive with man."*

Is this not the Spirit of the Father? Likewise, Jesus must be referring to the Father in Luke 4:18 where He speaks of *"The Spirit of the Lord"* being upon Him, anointing Him to preach the gospel to the poor and heal the broken hearted, etc.

Referring to the blindness of unbelieving hearts in relation to Christ, in 2 Corinthians 3:15-17 Paul explains how the Lord brings enlightenment to those who seek the Lord, and also reveals how the *"Lord is that Spirit."*

The Spirit of the Lord and the Spirit of the Father must have equal application as is proved by the following Scripture of Luke 10:21, 22:

"In that hour Jesus rejoiced in spirit, and said, I thank thee, O Father, Lord of heaven and earth, that thou hast hid these things from the wise and the prudent, and hast revealed them unto babes: even so, Father; for so it seemed good in thy sight."

Romans 8:9, shows how the Spirit of God and the Spirit of Christ are one and the same by saying:

"But ye are not in the flesh, but in the Spirit, if so be that the Spirit of God dwell in you. Now if any man have not the Spirit of Christ, he is none of his."

The significance of all this text proves that it is unwise to conjure up a situation whereby an attempt is made to separate the Godhead; to create in the mind another God of the Spirit who is not connected to the Father.

There is so much Bible evidence that can be used guiding one to truth on this matter, of which the following are further examples:

Galatians 4:6: *"And because ye are sons, God hath sent forth the Spirit of his Son, into your hearts, crying, Abba, Father."*

Ephesians 4:4-6: *"One Lord, one faith, one baptism One God and Father of all, who is above all, and through all, and in you all."*

The Lord God is our heavenly Father, for Romans 8:14 says: *"For as many as are led by the Spirit of God, they are the sons of God."*

Speaking of The Lord God, we are called the sons of God. Nowhere in Scripture are we called sons of the Spirit.

1 Corinthians chapter 2 informs us of the power, wisdom, glory and mystery of God. The Spirit of God reveals these truths to us. Is this not the Father?

Acts 2:14: *"And it shall come to pass in the last days, saith God, I will pour out my Spirit upon all flesh."*

Again, is this not the Father? As is the following:

John 15:26: *"But when the Comforter is come, whom I will send unto you from the Father, even the Spirit of truth, which proceedeth from the Father, he shall testify of me."*

Showing the link between God the Father, the Son and the Spirit, it says in 1 John 3:22-24:

"And whatsoever we ask, we receive of him, because we keep his commandments, and do those things that are pleasing in his sight. And this is his commandment, That we should believe on the name of his Son Jesus Christ, and love one another, as he gave us commandment. And he that keepeth his commandments dwelleth in him, and he in him. And hereby we know that he abideth in us, by the Spirit which he hath given us."

"But he that is joined unto the Lord is one spirit" 1 Corinthians 6:17.

In Psalms 51:10, 11, David is on record as praying: *"Create in me a clean heart, O God; and renew a right spirit within me. Cast me not away from thy presence; and take not thy holy spirit from me."*

Is this not David praying to the Father that he might have a holy mind by the Spirit from the Father?

Whoever is blessed with the Holy Spirit reflects the character of God within his own personality. In essence each spirit has a personality, and each personality is in possession of a spirit.

Chapter 27
Eternal & Immortal

He who has Christ has eternal life (John 6:54). This means that whenever a Christian dies, he or she will rise to immortality. However, this eternal life (immortality) is conditional on those concerned remaining faithful to Jesus.

One is inevitably led to the next question as to whether there is a difference in meaning between the eternal Spirit and the immortal Spirit. The word *"eternal"* has to do with time; the word *"immortal"* has to do with nature.

If the word *"eternal"* had the same meaning as the word *"immortal"*, it would mean that people, blessed with the eternal, immortal spirit could not die. It is important to recognise the subtle difference in meaning between the words *"immortal"* and *"eternal"*.

Both words are not intended to convey precisely the same meaning. Yet it is common for people to conclude that both words mean immortal in the form of a noun. In a dual form this could lead to an erroneous teaching that there are two Gods.

Claiming that the eternal Holy Spirit is an immortal Being separate from God the Father opens the door to error. Believing that the Spirit is both eternal and immortal it becomes easy for false teachers and false Christians to promote the false doctrine of baptism in death. It would then logically follow, that there could exist a place of eternal torment for the wicked because they are not subject to death.

If the words eternal and immortal had the same meaning the doctrines of baptism in death and eternal torment would become more plausible. In addition, believing in a separate Being of the Spirit we would need to be made in the image of the Father and also the Spirit in order to establish what would appear to be the truth of Scripture.

If the Holy Spirit is not an integral part of God, but separate, how can we be made in God's image? Alternatively, if there is another God of the Spirit, in the image of which God are we made?

The doctrine of the dead knowing nothing is not totally compatible with the belief that an immortal Holy Spirit exists without the Father or vice versa because we are made in the image of God. Therefore, what constitutes human creation must basically reflect the Creator including, if applicable, a spirit separate from the body.

Also, if the eternal Holy Spirit represented immortality this would mean that once having accepted salvation, because the eternal Holy Spirit is involved, the Spirit itself would confirm eternal life regardless of future decisions on the part of the person who had accepted Christ. A false doctrine of once saved always saved could then be substantiated by Scripture. It would also mean that Satan and the fallen angels would not be subject to death, they having once been filled with the eternal Holy Spirit.

At death, human beings are separated from their spirit to exist in the mind of God. God cannot be separated from His Spirit. He alone is immortal. Endeavouring to establish the Spirit as a completely separate identity can lead to conclusions fraught with error.

Assuming that the singular title "Spirit" is indigenous to the Holy Spirit then why should references be made to the Spirit of the Father, and the Spirit of Jesus? Also, why should not the Spirit speak of, and glorify, Himself? (John 16:13, 14).

Is it because the Spirit is then in the servants of God who, by the Spirit, are praising and glorifying Jesus?

In mankind the eternal Spirit does not confirm immortality. At death of the body, the human spirit (breath) is withdrawn and returns to God. This is also true of the eternal Holy Spirit.

The word "immortal" when used as an adjective also applies to God, for He is an immortal God.

The dictionary also defines the eternal "spirit" as a noun, which, though abstract, is part of the body, just as an arm or a leg is part of the body.

If the meaning of the eternal spirit were changed to immortal, as a noun, it would still become part of the body just like any other part of the body.

The significant difference would be that whereas the body would decompose after death, there could remain reason to believe that the immortal indestructible spirit continued to live on as part of the person concerned rather than return to God.

Including those on whom He chooses to bestow this gift, only God has the power to separate His body, and His Spirit from His body. Thus can God be a God of the Spirit and a God of substance. As God He holds all of creation in His Being as one seen and unseen.

To make an inadequate but simple illustration, John could be a carpenter, a teacher, a husband and father. Yet he would still be John.

Miraculous evidence of how God can separate, or displace His body can be found in the fifth chapter of Daniel where is found evidence of an unseen hand extending a finger to write upon the wall.

Mankind could not accurately be described adjectivally as eternal or immortal beings. God can bless us with immortality possessing an eternal Spirit.

So, immortality brings the blessing of the eternal Spirit. But the blessing of the eternal Spirit does not guarantee immortality.

When one becomes a born again Christian, one does not acquire immortality. Even just prior to the return of Jesus, when the saints are filled with the eternal Holy Spirit and imparted righteousness of Christ, Christians are not immortal.

The word *"immortal"* can be an adjective or a noun, but as an adjective cannot ever accurately describe a Christian. It is by God's grace, imparting His Spirit as a noun that Christians become immortal. According to the apostle Paul, the change from corruption to incorruption, and mortality to immortality, takes place in the twinkling of an eye, at the last trump when the dead in Christ are raised. (1 Corinthians 15:50-54)

In truth, to every Christian, immortality will mean a consolidation in individuality to the body of Christ. To the body of Christ the eternal Holy Spirit will bring a collective purpose in compatibility to every Christian.

If the word *"eternal"* had the same meaning as *"immortal"* then the doctrine of the dead know nothing would lose its credibility and be logically unsustainable. Scripture cannot therefore support giving these words the same meaning.

Everyone is blessed with a spirit in the form of breath; the Christian being blessed with the eternal Holy Spirit. God imparts this Spirit in order to sanctify His people.

At death the eternal Spirit returns to God until the appointed time for the church to be made one in Christ. At the return of Jesus, all Christians are again blessed with the eternal Holy Spirit; this time accompanied by immortality defined as a noun, which will be an integral part of the body.

The word *"eternal"* as an adjective can apply only to one Being. He is the eternal God, who is without beginning and without end. Likewise only God is an eternal Spirit. *"God is Spirit"*.

Both the Father and the Son are now in the heavenly sanctuary. However, this does not prevent them also being present with the church on earth. This is why the Bible speaks with no distinction between the Spirit of Christ and the Spirit of the Father or the Holy Spirit. It always has the same meaning.

The Holy Spirit is the invisible presence of God who accompanies His people on the heavenly journey.

The Lord's Prayer of Matthew 6:9-13 reveals that the Father *"...is the kingdom, and the power, and the glory, for ever, Amen."* This passage, like so many other passages of Scripture, is obviously teaching that there is provision by the power of God for the existence of another Person of the Spirit by the power of the Father but not another God of the Spirit in addition to God the Father.

Even though both are self-existent, it is God the Father who makes possible the fact that there is a God of the Spirit, and vice versa. It is also true to say that the Holy Spirit is a Person with a Personality because He and the Father are one and the same God.

There is no reason to suppose that the spirit within man has life separate from the body. One does not exist without the other. Man and his spirit are one. God and His Spirit are one.

The big difference with God is that He is the eternal Spirit. So the Spirit can be said to be always in Him. He is also in His Spirit. By His Spirit God is Omnipotent, Omniscient and Omnipresent.

Chapter 28
Church Doctrine – Bible Doctrine

Any true church of God believes the following fundamental truths:
1 We are made in the image of God.
2 The Holy Spirit is a Person.
3 The dead know nothing.

Conviction regarding the above truths cannot be reconciled with logic or sustained by Scripture if this message now being presented is rejected. I am not challenging all aspects and validity of the above doctrines.

What I do challenge is the status quo regarding the general church concept of the Trinity, which makes impossible a sensible belief in the above doctrines.

There does not exist a God of the Spirit in addition to God the Father. The Spirit of the Father is one with the Father. There is one Spirit. He has a Personality. How else could God work on earth by His Spirit without a Personality? Yes! The Godhead is made up of a Trinity consisting of three great powers, God the Father, God the Son and Their Holy Spirit.

Because of plurality of function, of course, the Holy Spirit is a Person. The Father is a God of substance and the Spirit. But it is error to attempt fundamental separation between God the Father and His Spirit.

Once this truth is accepted sustainable reconciliation is achieved between the above doctrines and belief in the make up of the Trinity.

There are three Beings making up the Trinity. This is because although the Spirit is in God, God is also in the Spirit.

This gives another dimension to God. Yet because there is one Spirit, it still remains a fact that there is one God. There is no contradiction in claiming that there is one God that includes also a God of the Spirit.

By economy of function through the Spirit, it is God's plan to reflect His character by transposing His divine nature in His people. See 2 Peter 1:4.

In the new dispensation there will be God the Father, God the Son and members of the God family, His church, filled with one Spirit, with one divine nature reflecting the one character of God, yet consisting of many different personalities. Although the Holy Spirit is a Person, when He uses His power of conversion, He uses His Personality to change His people's character, not their personalities.

Let us allegorise by use of an analogy. Imagine the world as a very large garden, and all the people are trees, bearing different kinds of fruit. The trees are experiencing varying degrees of decay, and dying because of a deadly virus. What is needed is a systemic agent to combat the disease.

No two trees are quite the same (different personalities). The quality of the fruit reveals defects of character.

This is only an analogy, but imagine that God by His Spirit is the systemic agent working upon the trees of His church. By a combination of the will and power of God with the will of His subjects, the deadly decline is halted.

The trees begin to bear good, healthy fruit. The many different trees (personalities) begin to bear a variety of fruit of the same good character.

The purpose of the third Person of the Godhead is to reflect God's character image in His people. The conclusion is that the people of God attain to His character, to be as alike as two peas in a pod, and in personality as individual as any two leaves on a tree.

If we were to so violate Scripture as to exaggerate the separation between the Father and His Holy Spirit it would be difficult to avoid the conclusion that personalities would be changed by the Spirit rather than character. The personality is the vehicle used to reveal character.

Such text as Matthew 10:20 should not be ignored. *"For it is not ye that speak but the Spirit of your Father which speaketh in you."* The Spirit of the Father is a reflection of His character.

The Holy Spirit plays an essential role in the conversion of man. Combined with the intellect of man it is the agent that searches for truth. The Spirit bears witness to the truth and majesty of God.

It is not in harmony with God's will that we obscure truth because of a blind attitude of mind. It is wiser to be guided by logic in harmony with God's word than bog down the mind with an inconsistent idea that something must be right because it appears at first glance to be so. In Isaiah 1:18 God is on record as saying:

"Come now, let us reason together."

The Holy Spirit has a Personality, *"else He could not bear witness to our spirits and with our spirits"* that we are the children of God. (Romans 8:16). He must also be a Divine Person. If He were not, He could not search out the secrets, which lie hidden in the mind of God.

God is Spirit. He is a Person. He is also in possession of a Personality. But there are not two Gods. It is as a divine Person in man that the Spirit searches out secrets that lie hidden in the mind of God. It could be that your mind is being influenced, and by the Spirit, the Father is searching and seeking in you and for you (Matthew 10:20).

When making an assessment of the Holy Spirit searching the mind of God, it is also wise to consider the context Jesus used in His address to Peter who was at that time under the influence of Satan. It reads:

Matthew 16:23: *"Get thee behind me, Satan: thou art an offence unto me: for thou savourest not the things that be of God, but those that be of men."*

In the same way, man could be addressed as the Spirit when in harmony with the Spirit of God; he is searching the mind of God. It is no strange fact that a Spirit God should have a Personality. Neither is it strange that in God, mind and Spirit would be in unison when there is need to cogitate on matters that are beyond human understanding.

There is one God with one mind and one Spirit at a compatible level of majesty. Thus both mind and Spirit are in perfect harmony. This is true of God the Father and God the Son. Paul explains that no man can know anything about the Father except by the *"Spirit of God"*. See following from 1 Corinthians 2:11:

"For what man knoweth the things of man, save the spirit of man which is in him? Even so the things of God knoweth no man, but the Spirit of God."

The apostle is plainly stating that the Spirit has no need to search out *the secrets which lie hidden in the mind of God* to complete His understanding. The Spirit of God already knows all about God. The Spirit is God. In the Good News version it is even more plainly stated: *"Only God's Spirit knows all about God."*

Verse 10 makes it clear that God the Father reveals things to His people by His Spirit, explaining, *"the Spirit searcheth all things, yea, the deep things of God."*

There is a distinction between the spirit and the mind; every mind being under the influence of a spirit. A discerning mind that is not holy can consider it expedient to do what is right for selfish reasons.

How much better when the mind is holy and in harmony with the Holy Spirit, bringing God and man into perfect symphony. Man knows what motivates his spirit regardless of how it is assessed within the mind.

If the Holy Spirit is a Person then He must possess a Personality. He must also be a Divine Person else He could not search out the secrets that lie hidden in the mind of God.

It is correctly declared that it takes a Divine Person, or Spirit to search out the secrets that lie hidden in the mind of God. This is a fact that can be fully appreciated.

Nevertheless, it would be absurd to conclude that we are presented with a situation where the Holy Spirit is searching out the secrets hidden in the mind of God as if the Spirit needs knowledge of God.

The Spirit is God. Scripture tells that God is Spirit. Paul's conveyance about the Spirit clearly states, *"Only God's Spirit knows all about God."*

Paul further explains in 1 Corinthians 2:12, 13:

"Now we have received, not the spirit of the world, but the spirit which is of God, that we might know the things that are freely given to us of God. Which things also we speak, not in the words which man's wisdom teacheth, but which the Holy Ghost teacheth; comparing spiritual things with spiritual."

From the above quotation it is obvious that the Holy Spirit's presence is essential in order to enable man to understand the hidden secrets in the mind of God. However, to conjure up a situation where there is a suggestion that the Holy Spirit of God is searching the mind of God for His own edification is not sensible.

The apostle Paul has fully explained the truth regarding such a false assumption. He has clearly stated, expressed in language simple to understand that in order to extend His knowledge, the Spirit of God has no need to search the hidden secrets of God. Here it is repeated:

"For what man knoweth the things of man, save the spirit of man which is in him? Even so the things of God knoweth no man, but the Spirit of God." (1 Corinthians 2:11).

Because the Spirit of God is cited as having knowledge of God, the above verse is often quoted as proof that the Spirit of God is a separate God. However, the same verse gives the same evidence regarding the spirit of man.

When making an interpretation of each half of the above verse, we should be consistent and apply the same logic to both. The spirit of man knoweth man. And the Spirit of God knoweth God. The Being of God is complete with His Spirit. And the being of man is complete with his spirit.

It is not in harmony with common sense or Scripture to make a separation between a person and his spirit. Man is made in the image of God.

No one would seriously consider that man and his spirit are separate beings. So why should we consider erroneously that God and His Spirit are separate Beings except in the context of God's plurality?

The above text gives conclusive proof that any reference to a Divine Person searching out the secrets hidden in the mind of God is not revealing a need of the Holy Spirit to learn secrets. Rather, the Holy Spirit within man enables man, by the Spirit, to search out the secrets that lie hidden in the mind of God.

It could equally be said that the Holy Spirit searches out the secrets of God in order to convey them to man. However, it should be kept in mind that the Spirit is bringing enlightenment to the mind of man.

The Spirit of God has no need to search in order to further His knowledge. Following the line of this study on the Spirit in proper sequence it has been proved by the apostle Paul, that it is not a matter of a separate Spirit God exercising His power in order to understand the mind of a God of substance. Rather, it is the Spirit of God enabling man to explore secrets that lie hidden in the mind of God.

Conclusively it also takes a Divine Spirit to understand or make a divine self-assessment. Thus can a Divine Person search a divine mind. In the same kind of self-assessment man knows what motivates his spirit regardless of how it is assessed within the mind. But without God's Spirit, man is unable to search the *"deep things of God."*

We know that the Holy Spirit has a Personality. This is a fact that could not reasonably be refuted. The Spirit could not be God without a Personality *"else He could not bear witness to our spirits."* It naturally follows that He must also be divine.

In essence, Paul is saying that the Spirit of God knows the mind of God, and the spirit of man knows the mind of man. Man needs the Spirit of God in order to search out what is in the mind of God. In support of this truth, Paul has recorded as much in 1 Corinthians 2:10:

"But God hath revealed them unto us by his Spirit: for the Spirit searcheth all things, yea, the deep things of God."

The Holy Spirit can be defined as a Divine Person with a Personality. However, we should not conclude from this that the mind of the Spirit is searching the mind of the Father, as if they were separate identities, unless it is in the manner that we all use to search our minds.

Rather, it can be that God the Father is searching His own mind, as human beings tend to do. Or it is the Spirit identifying with the man to the enlightenment of man.

As our study has proved, any other conclusion would place us in contradiction with the apostle Paul. Without the Holy Spirit, man would be incapable of searching the deep secrets of God.

Possession of the Holy Spirit elevates the mind to a higher level of discernment, understanding, and power.

There is intelligence in the Spirit that is independent of and in addition to the mind. This quality in man is limited. This is the reason why, in man, God bestows His Spirit in order for man to search the deep things of God.

Regarding baptism, it is only proper to baptise in the name of the Father, the Son, and the Holy Spirit, because more is involved in redemption than a purely intellectual decision on the part of the mind of God and His Spirit. The Spiritual aspect of God is also involved. It is important to be aware of the fact that both God and man can make a decision with the mind and with the spirit.

To acquire a clearer understanding of the Trinity it is helpful to appreciate the distinction between the spirit and the mind. A spirit in rebellion against God can find pleasure in breaking the law regardless of how actions are assessed in the mind. For example, people involved in adultery often ignore conclusive evidence of rebellion presented in the mind, choosing to be guided by a contrary spirit.

Of course, the Holy Spirit is a Person. God is Spirit and also Omnipresent and as such His presence can be everywhere.

Setting aside the fact that God is Omnipresent, on Bible evidence mankind appears not to mirror at any level the truthful account by respected scholars that the Holy Spirit is a separate Divine Person.

These scholars often give more credence to the belief in a separate God of the Spirit than the Bible. Because man is made in the image of God this would indicate a contradiction of Scripture.

This misconception of the true facts would seem to present us with a serious dilemma of impossible reconciliation between what appears to be two opposing truths. The problem is solved if the plurality of God is accepted together with potential for plurality of man.

So far in our study of the Holy Spirit there has been no evidence from the Bible that there is a duality in God. Such a belief would open the door to the satanic doctrine that the sinner cannot die because of the nature of the eternal spirit that resides in man who is made in the image of God.

To be in harmony with Scripture the only other way to explain the Person of the Father and the Person of the Spirit is to recognise the plurality of God.

This added dimension to His Being enables God to be both present in heaven and on earth. This fourth dimension also explains how on the mount of transfiguration Elias and Moses appeared to Peter, James and John (Mark 9:4).

To conclude this section: The Holy Spirit is either a Person in addition to God the Father and God the Son or not. If in the literal sense He were a separate Person it would indicate duality in some form, and definitely a separate God of the Spirit. Such a doctrine would rule out the Bible truth that we are made in the image of God. The alternative is that the Holy Spirit is a Person in God's plurality.

Chapter 29
Personality and Character

With an increase of light this message should have dispelled any dilemma regarding reconciliation between what can appear to be conflicting views on the Trinity. *For "the path of the just [is] as the shining light, that shineth more and more unto the perfect day."* (Proverbs 4:18).

As we have already learned from the Bible it is possible to gather information that sometimes appears to be contradictory. From the above quotation it can be seen that it is not God's will that His people be left in darkness.

For an example of apparent contradiction let us consider the following quotations from the Bible. The first quotations plainly indicate that God is in the heavenly sanctuary throughout the duration of the seven last plagues. The last quotation equally indicates that God is walking the earth at the same time.

Revelation 15:8: *"And the temple was filled with smoke from the glory of God, and from his power; and no man was able to enter into the temple, till the seven plagues of the seven angels were fulfilled."*

Revelation 6:1: *"And I heard a great voice out of the temple saying to the seven angels, Go your ways, and pour out the vials of the wrath of God upon the earth."*

Revelation 16:17: *"And the seventh angel poured out his vial into the air; and there came a great voice out of the temple of heaven, from the throne, saying, It is done."*

Isaiah 26:21: *"For, behold, the LORD cometh out of his place to punish the inhabitants of the earth for their iniquity: the earth also shall disclose her blood, and shall no more cover her slain."*

Along with other important conclusions, it has surely been proved how the fact of God being present in the sanctuary during the plagues, while also walking the earth is a belief perfectly sustainable with One God Omnipotent, Omnipresent and Omniscient.

Remember, according to the apostle Paul (1 Corinthians 2:14) there is more discernment by the Spirit than an unsanctified mind. Therefore, to function properly, the servants of God need the mind of Jesus by the Spirit of Jesus (Philippians 2:5).

In Satan there is one evil mind and one evil spirit. With his supporters there are a multiple of minds but in purpose and motivation, one evil spirit.

In 1 Corinthians 12:12-26, the apostle Paul has recorded a message about the body. Although Paul makes reference to a physical body, in context he is speaking spiritually. For example, physical pain registered in the mind can in turn have an effect upon the spirit. One person cannot share another's physical pain but can be affected in spirit. Thus could Paul truthfully say:

"And whether one member suffer, all the members suffer with it; or one member be honoured, all members rejoice with it." Verse 26.

It is by the spirit that it is possible to *"Bear... one another's burdens, and fulfil the law of Christ."* (Galatians 6:2).

It is by the Spirit that an Omnipathic God suffers with His people. Do we dare attempt to disassociate God the Father and the Son from the Spirit and thus negate the sufferings of part of the Godhead compared to another part?

Mankind consists of mind, character, and personality. A particular personality will not necessarily make a bad character, but a defective character will adversely affect a personality. In the same way a defective character in fruit will adversely affect the taste.

There is a personality of the natural mind, or character, and there is a personality aspect to the spiritual mind or character. So in this respect some aspects of every personality will be a reflection of the mind or character. Any reference to the Spirit of God, the Person of God, or the Spirit, or the Personality of the Spirit, encompasses the one Spirit God. God's Spirit and the Personality of His Spirit is a reflection of His character.

In the earth made new there will be one character in the fruit of the earth. Just as there will be many beautiful personalities with one Spirit in God's church, so will there be many deliciously tasting fruits, (pears, apples, grapes etc.) with one good character.

Whatever the fruit, (personality) the condition of its character will have an effect upon its taste. Equally, in man, a defective character will adversely affect the fruit or personality. No matter what the fruit that is under discussion will not change the fact that there is just one fruit.

In the same way, whoever is the person under discussion, will not change the fact that essentially there is just one person. In plainer words: The character and the personality make up one person. This applies equally to man and God.

Except as they have been affected by a defective character, it is not God's will that the many varieties of fruit be changed in taste. (In the beginning *"it was good."* (Gen. 11:2).

It is God's will that the character (spirit) of mankind be changed, but not the personalities except as they have been affected by a wayward spirit.

As was commented on earlier, if too much emphasis is placed on the Personality of the Spirit in connection with conversion there is the danger of concluding that personalities would be changed rather than character.

By the Spirit, God is love and holy, which is the character of the Godhead bodily.

Consider the following list:
God desires *"an holy nation."* Exodus 19:6.
Paul refers to *"holy brethren."* 1 Thessalonians 2:7.
God's prophets are holy. Luke 1:70.
The unfallen angels are holy. Mark 8:38.
Jesus was a holy child. Acts 4:27.
The Redeemer is the *"Holy One of Israel."* Isaiah 54:5
The Father is Holy. John 17:11.
The Lord our God said, *"I am holy."* Leviticus 11:44, 45

With this list in mind, the simple truth is, there can be no one more holy than the Holy Spirit. Yet Hannah prayed, and said: *"There is none as holy as the Lord: for there is none beside thee. Neither is there any rock like our God."* (1 Samuel 2:1, 2)

Confronted with all such seemingly confusing text it can surely be seen that the only reasonable explanation is that any reference to the Holy Spirit is also a reference to the Father or the Son.

It is not given to man to understand the mystery of God, but this kind of assessment coupled with previous reasoning does partly explain the following Scripture references of how, by the Spirit, Jesus can be all things. Also of how, by the Spirit, it is possible to be adopted into the God family.

In this context, Jesus quoted Psalms 82:6, when He *"answered them, Is it not written in your law, I said Ye are Gods?* (John 10:34).

Also there is this text:

Psalms 82:1: *"God standeth in the congregation of the mighty; he judgeth among the gods."*

Isaiah 9:6: *"For unto us a child is born, unto us a son is given: and the government shall be upon his shoulder: and his name shall be called Wonderful, Counsellor, The mighty God, The everlasting Father, The Prince of Peace."*

The above text shows how by the Spirit, Jesus can identify with His servants or with the Father. Hence could Jesus claim all the above titles and also claim: *"He that hath seen me hath seen the Father; and how sayest thou then, Shew us the Father?" (John 14:9).*

Logic is one of the great hallmarks of the Bible. With this in mind it does not seem to be sensible that without reference to one's character, and the need for change, one could claim eternal life just based on believing that Jesus died for our sins.

Yet it is quite common that on the basis of one text misunderstood, taken in isolation, with doubtful interpretation (such as Acts 16:31) many believe it possible to sail in God's kingdom regardless of the kind of character that has been developed. *"And they said, Believe on the Lord Jesus Christ, and thou shalt be saved, and thy house".*

The virtue is not in belief alone but in good behaviour because of belief. To believe on the Lord Jesus Christ is to be guided by His Spirit and live in harmony with His holy purpose.

Conversely there are others who are in despondency because of the fear that they are lacking in faith. By the Spirit, God is love, and as such is perfectly fair and beyond reproach of any kind. There is absolutely no merit in mankind that can commend itself to God.

For an example of a text that some might find confusing, in Hebrews 11:6, regarding God we are told that: *"without faith it is impossible to please him: for he that cometh to God must believe that he is, and that he is a rewarder of them that diligently seek him."*

To the sceptic this portion of Scripture would seem to suggest that man has a more dominant and meritorious role to play in salvation than is true in fact. The sceptic could point to suffering as a reason for unbelief and claim therefore that God is unkind in condemning such a one who is weak in faith.

In truth God does not condemn but offers His Spirit of understanding that any in all circumstances might believe and enjoy a measure of faith. His Spirit makes faith and belief in God possible.

When the reason for unbelief is analysed, lack of the Holy Spirit is revealed to be the basic problem. In essence, the above message taken from the book of Hebrews is simply saying: Without the new birth by God's Spirit, it *"is impossible to please Him."*

We are admonished to believe in God. Yet *"the devils also believe, and tremble."* (James 2:19). What is the explanation? It is possible to be convinced about something spiritual and believe in the calculating section of the mind but it is far better to be convicted and believe in the spirit, or spirit of the mind. *("And be renewed in the spirit of your mind" Ephesians* 4:23).

On a basic level the brain is a calculating memory which is able to sense warmth, pain and hunger, etc. Beyond this we are blessed with a mind with a spiritual dimension capable of wonder and to be able to appreciate the mystery and wonders of creation.

One can believe with the mind in the existence of God but it is possible for this belief to be incompatible with the desire of the spirit, therefore bringing the believer's heart into discord with the Creator.

By the same token it is also possible that great trials could raise obstacles to an establishment of a firm belief with the mind while at the same time the desire of the spirit brings compatibility between God and His subject.

This is a belief with the mind of the spirit. An example of this apparent contradiction of convictions can be found in Mark 9:17-24:

"17 And one of the multitude answered and said, Master, I have brought unto thee my son, which hath a dumb spirit; 18 And wheresoever he taketh him, he teareth him: and he foameth, and gnasheth with his teeth, and pineth away: and I spake to thy disciples that they should cast him out; and they could not. 19 He answereth him, and saith, O faithless generation, how long shall I be with you? how long shall I suffer you? bring him unto me. 20 And they brought him unto him: and when he saw him, straightway the spirit tare him; and he fell on the ground, and wallowed foaming. 21 And he asked his father, How long is it ago since this came unto him? And he said, Of a child. 22 And ofttimes it hath cast him into the fire, and into the waters, to destroy him: but if thou canst do any thing, have compassion on us, and help us. 23 Jesus said unto him, If thou canst believe, all things [are] possible to him that believeth. 24 And straightway the father of the child cried out, and said with tears, Lord, I believe; help thou mine unbelief."

In the section of his mind predominantly governed by his calculating intellect, the man in the story could not reconcile the anguish of his family's life, with a God who cared.

In the darkness of the spiritual dimension of his mind the distraught father was looking for a sign that would inspire hope to lift his despair.

The man's voice was pregnant with doubt and hope as he implored: *"If thou canst do any thing, have compassion on us and help us"* (verse 22).

Jesus answered: *"...If thou canst believe, all things are possible to him that believeth."* (Verse 23). Realising that even for this measure of belief, he needed the power of God, the man cried out *"I believe; help thou mine unbelief."* (Verse 24).

There are many Christians who daily utter this same despairing cry. Physical Israel faced giants before they entered the Promised Land. Many of God's people, (spiritual Israel) will also encounter giants before crossing the river Jordan into Canaan. These giants will be spiritual, taking many forms including all types of sickness.

Matthew 5:10: *"Blessed are they which are persecuted for righteousness sake: for theirs is the kingdom of heaven."*

The reason for persecution is not always obvious because many battles are waged as spectacles to be witnessed in heavenly places. Christianity is not a game to be indulged at whim. There are serious consequences of an eternal dimension being decided as the drama of the conflict unfolds.

In spite of the awful suffering of Jesus, filled with the Spirit He could not deny the principle of love and justice. To do so He would have been denying Himself.

So will it be with God's servants. Despite the pain inflicted by Satan, they cannot deny the thoughts of harmonisation with the Holy Spirit. In their agony they could intellectually doubt the existence of God, and even voice these doubts, but because of a holy desire for righteousness they could never oppose the Holy Spirit.

This truth is the reason for the following Scripture taken from Matthew 12:31:

"Wherefore I say unto you, All manner of sin and blasphemy shall be forgiven unto men: but the blasphemy [against] the [Holy] Ghost shall not be forgiven unto men. 32 And whosoever speaketh a word against the Son of man, it shall be forgiven him: but whosoever speaketh against the Holy Ghost, it shall not be forgiven him, neither in this world, neither in the [world] to come."

This text is plainly stating that God is not waiting to pounce on anyone who is so distressed as to doubt His existence. There is no need to fear God in such circumstances.

There is no condemnation for those of God's servants who display a lack of faith in the face of adversity. We are not to be judged on our doubts but on our spiritual commitment to Christ.

Righteousness will bring its reward whether one is conscious of its significance or not. By the same token, sin will be brought into judgement whether one is fully conscious of sin or ready to admit of its significance or not.

When seeking salvation it is essential to believe in the principles of God rather than the existence or substance of God. Believing in the substance or existence of God is an intellectual exercise whereas believing in the righteous principles of God is a spiritual exercise.

It might appear to the unlearned in the ways of God that He is not making enough allowance for our ignorance. But God has not left us in darkness regarding salvation.

It is given to everyone to know deep within our souls whether we are in harmony with God or not. For the apostle Paul has written that man knows by what spirit he is motivated. *"for what man knoweth the things of man, save the spirit of man which is in him."* (1Corinthians 2:11).

This text is a revelation that by the spirit disharmony with God brings about it own condemnation. In order to provide a confirmed rebel with a means of escape from self-condemnation, God allows the rebel to be deluded as can be seen from the following Scripture reference:

"And for this cause God shall send them strong delusion, that they should believe a lie." (2 Thessalonians 2:11).

From the above text it is shown how humanity can be in the strange situation where the spirit acknowledges rebellion while the intellect practices self-deception. Thus can we rightly condemn ourselves when wrong, and wrongly justify ourselves against right.

Emphasis has been placed upon the fact of there being one Spirit in Christ, and one spirit of rebellion. It is hoped that the reader will not split hairs and miss the whole thrust of this message by quoting such Scripture references as Mark 5:13, with its mention of *"spirits"*.

Of course, it can be claimed that there are many individual spirits in Satan's army of rebels, but there is just one rebellion, and one spirit of rebellion. In the same way, there is just one Spirit in harmony with Christ.

The same logical explanation applies to the body and church of Christ. There are many individual bodies that make up the body, but in Romans 12:5, Paul refers to these *"many members"* as *"one body"*.

When the apostle Paul prayed for the Spirit, he did not make a separation between the Father and His Spirit but prayed that He would grant *"according to the riches of his glory. To be strengthened with might by his Spirit in the inner man."* (Ephesians 3:16).

Regarding the Father, the Son and the Holy Spirit, these are the simple Bible truths:

1. In Ephesians 4:6 we are told that there is *"one God and Father of all, who is above all, and through all, and in you all."*
2. Jesus identified Himself with the Father when He said; *"he that hath seen me hath seen the Father."* (John14:9).
3. We are informed in John 4:24, that *"God is a Spirit."*
4. Ephesians 4:4 says: *"There is one body, and one Spirit, even as ye are called in one hope of your calling."*
5. It is *"by one Spirit are we all baptized into one body, whether we be Jews or Gentiles, whether we be bond or free; and have been all made to drink into one Spirit."* (1 Corinthians 12:13).

None of the above references make any allowances for the existence of a separate God of the Spirit.

In 1 Timothy 1:17 there is reference *"...unto the King eternal, immortal, invisible, the only wise God."* This text testifies to the oneness of God including His immortality and the invisibility of His Spirit. But it does not indicate that there is another immortal God of the Spirit.

In the fullness of time Christians become *"...partakers of the divine nature...."* (2 Peter 1:4). It is then that God's people inherit immortality together with the eternal Spirit of God.

With reference to the Trinity, we can believe in the duality of God (separate Spirit God) that could include that mans spirit lives on after death of the body.

This is the doctrine of Babylon. Or we can believe in the plurality of one God that encompasses another dimension of the eternal spirit that remains in God's power to bestow or withdraw.

Before concluding, let us recap on some important points. To mankind the Trinity is a mystery. However, this is no reason to add confusion to the mystery.

We are all spiritual beings and there is no more mystery in the fact of God searching His Spirit or mind than with us when we search our spirits or minds. But with us that is where the power stops. God has the power that enables Him to search all spirits and all minds.

This is the wonder and mystery of God. This mystery cannot be explained away with the invention of an additional God of the Spirit.

Regarding the Personality of the Holy Spirit, as spiritual beings we are also in possession of a personality. With the spirit it is the vehicle, which gives lustre, and adds a zest to life. It is the will of God that our personalities also become portraits of the divine character.

By the Spirit we are meant to be channels of love. Thus can we share with Jesus in living and giving of life *"more abundantly"* (John 10:10). Conversely we can choose by the spirit to become obstacles of the Spirit. Then do we stifle the lustre of life in the living and the giving, to share with Satan who *"was a murderer from the beginning."* (John 8:44).

The present incomplete teaching on the Trinity by most churches leaves a weakness in the doctrine, which is not totally incompatible with the belief, which promotes baptism of the dead.

It would be incorrect to claim that the doctrine of the churches is always at fault. It would be more appropriate to say that with certain aspects there has been a lack of light.

It is fitting to close this study with some relevant quotations from Scripture.

1 Corinthians 8: 4-6, Ephesians 4:4-6, 1 Corinthians 6:17 teach us that *"there is but one God the Father, and one Lord, Jesus Christ, and one Spirit."* To attempt conjuring up a separate God of the Spirit is not in harmony with Scripture.

Galatians 2:20: *I am crucified with Christ: nevertheless I live; yet not I, but Christ liveth in me; and the life which I now live in the flesh I live by faith of the Son of God."* Is not Christ living in His servants by His Spirit?

In this section there has been an exposition, qualifying the identity of the third Person of the Godhead. It has been proposed that the Spirit is in God and that God is in His Spirit. This plurality explains how there is a third Person of the Godhead.

In like manner, the beloved disciple John was in the Spirit on the Sabbath day as Jesus opened to the disciple the wonders of Revelation. See Revelation 1:10, and Revelation 4:2. Of course, the Spirit was also in John.

Born of human nature the only hope for humanity is to be transformed into the nature of Christ. The old man of sin must die to make place for the new.

The third Person of the Godhead, which is the Spirit of the Father and the Son, is to sanctify God's people. Then will Christ be glorified through His Spirit of grace.

The doctrine that teaches a separate God of the Spirit is not in harmony with Scripture and portrays the Creator God in diminished majesty and glory. This is because a separate God of the Spirit would logically be worthy to share in the worship that is the prerogative of the one Creator God.

In these circumstances it would also be necessary for Scripture to change its way of identifying God. This could be the reason why Scripture does not identify God as "a" Spirit. In John 4:24 in the Greek it says: "God **is Spirit**".

In the description of God given above, it can be seen that there is a subtle difference between identifying "God as a Spirit", and saying that "God is Spirit".

If God were to be identified using the definite article of "a" Spirit it would give credence to the claim that the Spirit of God was another separate Person. Also, if God were to be identified solely as "a Spirit" it would be suggesting that God was without a physical form.

To claim that God the Father is not the Spirit or that the Spirit is not the Father is to place a limit on the fullness of the Godhead bodily.

Attempting to conjure up a separate tangible visible form of the Holy Spirit is not in harmony with Scripture. As seen in the following quotation taken from Luke 24:39, Jesus gives clear evidence that the Holy Spirit is not a tangible second separate identity in addition to God:

"Behold my hands and my feet. That it is I myself: handle me, and see; for a spirit hath not flesh and bones, as ye see me have."

Although Jesus has instructed us that in normal circumstances *"a spirit hath not flesh and bones,"* this does not mean that according to His will, the Spirit of God is not able to appear in another form as shown in the following quotation taken from Matthew 3:16:

"And Jesus, when he was baptized, went up straightway out of the water: and, lo, the heavens were opened unto him, and he saw the Spirit of God descending like a dove, and lighting upon him."

At the beginning of this study, mention was made as to the possible simplicity of an answer to some important questions. In spite of many in-depth expositions of the Holy Spirit in connection with the Trinity the reader is invariably left without a satisfactory conclusion.

The above explanation is simple, and as reasonable a conclusion that one is likely to acquire this side of eternity.

God the Father is both a God of substance and Spirit. If accepted, this proposal of plurality brings about reconciliation between the doctrine of one God and a Trinity.

Making the claim that the Holy Spirit is the third Person of the Godhead without such qualification is the same as introducing another God. But it does not bring reconciliation between the doctrine of one

God and a Trinity. By accepting the plurality of God it can be seen how the adjective "Holy" could appropriately describe the noun "Spirit" that could be Omnipresent, while at the same time, the physical presence of the same Spirit God could be present on the throne in heaven.

Chapter 30
The Anointed Cherub

It is difficult for human beings to comprehend how, in the beauty and holiness of heaven, there could have occurred rebellion against a God of love.

In Ezekiel chapter 28 is the record of a message being given to the prophet concerning the prince and the king of Tyrus. However, from the contents of the message it can be seen that more than an earthly king is involved.

The king of Tyrus was never in the Garden of Eden, nor was he ever *"upon the holy mountain of God"*. The following verses of 13-15 make it clear that reference is being made to Satan or Lucifer as follows:

*Thou hast been in Eden the garden of God; every precious stone [was] thy covering, the sardius, topaz, and the diamond, the beryl, the onyx, and the jasper, the sapphire, the emerald, and the carbuncle, and gold: the workmanship of thy tabrets and of thy pipes was prepared in thee in the day that thou wast created. Thou [art] the anointed **cherub that covereth**; and I have set thee [so]: thou wast upon the holy mountain of God; thou hast walked up and down in the midst of the stones of fire. Thou [wast] perfect in thy ways from the day that thou wast created, till iniquity was found in thee.*

Speaking of Lucifer, in verse 15 above it says: *"Thou wast perfect in thy ways from the day that thou wast created, till iniquity wast found in thee."*

How could a perfect being filled with the Spirit, rebel?

When under the direction of God, Moses instructed Israel to erect the tabernacle with its contents; a shadow or type of that in heaven was made. The Ark of God's Covenant and the mercy seat was placed in the inner sanctuary of the temple.

The types of cherubim above the ark were depicted as guardians and expositors of the Decalogue. This is not to say that in heaven the ark is in danger of being stolen.

We are told in Ezekiel 28:14 that *Lucifer "art the anointed cherub that covereth."*

Portrayed in Exodus 25:18, above the Ark of the Covenant were the types of two cherubim that cover the mercy seat in heaven. At each end of the ark was a cherub with its wings outstretched to protectively cover God's Ark of the Covenant and His Law of Ten Commandments.

Understanding that Lucifer, as the *"anointed cherub that covereth"* was one of the cherubim that covered the Ark of the Covenant in heaven, it is eminently possible that in heaven the one with Lucifer in dealing with matters of the Decalogue was Jesus or maybe the angel Gabriel.

As expositors of the law, the two that included Lucifer would be in a position that enabled them to answer questions arising from the workings of God's government.

It does not seem possible that one filled with the Spirit of God would ever desire to rebel against his Creator.

In this elevated office it is apparent that Satan became intellectually convinced that he did not need the Holy Spirit of God in order to live in harmony with the law, of which he was an expositor. Then began Lucifer's insistent requests to be allowed to stand independent of God.

The kingdom of God is established on love, which includes the consent and support of it subjects. The strength of such a kingdom requires it to function in total harmony.

In these circumstances, after much serious discussion over a long period of time, God would finally accede to Satan's request and withdraw His Spirit from the anointed cherub.

Being filled with the Holy Spirit of God is to be undivided from the loving purpose and disposition of holiness. Such a kingdom cannot be divided against itself lest part of that kingdom fall. By the same token Satan cannot be cast out from the kingdom of Satan lest that kingdom fall.

Based upon the truth of Scripture, and applying this logic, it can be seen that Lucifer could not have desired to rebel against the kingdom of God while he was filled with God's Holy Spirit.

Once the Spirit was withdrawn, Satan would find himself in rebellion against his Creator, yet enjoy this agitated state that he would call freedom. He would then become unwilling to be reverted to his original beauty.

It is then that he would make the audacious claim that God was responsible for his present condition and insist that having been granted his apparent freedom it was no longer possible for him, or anyone else in this position, to desire a change to the original state. Thus began the great controversy and Satan's attack on the law of God.

Satan is now making the claim that it is not normal for created beings to be truly content by living in harmony with one Spirit. To refute this claim God requires that His people on earth should become holy by choice, and have the desire to remain so.

When God has a predetermined number who have become holy, and have the intellectual and spiritual desire to remain so, the controversy between good and evil is ended.

We do not know at what stage in his rebellion that Satan reached a point of no return. But it seems that there was never a time when he desired to become one again with God. It is also unlikely that God would be able to allow him back into the fold once a human being had lost eternal life.

To believe that it is possible for a holy being to rebel against a Holy God is to ignore the teachings of Jesus as set out in Matthew 12:22-27 as follows:

*"12:22 Then was brought unto him one possessed with a devil, blind, and dumb: and he healed him, insomuch that the blind and dumb both spake and saw. 12:23 And all the people were amazed, and said, Is not this the son of David? 12:2 But when the Pharisees heard [it], they said, This [fellow] doth not cast out devils, but by Beelzebub the prince of the devils. 12:25 And Jesus knew their thoughts, and said unto them, Every kingdom divided against itself is brought to desolation; and every city or house divided against itself shall not stand: 12:26 **And if Satan cast out Satan, he is divided against himself; how shall then his kingdom stand?** 12:27 And if I by Beelzebub cast out devils, by whom do your children cast [them] out? therefore they shall be your judges."*

As seen above, a divided kingdom cannot stand. It is against an inherent nature to rebel against self. This fundamental truth applies to the kingdom of God, and the kingdom of Satan.

The fundamental rule of living in harmony with the desires of self, will always apply. This truth cannot change. It is for this reason that the nature of self must change in order for there to take place a restoration of harmony with God's law of love. In this way the nature of self is replaced with the nature of Christ. (2 Peter 1:4). Christ becomes the new self.

The truth proclaimed above, is proof that in the beginning of the great controversy between Christ and Satan, Satan made a choice to adopt a nature apposed to Christ. The controversy between Christ and Satan always hinges on a matter of choice. In this conflict between the two powers, the justice of a loving God cannot deny Himself by stifling the freedom of choice.

Eminent scholars have made the claim that in coming to earth as a human being, God took a calculated risk and that the plan of salvation could have failed. Using the criterion that there is an element of risk in most actions involving conflict I would not be in contradiction with these scholars. For, if Jesus was not tempted in all things as we are He could not be our Saviour and a perfect propitiation for sin.

Our previous study has shown that it appears to be unlikely that one filled with the Spirit of God could ever find himself in rebellion against the Spirit. It would be like rebelling against self. For Jesus to successfully engage in His mission of salvation, He first needed to yield to the nature of His mother and consent to temptation.

Thus for our sakes, Jesus placed Himself in submission to Satan's attacks. Enduring temptation far in excess of humanity, Jesus was faced with choice. In this respect when tempted we are all faced with a choice. However, because of Satan's extraordinary efforts to defeat the world's Redeemer, our temptations are light by comparison to those experienced by Jesus, as shown by observations taken from Isaiah 52:14 as follows:

"As many were astonied at thee; his visage was so marred more than any man, and his form more than the sons of men."

Jesus was born after the human race had endured four thousand years of abuse. This meant that at that time human nature was in a far weaker state than that which Adam and Eve enjoyed. From His mother, Jesus inherited a fallen human nature. Because of this inherited fallen nature Jesus could have failed in His mission to defeat sin. Yet from His Holy Father, Jesus inherited the perfect character of God that alone could provide a sure barrier against sin.

Thus we have a seemingly contradictory situation where because of His fallen human nature inherited from His mother, Jesus was in all ways tempted as we are and could have fallen. Yet being filled with the Holy Spirit, would suggest that it was not possible for Him to fall into sin. However, there is no contradiction. Jesus needed to place Himself in the weakened position of a sinner in order to gain the victory over sin. In this way He therefore became a perfect sacrifice for the human race.

Being born of the Spirit, it seems that with that Holy nature it would have been impossible for Jesus to sin. Although it would not be against His human nature it would be against the nature He had inherited from the Father.

(Applying the same logic regarding Adam and Eve it seems that without seeking the protection of God's word, and not fully protected by the Holy Spirit it would have been impossible for them to be able to resist sinning). Yet in order to bring salvation to a lost humanity Jesus consented to expose Himself to Satan by subjecting Himself to the weakness of human nature. In so doing Jesus gained the victory over sin.

The question now arises as to what was the different circumstance that resulted in Adam and Eve being defeated by Satan, but brought victory to Jesus Christ? It seems that once again we are faced with the matter of choice. Adam and Eve chose not to depend on the word and promises of God. In this way they had separated themselves from the power that lay in the word of God. On the other hand, Jesus always countered Satan's accusations and promises by quoting Scripture such as *"it is written."* In a time of crisis His mind was fastened on God's word.

In answer to the temptation to turn stones into bread in order to appease His hunger, Jesus answered as recorded in Matthew 4:4: *"Man shall not live by bread alone, but by every word that proceedeth out of the mouth of God."* Jesus always answered Satan's temptations in the same vein.

In the wilderness of temptation, a hungry and despondent Jesus faced every conceivable weapon in Satan's armoury, sustained only by the word of God.

To be bereft of God's word and His Holy Spirit is to be cast adrift upon the storm tossed sea of life without a rudder and without His stabling presence. It could be a fatal mistake to deliberately neglect the moral support given in God's word or any part of the law of Ten Commandments. In so doing we lose the confidence that adherence to the word inspires.

Until fully revealed by heaven, it is impossible for human beings to fully appreciate or understand the fathomless depths of the sacrifice paid by Jesus on behalf of the sinful race. Jesus willingly left the glory of the heavenly courts to present Himself as a sacrifice that could have failed bringing eternal death.

The lesson taught by the typical service of the earthly sanctuary was that every sin offering had to be without blemish typifying the projected perfect sinless sacrifice of Jesus Christ our Saviour.

We learn from Romans 6:23 that *"the wages of sin is death"*. But through divine favour we are promised in the same verse *"the gift of God is eternal life through Jesus Christ our Lord."* This means that eternal death is the price to be paid for sin. This is the eternal decree proclaimed by the God Jehovah, and can in no way be gainsaid.

Thus we have absolute proof proclaimed in the divine word of God that had Jesus failed in His battle against the temptations of Satan, the human race would have been eternally lost.

By dying in the place of sinners it can be appreciated to some degree that in the suffering of what seemed like eternal separation from the Father, Jesus endured the pain of the eternal second death.

However, it is not within the scope of human intellect to comprehend how the divine Son of God could be placed in the vulnerable position of a human being subjected to the temptations of Satan and possible failure bringing eternal death. But that would have been the consequence of Jesus' failure as proved by the decree regarding the sinner as proclaimed from the word of God.

In the beginning, in the Garden of Eden before the fall, Adam stood in the glory of a new creation untainted by the discordant seed of Satan's sin. His nature was free from any debilitating effects. By comparison, when Jesus went into the wilderness of temptation, He stood in the resulting weakness that followed four thousand years of degeneration in human nature.

When Adam succumbed to the temptation of appetite he was not plagued with hunger. Contrasting the comforting circumstances of Adam's test, at the time of His big temptation, Jesus had been fasting for forty days and forty nights. It was in human weakness wrought by four thousand years of inherited accumulative debilitating indulgence to appetite that Jesus defeated all of Satan's efforts and temptations. In His humanity Jesus could have yielded but, in exercising self control and being sustained by the word of God, He gained a victory that overshadowed the battle lost through Adam's self indulgence to appetite.

Jesus defeated Satan in His humanity that He might bestow upon us a victory by His divinity.

Adam and Eve were created perfect, pure and sinless, yet their fall from grace proved that they had no inherent defence against sin. The consequential fallen nature of their descendants gave them the propensities of sin.

The only sure way that Adam and Eve could have resisted Satan, and be at peace, was by being filled with the Spirit of God. However, God could not bring about this Holy State against the will of His subjects. This means that without divine help it is not possible for mankind to avoid sinning *"For all have sinned, and come short of the glory of God."* (Romans 3:23).

The same help of God's word that strengthened Jesus was available to Adam and Eve. However, in believing the promises of Satan, they rejected the warnings of God.

Like the father of the human race every living descendant of Adam is faced with a choice. We can all choose every day to be guided by the word of God, and be blessed with the Spirit of God, developing an abhorrence of sin in harmony with the Spirit of Jesus. Or we can choose to be in a fallen state and develop a love for sin.

Adam made a choice that led to rebellion and sin. To sin or not to sin has always been a matter of choice that began with Satan and the fallen angels; the choice carried on through Adam and the whole human race to end with the last generation.

Jesus made a choice that gained a victory over sin. There is another lesson in Scripture, which reveals the inevitability of sin, and the inability of the church to refrain from sin without choosing to follow Christ.

To learn this lesson it is necessary to understand something of the way symbols and types are used in the Bible. A woman can represent a church in both a fallen and pure state.

In the book of Leviticus chapter 15 verse 19 it says that during her monthly period a woman is unclean. The lesson is taught in verses 25-31 that as long as an issue of blood lasts the woman will remain unclean, and reads as follows:

"And if a woman have an issue of her blood many days out of the time of her separation, or if it run beyond the time of her separation; all the days of the issue of her uncleanness shall be as the days of her separation: she [shall be] unclean. 15:26 *Every bed whereon she lieth all the days of her issue shall be unto her as the bed of her separation: and whatsoever she sitteth upon shall be unclean, as the uncleanness of her separation.* 15:27 *And whosoever toucheth those things shall be unclean, and shall wash his clothes, and bathe [himself] in water, and be unclean until the even.* 15:28 *But if she be cleansed of her issue, then she shall number to herself seven days, and after that she shall be clean.* 15:29 *And on the eighth day she shall take unto her two turtles, or two young pigeons, and bring them unto the priest, to the door of the tabernacle of the congregation.* 15:30 *And the priest shall offer the one [for] a sin offering, and the other [for] a burnt offering; and the priest shall make an atonement for her before the LORD for the issue of her uncleanness.* 15:31 *Thus shall ye separate the children of Israel from their uncleanness; that they die not in their uncleanness, when they defile my tabernacle that [is] among them."*

At this time of the month the woman's condition is likened unto one of sin. Yet common sense dictates that at such a time there is no reason to suggest that a woman is more sinful than a man. In Mark 5:25-34 is the following story of a woman *"which had an issue of blood"*.

"And a certain woman, which had an issue of blood twelve years, 5:26 And had suffered many things of many physicians, and had spent all that she had, and was nothing bettered, but rather grew worse, 5:27 When she had heard of Jesus, came in the press behind, and touched his garment. 5:28 For she said, If I may touch but his clothes, I shall be whole. 5:29 And straightway the fountain of her blood was dried up; and she felt in [her] body that she was healed of that plague. 5:30 And Jesus, immediately knowing in himself that virtue had gone out of him, turned him about in the press, and said, Who touched my clothes? 5:31 And his disciples said unto him, Thou seest the multitude thronging thee, and sayest thou, Who touched me? 5:32 And he looked round about to see her that had done this thing. 5:33 But the woman fearing and trembling, knowing what was done in her, came and fell down before him, and told him all the truth. 5:34 And he said unto her, Daughter, thy faith hath made thee whole; go in peace, and be whole of thy plague."

Just as a woman can symbolise a church, blood can be a symbol of life. The blood of *"it is the life of all flesh; the blood of it is for the life thereof."* (Leviticus 17:14).

Losing the blood of life is symbolic of losing life through the contamination of sin.

The above accounts in the book of Leviticus and the story of the woman in the gospel of Mark are teaching that without the presence of Christ, sin is inevitable. The only way that it is possible to avoid its curse is to be in constant touch with Jesus.

The lesson in the book of Mark is teaching that the woman (Church) needs continued contact with the Saviour. As inevitable as is the time of the month for a woman so is the ever presence of sin ready to pounce on those out of touch with Jesus.

The Bible does not teach that the pathway to Christ is always easy. The woman of the story had to do a lot of manoeuvring, pushing and weaving in order to reach the Saviour. Having achieved her objective she was granted healing and peace.

There are those who reject all but an easy way of seeking salvation believing to be under the grace of a loving God regardless of conduct in life.

Chapter 31
This Generation

In spite of the fact that the timing of Jesus' return to earth is shrouded in mystery, He has given signs to help us know when His appearance is near.

Probably the clearest example of an explanation in connection with the return to earth of Jesus is found in the 24th chapter of Matthew. In this chapter Jesus described a swathe of time that began with His day and ended with His return as *"King of Kings and Lord of Lords."*

There could be an important truth in Matthew chapter 24 that throughout the ages has been obscured by the parentheses that were used by Jesus. In order to ascertain the full message of this chapter, I believe there is a need to detach these parentheses used by Jesus from the rest of His discourse. By so doing, it is possible to obtain a more comprehensive picture of end time events.

A number of the prophecies in Matthew chapter 24 have already been fulfilled. Firstly, there was the *account detailing the* destruction of Jerusalem *and its temple*, involving tremendous detail of stone structure being laid bare. As prophesied by Jesus, Jerusalem was destroyed by Rome seventy years later.

Many people have been, and are still being deceived by false Christs. There have been wars and rumours of wars. There has been the 1260 years of persecution that in Scripture is mentioned seven times. The sun has been darkened and the moon has failed in the giving of light.

Reference to a great earthquake, the darkening of the sun, falling stars, and the moon as blood can be found in Revelation 6:12,13 at the opening of the sixth seal which is now in the past.

History records what is known as the earthquake of Lisbon, which took place in November 1, 1755. In May 19, 1780 there occurred a darkening of the sun *that* extended over New England. On November 13, 1833 there also occurred a meteoric shower of stars, which extended throughout much of the U.S.A.

Among all the phenomenal events recorded in the 24th chapter of Matthew, there are two verses, which in their attraction and significance, seem to leap out from the pages. They are verses 7 and 34 that say:

"For nation shall rise against nation, and kingdom against kingdom:"
"Verily I say unto you, This generation shall not pass till all these things be fulfilled."

I believe that these two verses are significant in our search for truth in connection with the end of time. From the verse below we learn that God did not intend that His followers should know exactly when He would return.

Matthew 24:36: *"But of that day and hour knoweth no man, no, not the angels of heaven, but my Father only."*

Yet I believe that Jesus did leave a clue intended for the last generation to help recognise the nearness of His return.

Matthew 24:34 supplies the clue with these words just referred to: *"This generation shall not pass, till all these things be fulfilled."*

Verse 34 is written in the context of verses 27-51 that deals exclusively with the Second Coming of the Son of Man at the end of the world.

In Matthew chapter 24 the salient points of Jesus' discourse are these: *"Many shall come in my name; saying I am Christ"* (verse 5) In verse 6 Jesus records that there will be *"wars and rumours of wars"* but that this would not signify the end.

In verse 7 there is the forecast that *"nation shall rise against nation, and kingdom against kingdom."* From world history we learn that this has happened twice. Firstly there was the 1914-1918 "World War". Then in 1939-45 there was a repeat of nation rising up against nation and kingdom against kingdom.

Because Jesus made reference that could apply to two wars that involved nations and kingdoms, there is a need to ascertain which one He was referring to. He would hardly confuse the issue by ignoring the First World War in favour of the second, so the logical conclusion must be that when saying, *"nation would rise against nation"* He was referring to the First Word War. Jesus ends verse 7, describing a now well-catalogued description of pestilence and earthquakes.

In verses 15-22 Jesus foretells of the fall of Jerusalem and the persecution of the saints during the great 1260 years tribulation of Daniel 7:25.

Jesus then continues giving a further account of *"false Christ, and false prophets"* as He takes us to the time of the end in verses 24-27.

In verse 29 Jesus refers again to the tribulation of verses 21,22 before drawing our attention to the date of May 19 1780 at the darkening of the Sun, and the falling stars of November 13,1833.

We are told that the signs mentioned in these verses and in Luke 21:25 would take place near the day of Christ's return. There is also the declaration, referred to above, that the generation that is alive to see these signs would not pass away before *"all these things be fulfilled."*

When the disciples approached Jesus with the question about the foretold destruction of Jerusalem, they asked Him *"when shall these things be? And what shall be the sign of thy coming, and the end of the world."* Jesus gave a general answer with a sweep of time beginning in verse 4, and ending in verse 27.

In verse 13 Jesus comes to the end of time with these words: *"But he that endureth to the end, the same shall be saved."*

Yet this verse did not indicate the end of Jesus' reply. Within this general answer Jesus gave a parenthetical account of the fall of Jerusalem (verses 15-20). He then carried on with another parenthetical description of events preceding His return ending in verse 34, and His statement that *"This generation shall not pass, till all these things be fulfilled."* (What generation? World War One generation).

So within this sweeping statement, Jesus departed from the main theme with the use of several parentheses that included a specific reference to the 1914-1918 Great War, which reads in verse 7:

"For nation shall rise against nation, and kingdom against kingdom ..." (Historians describe it as World War One).

There have always been wars, generally between two opposing armies, and armies have overrun nations. But until what has become to be known as the first "World War" or "Great War", there had never been war which involved whole nations and kingdoms rising up against each other.

After this parenthesis of the Great War, Jesus carried on with the main theme to include the key verse 34. To repeat: *"Verily I say unto you, This generation shall not pass, till all these things be fulfilled."*

As if to impress our minds with their significance, Jesus also emphatically draws our attention to specific events with repeated use of the preposition *"For."*

Here are some examples:

Verse 5, **"For** *many shall come in my name."* Verse 6, **"For** *all these things must come to pass."* Verse 7, **"For** *nation shall rise against nation."* (World War One).

Jesus was warning the disciples then present and future, against deception (for) because many would come and claim to be Christ. He also said that the end would not come at a time expected (for) because there fist had to take place a time when nation would rise against nation. This is an apt description of the First and Second World Wars. When Jesus was describing the great conflict involving whole nations He was so specific regarding the importance of the relevant date indicating its importance in connection with His return to earth.

With the conclusion that the account of nation rising against nation recorded in verse 7 is inserted parenthetically it would logically mean that verse 8 chronologically follows verse 6. In verse 8 Jesus says that *"All these are the beginning of the sorrows."*

Because Jesus was answering a question about the end of the world then it must mean that Jesus will be returning before the generation that witnessed The First World War passes away. This means that the last generation will include those who were alive during the First World War, see the fulfilment of the prophecies and will of course also witness the return of Jesus.

All the events that led up to the "Great War", together with their generations have passed away. This war is also historically behind us, but the generation that witnessed this event cannot pass away before Jesus returns because He has so prophesied.

Considering that no one knows the day or the hour of Jesus' return, then the longer it is delayed the easier it becomes to attempt an answer by reckoning the ages of those left alive of the generation that has seen *"all these things fulfilled."* (I.e. who were born before or during the Great World War).

This must surely mean that the return of Jesus should always be regarded as imminent. Not everyone will find it easy to accept the conclusion that has been reached on this subject, so let us recap.

Jesus did declare how nation would rise against nation and kingdom against kingdom. He also connected this catastrophe with a time before the end of the world by stating that the *"end is not yet"* for there had to take place this Great War. There seems to be no reasonable conclusion other than that Jesus was referring to "The First World War."

If it is accepted that this is true, the only fact that has to be fitted into the jigsaw is to learn which generation that Jesus had in mind when He said that they would not pass *"till all these things be fulfilled."* It could not be His generation because they have all passed away before the events referred to have been fulfilled. This is also true of every other generation since then to include all those who have lived and died before the "First World War".

Neither could Jesus have been referring to any generation living after the death of the generation who saw the "Great War" because this would mean that the World War generation had also passed away who were to see all these things *"fulfilled"*, including the return of Jesus.

On this matter another alternative left for us to consider is to ignore Jesus' important predictions in connection with His return and believe that Jesus said that the last generation then alive would not pass away before all things are fulfilled and witnessed His return. This conclusion, although obviously true, is not a sensible answer.

It has been suggested that Jesus was referring to the 144,000 from the last generation not passing away before His return. Although it would not be reasonable to refer to the whole generation not passing away, it is an obvious truth that the especially chosen 144,000 of God will not see death. However, considering the contents and context of Jesus' message the explanation as regards the World War One generation is more plausible

It would not be a wise thing to delay seeking the Lord under the illusion that there remains more time available, because the Lord is to cut His work short. Is this because of the imparted righteousness of the saints being developed quickly, and short of the allotted time span of the prophecy? I refer again to the following:

Romans 9:27: *"Esaias also crieth concerning Israel, Though the number of the children of Israel be as the sand of the sea, a remnant shall be saved: 9:28 For he will finish the work, and cut [it] short in righteousness: because a short work will the Lord make upon the earth."*

Chapter 32
The 2520 Curse

When giving a Christian message it is possible to give a biased view based upon ones own convictions. Unless writing on behalf of a particular body, in order to avoid giving the impression of bias, the tendency for a writer is to avoid controversy and to steer clear of spiritual matters that tend to project a particular church doctrine. The problem with this thinking is that there then develops the danger of omitting important truth in order to escape the accusation that one is projecting a certain doctrine for some biased reason.

I consider the truth for this time to be so important that it must be told as it is. This means that in the message to follow there will be a need to mention the Seventh Day Adventist Church by name, not because I have any personal axe to grind but because of the need to speak the gospel truth.

Because the present world spiritual climate shows a lack of spirituality or keen interest in general towards any form of religion, it is difficult to visualise a situation when there is going to be a threat to anyone who refuses to have the mark of the beast.

It must appear to be all the more strange when the Bible makes the prophecy that those under threat are the ones who are said to be doing the will of God. The threat is portrayed as being against those who represent the government of God.

For example, in the book of Revelation it states clearly that before the return of Jesus, there is going to be a short time of persecution when the people of God will face a threat to their lives if they don't accept the mark of the beast.

We read in previous chapters of the rise and fall of the Papacy, and the significant role to be played at the time of the end by the United States of America.

Armed with this basic information in conjunction with a message from the book of Revelation it is possible to gain an insight into events that are to befall the world before the entrance onto the world scene of Jesus Christ.

Speaking of the threat that is to be posed by the by the U.S.A and the Papacy in the time nearing the end, it says in Revelation 13:14-18:

"And deceiveth them that dwell on the earth by [the means of] those miracles which he had power to do in the sight of the beast; saying to

them that dwell on the earth, that they should make an image to the beast, which had the wound by a sword, and did live. And he had power to give life unto the image of the beast, that the image of the beast should both speak, and cause that as many as would not worship the image of the beast should be killed. And he causeth all, both small and great, rich and poor, free and bond, to receive a mark in their right hand, or in their foreheads: And that no man might buy or sell, save he that had the mark, or the name of the beast, or the number of his name. Here is wisdom. Let him that hath understanding count the number of the beast: for it is the number of a man; and his number [is] Six hundred threescore [and] six."

We studied in chapter 6 about the sign of God. Understanding that the sign of God is the seventh day Sabbath, it logically follows that the mark of the beast would be a sign that is opposed to the sign of God. This means that to bestow honour on another day contrary to the sign of God would be a sin of violation against the Sabbath commandment, and would constitute the mark of the beast.

A sincere and honest study of the doctrines projected by Christendom will prove beyond any reasonable doubt that there is just one church that represents the message of Jesus and is teaching doctrines that are in harmony with the will of God manifested in His law of Ten Commandments, and that is the Seventh Day Adventist Church.

Sin is transgression of God's law. Therefore, any doctrine that is in violation of this basic truth is not in harmony with the will of God.

Having established the basis of truth above we can proceed further.

There is a long prophecy known as the *"Seven times"* or the *"2520 curse"*, and is to be found in the book of Leviticus chapter 26.

In this chapter there was set before the people of Israel a choice of *"life and death, blessing and cursing."*

The following quotation taken from Exodus 19:1-6 is a record of God's covenant with His people:

"In the third month, when the children of Israel were gone forth out of the land of Egypt, the same day came they [into] the wilderness of Sinai. For they were departed from Rephidim, and were come [to] the desert of Sinai, and had pitched in the wilderness; and there Israel camped before the mount. And Moses went up unto God, and the LORD called unto him out of the mountain, saying, Thus shalt thou say to the house of Jacob, and tell the children of Israel; Ye have seen what I did unto the Egyptians, and [how] I bare you on eagles' wings, and brought you unto myself. Now therefore, if ye will obey my voice indeed, and keep my

covenant, then ye shall be a peculiar treasure unto me above all people: for all the earth [is] mine: And ye shall be unto me a kingdom of priests, and an holy nation. These [are] the words which thou shalt speak unto the children of Israel."

The covenant between God and His people was based upon the law of Ten Commandments that is a transcript of the Holy character of God.

Based on the covenant, there were to be blessings or curses. In Leviticus 26:3-7 is the following record of God's promise to Israel providing they kept His commandments:

"If ye walk in my statutes, and keep my commandments, and do them; Then I will give you rain in due season, and the land shall yield her increase, and the trees of the field shall yield their fruit. And your threshing shall reach unto the vintage, and the vintage shall reach unto the sowing time: and ye shall eat your bread to the full, and dwell in your land safely. And I will give peace in the land, and ye shall lie down, and none shall make [you] afraid: and I will rid evil beasts out of the land, neither shall the sword go through your land. And ye shall chase your enemies, and they shall fall before you by the sword. And five of you shall chase an hundred, and an hundred of you shall put ten thousand to flight: and your enemies shall fall before you by the sword."

In the important circumstances of life and salvation there are always two choices set before the people. The one is to follow God and enjoy His promised blessings culminating in eternal life. The other choice is to live in rebellion against His government and come under the curse associated with the rebel government of Satan. If the nation of Israel broke the covenant with God they were told in verses 14-:24:

*"But if ye will not hearken unto me, and will not do all these commandments; And if ye shall despise my statutes, or if your soul abhor my judgments, so that ye will not do all my commandments, [but] that ye break my covenant: I also will do this unto you; I will even appoint over you terror, consumption, and the burning ague, that shall consume the eyes, and cause sorrow of heart: and ye shall sow your seed in vain, for your enemies shall eat it. And I will set my face against you, and ye shall be slain before your enemies: they that hate you shall reign over you; and ye shall flee when none pursueth you. And if ye will not yet for all this hearken unto me, then I will punish you **seven times** more for your sins. And I will break the pride of your power; and I will make your heaven as iron, and your earth as brass: And your strength shall be spent in vain: for your land shall not yield her increase, neither shall the trees of the land yield their fruits. And if ye walk contrary unto me, and*

*will not hearken unto me; I will bring **seven times** more plagues upon you according to your sins. I will also send wild beasts among you, which shall rob you of your children, and destroy your cattle, and make you few in number; and your [high] ways shall be desolate. And if ye will not be reformed by me by these things, but will walk contrary unto me; Then will I also walk contrary unto you, and will punish you yet **seven times** for your sins. And I will bring a sword upon you, that shall avenge the quarrel of [my] covenant: and when ye are gathered together within your cities, I will send the pestilence among you; and ye shall be delivered into the hand of the enemy. [And] when I have broken the staff of your bread, ten women shall bake your bread in one oven, and they shall deliver [you] your bread again by weight: and ye shall eat, and not be satisfied. And if ye will not for all this hearken unto me, but walk contrary unto me; Then I will walk contrary unto you also in fury; and I, even I, will chastise you **seven times** for your sins."*

Having disobeyed God, the nation of Israel came under the seven times curse. We are already familiar with the Bible rules that apply regarding prophetic time and the significance attached to something when it is repeated three times. It will be noted that the terminology used to describe the *"***seven times***"* curse is repeated **four times** above.

In Daniel chapter 4 is a record of the boastful Nebuchadnezzar having his kingdom taken away and suffering the punishment of seven times or seven years before, when contrite of heart, his kingdom was returned to him.

From this record, in connection with Nebuchadnezzar, it can be seen that in the Bible one time is equal to one year and seven times is equal to seven years.

As previously noted, from Numbers 14:34 and Ezekiel 4:6 we learn that in prophetic time one day equals one Bible year of 360 days. A year for a day means that 360 days is thus equal to 360 years. Seven times 360 years is equal to 2520 years.

Understanding that literal Israel broke the covenant with God means that they came under the curse that is plainly set out in Leviticus chapter 26.

Nebuchadnezzar was punished seven times, or 2520 literal days, whereas the people of God came under the curse for 2520 literal years. This is because 2520 prophetic days are equal to 2520 years.

Nebuchadnezzar's return to glory is an allegory of God's people being returned back to Him in the blessing of gathering back to Him after the curse of the scattering has ended.

Because of the sins of Solomon, the nation of Israel was divided into two nations--the Northern and Southern kingdoms. Each one was in rebellion against God's commandments and thus forfeited the conditional promised blessings and, therefore, came under the curse of Leviticus. Thus there were two lines of rebellion and two lines of the 2520 curse.

The 2520 curse began for the Northern tribes with King Hoshea when Israel was taken into captivity by Babylon in 722 B.C. (See 2 Kings 17:1-8,13,16-18).

The 2520 curse for the Southern kingdom began when King Manasseh went into captivity in 677 B.C. (See 2 Chronicles 33:11, 2 Kings 21:16).

The Bible ties the two *"seven times"* curses together. In 2 Kings 21:13 it says that God would *"stretch over Jerusalem the line of Samaria, and the plummet of the house of Ahab: and I will wipe Jerusalem as a man wipeth a dish, wiping it, and turning it upside down."*

The Bible is saying that the 2520 plummet measuring the rebellion of the Northern line and its curse was to be stretched over the Southern line. This means that the two lines of prophecy would be interrelated by joining together.

The Northern line of 2520 curse reaches from 722 B.C. in the reign of King Hoshea to 1798 A.D. when the Papacy suffered its deadly wound. The time scale of this 2520 is split exactly in half by the date 538 A.D. when the Pope became head of the churches. Thus included in this 2520 curse of the Northern line there is a 1260 days (years) prophecy from 722 B.C. to 538 A.D. at the time of the ascension of the Papacy, and 1260 days (years) from 538 A.D. to the demise of the Papacy in 1798 A.D.

These two 1260 years represent two desolating powers. The one is Pagan desolation. The other is Papal desolation brought about by the union between church and state.

The Southern line of the 2520 curse reaches from 677 B.C. in the reign of King Manasseh to 1844, which was the date that Jesus entered the heavenly sanctuary as recorded in Daniel 8:14. In the heavenly sanctuary, Jesus is now investigating the records of those who claim to be His people, and cleansing the records of those who are faithful. This cleansing in heaven is the anti-type to the Jewish Day of Atonement that was the cleansing of the earthly sanctuary.

Just as there were two lines of a *"seven times"* 2520 curse involving two times of scattering so are there two times of gathering of God's people. The first gathering began in 1798 at the demise of the papal government. The second gathering began with a new understanding of the judgement message when Jesus entered into the heavenly sanctuary in 1844.

When referring to the time that it took to re-build the temple in Jerusalem, it was said, as recorded in John 2:20 that it took 46 years. This period of time is confirmed in our previous study of the re-building of the Jewish temple as decreed by King Artexerxes in 457 B.C.

It will be noted that in our previous study the record shows that the re-building took 49 years. This is 3 years more than that stated by John. However, Daniel 9:25 speaks of the re-building time to include the streets and the wall. This added building work took a further 3 years, but the building of the temple took 46 years.

The first gathering began at the end of the Northern 2520 curse in A.D.1798. There was another gathering in A.D.1844 at the completion of the Southern 2520 curse.

It will be seen that 46 years separated the two gatherings. This means that it took 46 years from 1798 to 1844 to prepare the seed leading to the development of a people who recognised the validity of the Ten Commandment, and were ready to proclaim the three angels' messages of Revelation chapter 14. That this has been proved to be true is made evident by the record showing that there were people proclaiming the 1844 message at the relevant time.

Thus, there were 46 years in the re-building of the physical temple in Jerusalem, and 46 years in the formation of a people who bestowed honour on God's law which eventually led to the formation of the Seventh Day Adventist Church, equipped to proclaim the judgement message of 1844.

There is some significance in the repeated use of the number three in connection with the building of the physical temple in Jerusalem and the spiritual temple, which is God's church. It is an established fact that there is added importance attached to a statement that is repeated in the Bible three times.

In John 2:19 Jesus makes reference to His resurrection and the length of time that His body would be in the grave when He said: *"Destroy this temple, and in three days I will raise it up."*

It is interesting to note that just as there were three days before the raising of the temple of His physical body, there were also three decrees before the raising of the temple in Jerusalem.

There was also the same number of decrees involved in the 1844 message that was the beginning of a body that led the building of God's final church.

These three kinds of decrees were the three angels' messages of Revelation chapter 14. In verse 7 the first angel is *"Saying with a loud voice, Fear God, and give glory to him; for the hour of his judgment is come (1844) and worship him that made heaven, and earth, and the sea, and the fountains of waters."* In its reference to worship the God who made heaven, and earth, this verse is a definite instruction to bestow honour on the God of creation by worshipping on His seventh day Sabbath.

The seventh day Sabbath message has been faithfully proclaimed by many of God's people as they have sought to bring to light the importance of remembering that the seventh day Sabbath is a sign of God's creation. Those faithful ones who die in this message will have part in the special resurrection to witness the victory of the 144,000.

This truth is established in the following quotation taken from Revelation 14:13: *"And I heard a voice from heaven saying unto me, Write, Blessed [are] the dead which die in the Lord from henceforth: Yea, saith the Spirit, that they may rest from their labours; and their works do follow them."*

In verse 8 the second angel refers to the spiritual fall of Babylon and also the fall of the Papacy in 1798 by *"saying, Babylon is fallen, is fallen, that great city, because she made all nations drink of the wine of the wrath of her fornication."*

In verses 9 and 10 is the record of the third angel speaking in *"a loud voice"* warning people not to receive the mark of the beast.

Showing the consistency and accuracy of Bible prophecy, the words of Isaiah 7:8,9 prophesied, *"within **threescore and five years** shall Ephraim be broken, that it be not a people."*

20 years later in 722 B.C. the northern kingdom (Ephraim) was broken when Hoshea was taken prisoner. 65 years after the prediction of Isaiah, and 45 years after the captivity of the northern kingdom, Manasseh of the southern kingdom was also taken captive making a total of 65 years as prophesied. Thus within the predicted 65 years both kingdoms of Israel were broken.

The promised blessings to the people who enter into a covenant relationship with God, and the resulting curse for those who reject this covenant is plainly taught throughout the Bible as is further evident in Jeremiah 11:1-4 where it says:

"The word that came to Jeremiah from the LORD, saying, Hear ye the words of this covenant, and speak unto the men of Judah, and to the inhabitants of Jerusalem; And say thou unto them, Thus saith the LORD God of Israel; Cursed [be] the man that obeyeth not the words of this covenant, Which I commanded your fathers in the day [that] I brought them forth out of the land of Egypt, from the iron furnace, saying, Obey my voice, and do them, according to all which I command you: so shall ye be my people, and I will be your God:"

Finally, in connection with the 2520 curse, there is a message of some significance in the writing that appeared on a wall on the night that the kingdom of Belshazzar was finished. In effect, the proclaimed curse of Leviticus chapter 26 is amazingly repeated, as follows in Daniel 5:25-28:

"MENE, MENE, TEKEL, UPHARSIN This [is] the interpretation of the thing: MENE; God hath numbered thy kingdom, and finished it. TEKEL; Thou art weighed in the balances, and art found wanting. PERES; Thy kingdom is divided, and given to the Medes and Persians"

The plain English of the message from God to Belshazzar, as recorded in the book of Daniel, states that in spite of Belshazzar's knowledge of the lesson that had been given to Nebuchadnezzar, in order for him to learn that it is the God of creation who holds the destiny of all in His hands, Belshazzar still revealed his contempt for God. He showed his contempt by the way that he desecrated the cups and bowls taken from the temple, and together with his wives and noblemen drank wine from the sacred vessels to the honour of gods of gold, silver, bronze, iron, wood and stone, who cannot see or hear, and that do not know anything.

However, in addition to the statement that the kingdom of Belshazzar was finished, God was proclaiming another message that relates to the 2520 curse that is recorded in Leviticus chapter 26.

Adding the numerical value of the currency of the day MENE, MENE, TEKEL, UPHARSIN mentioned above, we arrive at an interesting figure as follows:

MENE = 50 SHEKELS. MENE=50 SHEKELS. TEKEL=1 SHEKEL. UPHARSIN=25 SHEKELS. Total=126 SHEKELS.

In Ezekiel 45:12 it says: *"And the shekel [shall be] twenty gerahs...."*

See also Exodus 30:13, Leviticus 27:25, Numbers 18:16 and Ezekiel 45:12.

Multiplying 126 shekels by 20 gerahs we arrive at the figure of 2520 gerahs, which equals the seven times curse of 2520. It can be clearly seen that the message written on the wall in Babylon was a proclamation of the same 2520 curse that was recorded in Leviticus chapter 26.

Satan is responsible for introducing so much nonsense that has become woven into the gospel message causing it to be preached lacking the power of conviction or the power of God.

God has made a covenant with His people based upon His law of Ten Commandments. God cannot break this covenant, which is a blessing to His people. If those who profess to be God's people break the covenant they risk coming under the curse. When there is no recognition of the validity of the original covenant and the law of God, there is no substance in the message of salvation.

As always, the power of salvation is centred on separating the sinner from sin. God's message for today is the same as it was yesterday. Based upon restoring the original covenant, God is still offering the same blessings to the nation of spiritual Israel as He did to literal Israel.

From the above observations it can be seen that the people of God have reached the end of the curse, and that now is the time of the gathering before the return of Jesus.

Aware of the Bible rule that when something is repeated three times it takes on special significance, it should be noted that in connection with the 2520 curse, the *"seven "times"* message of Leviticus 26 is repeated four times.

In addition to this fact, we now have evidence of the 2520 curse being projected a further three times. There is the record of the 2520 curse being applied to the Northern kingdom. There is also the record of the 2520 curse being applied to the Southern kingdom. In the *"MENE, MENE, TEKEL, UPHARSIN"* message of Daniel there is further evidence of the same 2520 curse.

In harmony with human nature, there will be those who might be reluctant to accept this message of a repeated curse in the book of Daniel because of believing that this is a message instigated by the hand of man rather than the hand of God. However, the words and interpretation of *MENE, MENE, TEKEL, and UPHARSIN* did not originate in man but came from God.

It is time for God's people to wake up to the truth now being proclaimed in preparation for the conflict of the ages.

In chapter 14 of Revelation the message for this time is clear. John said, as recorded in verse 1: *"And I looked, and, lo, a Lamb stood on the mount Sion, and with him an hundred forty [and] four thousand, having his Father's name written in their foreheads."*

This number of 144,000 described by John is the final remnant of God's people who in the presence of a world in rebellion, are to vindicate God and His law of Ten Commandments.

In verses 6 and 7 is the message of the everlasting gospel being delivered to the entire world and also the message that the hour of God's judgement has come in the year 1844.

As if to show that some of the obstacles placed by Satan to thwart the message of the everlasting gospel are being removed, it says, as seen previously in Revelation 14:8: *"And there followed another angel, saying, **Babylon is fallen, is fallen**, that great city, because she made all nations drink of the wine of the wrath of her fornication."*

The fall of Babylon was spiritual and as a result of false doctrines and corrupting the truth. However, as it relates to the Papacy, Babylon also suffered a catastrophic physical fall in the year 1798 just at the time when God was preparing His church to take the everlasting gospel together with the proclamation that the hour of judgement had come.

Babylon has not yet recovered from this fall. This gives God's people the opportunity to finish the work that He has set by proclaiming the messages of the three angels of Revelation chapter 14.

Are God's people going to spurn the God-given opportunity to finish the work that He has set, by refusing God's power of love that will enable His people to enter into His rest?

If God's message of love is not proclaimed in a time of relative peace, how can it be properly proclaimed in a time of persecution? Although it remains possible to gain salvation while Jesus is present in the sanctuary, the time will come when it is too late for preaching or salvation. This is because holiness of character is the key to eternal life. An intellectual desire and decision for victory with Christ means nothing if one has not used the time of probation to develop a character in harmony with God's circle of love as portrayed in John 17:21.

In the time of the final persecution the preaching time gives way to the testing time. Now is the time when God is preparing His people. Just as the latter rain is invisibly falling upon the hearts of God's people and sealing them with the sign of the Father's name, so will the mark of Satan be formed in the character of rebellion.

God is now preparing the 144,000 for the final conflict with Satan. The message of the everlasting gospel is to present the character of God and His impartial love, which is a fulfilment of God's law.

The knowledge that before the end of time there is to be enacted laws against religious liberty and God's people can serve the cause of complacency. To believe that it is possible to await the coming of such laws and then make a meaningful decision for Christ is the height of folly. As recorded in 1 Corinthians 6:2, the apostle Paul said, *"now is the day of salvation."*

In this time of gathering, the latter rain falls as God gathers His people to Himself. We cannot be gathered if we choose to remain scattered under the curse of the 2520. God is calling people out of Babylon. It is possible to belong to a pure church and still be spiritually in Babylon.

There is real danger if in all circumstances we rely too much on the grace of God through the blessing of imputed righteousness.

The promise of God is that at the time of the end, in the strength of imparted righteousness, God's people will love the righteousness of God with all of their hearts and minds and their neighbours as themselves.

If there is no evidence of this heavenly love in the present, how can it be possible to wait until the last proverbial minute to acquire such a wondrous love?

Speaking for myself, I do confess at being troubled that the weakness of my sinful human nature could sever my links with God forged by the grace of His imputed righteousness.

If with the passage of time the sin of my human nature and the blessing of imputed righteousness are not replaced with the nature of Christ and the blessing of imparted righteousness then again speaking for myself I find this condition to be real cause for concern.

When faced with the dilemma of reconciling the desires of his sinful nature with his desire to serve God, Paul explained his dilemma as follows:

"We know that the law is spiritual; but I am a mortal man, sold as a slave to sin. I do not understand what I do; for I don't do what I would like to do, but instead I do what I hate. Since what I do is what I don't want to do, this shows that I agreed that the Law is right. So I am not really the one who does this thing; rather it is the sin that lives in me. I know that good does not live in me--that is, in my human nature. For even though the desire to do good is in me, I am not able to do it. I don't do the good I want to do; instead, I do the evil that I do not want to do. If I do what I don't want to do, this means that I am no longer the one who does it; instead it is the sin that lives in me." (Romans 7:14-20 Good News version).

In chapter 8 Paul then goes on to explain that what the law could not do because of the weakness of human nature, God is able to do by sending His Son enabling us to live according to the Spirit.

In verse 6 Paul gives a beautiful summation of the matter where he is recorded as saying: *"To be controlled by human nature results in death, to be controlled by the Spirit results in life and peace."*

Paul is clearly stating that a born-again Christian is born with abhorrence for sin that will lead to a complete freedom from acts of sin. When there is no evidence of such freedom, then the integrity of a claimed Christian birth is brought into question.

It is a sobering thought to realise that a lack of total commitment to the cause of Christ could result in a severed connection to Christ even before the edict of Jesus that is proclaimed thus in Revelation 22:11:

"He that is unjust, let him be unjust still: and he which is filthy, let him be filthy still: and he that is righteous, let him be righteous still: and he that is holy, let him be holy still."

Chapter 33
The Seven Thunders

In order to be more fully acquainted with events associated with the present truth we turn to Revelation chapter 10:1,2 where is the record of John saying:

"And I saw another mighty angel come down from heaven, clothed with a cloud: and a rainbow [was] upon his head, and his face [was] as it were the sun, and his feet as pillars of fire: And he had in his hand a little book open: and he set his right foot upon the sea, and [his] left [foot] on the earth."

This account given by John relates in verse 3 to the mighty angel who *"cried with a loud voice, as when a lion roareth."* We learn from Revelation 5:5 that Jesus is *"the lion of the tribe of Judah"*.

As observed in chapter 24 I believe that we can safely conclude that the mighty angel referred to above is none other than Jesus.

Further support for this belief is that in Scripture God is named as The Lord God Almighty. It is unlikely that any normal angel would be described with the same title.

The fact that the right foot of Jesus is depicted as upon the sea and His left foot upon the earth indicates the worldwide scope of the message. Verse 3 states that Jesus cried with a loud voice indicating the urgency of the message, which demands attention.

It is an established truth among students of God's word, that the open book referred to by John is a reference to the sealed message of Daniel as stated thus in Daniel 12:8,9: *"And I heard, but I understood not: then said I, O my Lord, what [shall be] the end of these [things]? And he said, Go thy way, Daniel: for the words [are] closed up and sealed till the time of the end."*

In Daniel 12:13 it says that he will stand in his lot *"at the end of the days"*.

Standing in one's lot can be interpreted in different ways. It can be a reference to being in the grave, or under judgement. But in the context used in Daniel, standing in one's lot is to fulfil a purpose. When the book of Daniel became unsealed it fulfilled its purpose. It can then be said that Daniel stood in his lot.

In some respects, the book of Daniel and the book of Revelation could be regarded as one book. The book of Daniel deals in prophecy, while the book of Revelation opens up the answers.

The proof of Scripture is thus developed and established line upon line, here a little, there a little.

We are told in Daniel that the sealed book was to be opened at the time of the end. The time of the end is widely accepted to begin in 1798 A.D. to include the present time. Encompassed in this time of the end is the culmination of the 2,300 days timed prophecy of Daniel 8:14 that extended to 1844 when Jesus entered into the heavenly sanctuary.

A record of this point in time is found in Revelation 10:6 and reads: *"And sware by him that liveth for ever and ever, who created heaven, and the things that therein are, and the earth, and the things that therein are, and the sea, and the things which are therein, that* **there should be time no longer***:"*

When saying that there **would be time no longer**, the writer is not referring to probationary time but to prophetic time. This means that there are no more prophesies beyond the 2,300 days prophecy of Daniel 8:14.

During this time of the open book that began with the time of the end, there has been an increase in understanding of God's word, which eventually led to the formation of the Seventh Day Adventist church.

From the year 1840 the people of God were led to a more comprehensive understanding of the messages given by the three angels of Revelation chapter 14. The first angel of verses 6,7 announced the hour of God's judgment, (1844) and a call to worship the God of creation. The second angel of verse 8 proclaims the fall of Babylon. The third angel of verses 9 and 10 gives the warning not to worship the beast.

However, the combined messages given at the relevant time were not fully understood, which resulted in some parts of the intended messages remaining sealed or closed. In keeping with a general misunderstanding of present truth at that time, it was widely believed that the judgement message of verse 7 indicated the return of Jesus.

Because of this lack of comprehension by God's people at the time of the 1844 message additional light was withheld. Just as John was about to reveal events related to the time of the end he was instructed as recorded in Revelation 10:4: *"And when the seven thunders had uttered their voices, I was about to write; and I heard a voice from heaven saying unto me, Seal up those things which the seven thunders uttered, and write them not."*

Verse 3 states that the *"seven thunders uttered their voices."* Verse 4 records that John was about to write of events that were to unfold as uttered by the voices of the seven thunders, but he was told not to reveal these events, *"and write them not."*

As a result of study from the word of God, many of His people expected the return of Jesus to take place in the year 1844. This was the message that in Revelation 10:10 was described as sweet *"as honey"*. Revealing the disappointment at the outcome of the message, the same verse describes the message as being bitter.

However, because the servants of God were not spiritually prepared and therefore not ready for God's final messages at that time, do not make void the messages. The messages proclaimed by the seven thunders still stand.

In Revelation 10:11 is the implication that regarding the fullness the messages of the seven thunders John had to "*prophesy again*". They were only to remain sealed, as recorded in verse 4, until additional light enabled the people of God to understand the messages in their full significance.

Because the messages of the seven thunders were only delayed until a more enlightened time it is important that the people of God acquire an understanding of these messages that were proclaimed by the voices of the seven thunders.

The truth that in the year 1844, Jesus was to enter into the heavenly sanctuary was misinterpreted by some to mean that He was to return to earth at that time. Others at that time did not believe anything about the message, and consequently could not by faith enter into the most holy place.

The truthful events that led to the year 1844 were the three angels' messages of Revelation chapter 14.

There is also the account of Jesus, the mighty angel of Revelation 10:1, being involved in the preparation of God's people. The evidence from Scripture points to the period of time that led to the year 1844 as being the time connected with the misunderstood messages of the seven thunders.

It is because God's people at that time were not spiritually prepared for the full truth voiced by the seven thunders that it is to be repeated, as described in Rev 10:11, where it says: *"Thou must prophesy again before many nations, and tongues, and kings."*

This must mean that there is to be a repetition of the messages that led to 1844 with the addition of more understanding by God's people.

It is widely believed by many people that had the servants of God been spiritually prepared in the year 1844 that Jesus would have returned. If this is true then it can be appreciated just how important it is for the saints to know what are the repeated messages of the seven thunders.

The messages from 1844 onwards included the three angels' messages of Revelation chapter 14 and the mighty angel of Revelation 10:1.

Added to these messages and as an answer to the continued fall of Babylon there is the record in Revelation 18:1 of another angel of great power proclaiming the fall of Babylon. This angel is said to have such great power as to light the earth with his glory. The concentrated efforts of heaven are multiplied in an effort to combat the increasing measure of sins perpetrated by Babylon.

In Revelation 18:4 there is the record of yet another angel calling God's people out of Babylon. This makes a total of six heavenly messages. The fact that the people are being called out of Babylon that they do *"not partake of her sins"* show that no one is lost until a specific time of decision is proof of guilt or otherwise.

In addition to these six heavenly agencies at work prior to the close of probation, there is also the proclamation of the established truth in connection with the 144,000 and the mystery of God.

An account of this very important truth can be found in Revelation 10:7 where it says: *"But in the days of the voice of the seventh angel, when he shall begin to sound, the mystery of God should be finished, as he hath declared to his servants the prophets."*

From Ephesians 1:9,10 we learn that the mystery of God is the will and purpose of God. In Ephesians 6:19 it says that the mystery of God is the gospel. In Colossians 4:3 it is declared to be *"the mystery of Christ."*

In Matthew 24:14 is the following message indicating that the end comes when the gospel is preached to all the world.

"And this gospel of the kingdom shall be preached in all the world for a witness unto all nations; and then shall the end come".

Of course the above message is true. However, another account of the gospel of Christ reaching fulfilment is found in Colossians 2:2, thus: *"That their hearts might be comforted, being knit together in love and unto all riches of the full assurance of understanding, to the acknowledgement of the mystery of God, and the Father, and of Christ."*

Of course the above message is true. However, an account of another aspect of the gospel of Christ reaching fulfilment is found in Colossians 2:2, thus: *"That their hearts might be comforted, being knit together in love and unto all riches of the full assurance of understanding, to the acknowledgement of the mystery of God, and the Father, and of Christ."*

Thus the mystery of God is shown to be the gospel of Christ. In addition to the gospel going to the whole world, the gospel of Christ is also finished on reaching fulfilment when through complete sanctification there is a full measure of imparted righteousness manifested in the saints. This takes place when the elected 144,000 have the Father's name written upon their foreheads as recorded in Revelation 14:1.

It can be seen that the most important aspect of the messages of the seven thunders is the fulfilment of the gospel of salvation as revealed in the full-imparted righteousness of the 144,000, who will have entered God's Sabbath rest. This is the time when through the 144,000 the mystery of God is finished, as demonstrated by a full measure of God's imparted and impartial love in God's remnant.

Within the messages of the seven thunders six celestial agencies are involved, together with the message of the 144,000.

In addition to these proclaimed seven truths, there is to be the huge disappointment for the wicked and inexpressible joy for the saints at the end of time.

It was also during this period of the end time of prophetic events that there took place the collapse of Islam with the fall of the Ottoman Empire on August 11th 1840. If the collapse of Islam is to be repeated as indicated by the words of Revelation10:11, there is to be another dramatic collapse of Islam before the return of Jesus.

From the above observations we know that the messages of the voice of the seven thunders will include a repetition of messages of the three angels proclaimed in Revelation chapter 14. There is also the mighty angel of Revelation 10:1, the angel of great power of Revelation 18:1, and the angel who calls people to leave Babylon in Revelation 18:4. It must logically also include a call to the 144,000 to enter into God's rest when the *"mystery of God should be finished"*.

In addition, one should not be surprised if in the not too distant future there is another collapse of Islam.

Of course, the messages referred to above have always been in the Bible. There is no change in the messages but the passage of time has brought an increase in understanding.

It seems to be very fitting that God's final messages, which parallels the 1840 message, should be described as the voices of the seven thunders. This description finds perfect harmony with other proclamations found in the book of Revelation in connection with God's final messages as follows.

The messages of 1840 regarding the three angels' messages etc. were accompanied by great heavenly power.

The angel of Revelation 14:7 spoke *"With a loud voice"*. The third angel of verse 9 also spoke *"with a loud voice"*.

Of the angel of Revelation 18:1,2 it says that he had *"great power, and the earth was lightened with his glory. And he cried mightily with a, strong voice saying, Babylon is fallen"*.

The quotations above are aptly mirrored in the voices of the seven thunders.

In summary, what was actually said about the sealed book of Daniel that was opened in Revelation? We know that as recorded in Revelation 10:2 that the mighty angel had *"in his hand a little book open."* We also know that the open book is a reference to the sealed book of Daniel that is now unsealed.

In Revelation 10:10 John wrote of the sweetness of the open book that brought joy to those who expected the return of Jesus, which changed to bitterness when they discovered their mistake.

John saw that Jesus was to enter into the heavenly sanctuary in 1844. Of this he wrote not. This was the reason that people at that time wrongly believed that Jesus was about to return to earth.

As recorded in Revelation chapter 14, John saw the importance of the seventh day Sabbath, and the need to worship the God of creation, but of it he wrote not. Neither did he open up the full truth in connection with the mark of the beast. Even though there was an increase of knowledge in connection with the first two angels' messages of Revelation chapter 14, there still remained truth that was sealed.

For example, John had a vision of the 144,000 as recorded in Revelation chapter 14, but the full truth in connection with the 144,000, John wrote not.

In his account in Revelation 10:7 of the mystery of God being finished, is the revelation of the importance of the Spiritual Sabbath, which is fulfilled when the people of God enter into His rest. Of this John wrote not. In other words, the people of God were not spiritually prepared for the full truth at that time.

Thus, as recorded in Revelation 10:4, the final message to God's people remained sealed.

The only record in Revelation that can refer to this message not being sealed is found in chapter 22 verse 10 where it says: *"Seal not the sayings of the prophecy of this book: for the time is at hand."*

Is this verse not a fulfilment of the prophecy of chapter 10:11 where, when speaking of the seven thunders, it says: *"Thou must prophesy again before many peoples, and nations, and tongues, and kings."*?

We have read from verse 10 above of the unsealing of the complete book of Revelation. Verse 11 relates to the close of probation where it says: *"He that is unjust, let him be unjust sill: and he which is filthy, let him be filthy still: and he that is righteous, let him be righteous still: and he that is holy, let him be holy still"*

It can be clearly seen from the above two verses that a revelation of the full truth takes place when the prophecy of Revelation is unsealed not long before the close of probation.

The verses following verses 10 and 11 state the soon return of Jesus who comes to reward those who keep God's commandments and *"have right to the tree of life."*

Many people believe that the closing controversy that is to take place between the people of God and the forces of Satan will be a long and protracted affair. They take comfort from the assurances of Satan that time is on their side.

However, we have read that this conclusion finds no support in the passages of Scripture that relate to the end of time.

There is first recorded the sealing of the messages of the seven thunders as revealed in Revelation 10:4. This is followed by the prophecy of Revelation 10:11 where it speaks of the unsealed messages being repeated and proclaimed to *"many peoples, and nations, and tongues, and kings."*

The only record of this prophecy being unsealed is found in Revelation 22:10. This takes place as stated in the same verse when *"the time is at hand."* Verse 11 then refers to the unchanging condition of the unjust and the righteous.

Not long after the prophecy of Revelation 10:11 becomes unsealed as recorded in Revelation 22:10, the end of time is at hand. This is confirmed in verse 12 where it says:

"And, behold, I come quickly; and my reward is with me, to give every man according to his work shall be."

This means that a short time after the unsealing of the messages of the seven thunders probation will close followed by the quick return of Jesus.

An important issue for would be Christians is one of belief. For this reason it seems to be an important issue to close with. As a prerequisite to salvation the subject of belief is often stressed in Scripture. Yet as we can observe *"the devils also believe, and tremble."* (James 2:19).

In times of ease it is not too difficult to believe that there is an all powerful God of love in ultimate control of the affairs of men. But in times of extreme stress and utter despair it can be difficult even for saints to cling to such a belief and reconcile belief in the presence of an all powerful God of love with a situation that appears to be without hope.

If we find no real evidence of God, how is it possible to love God? There is an answer to this apparent dilemma of reconciling belief in the presence of God with the apparent hopelessness of a particular situation. Even when it appears that there is no evidence of God it is still possible to love everything that is a representative of God.

When admonished in Scripture to *"believe"*, it is my conviction that we are intended to make a distinction between the Person of God and the principles and righteousness of God. By so doing it is possible to believe in the principles and righteousness of God when there seems to be no evidence of the Person of God. This was the situation as recorded in Mark 9:17-24 where it says: *"And straightway the father of the child cried out, and said with tears, Lord, I believe; help thou mine unbelief."*

There is no merit or virtue in believing in the presence of God. As previously noted, even *"the devils also believe, and tremble."*

Virtue and merit are found as a result of loving the principles and righteousness of God.

When joining any kind of club or organisation there is generally the expectation that one will make a total commitment by accepting the relevant rules. The ensuing benefits are commensurate with the commitment.

The same kind of conditions apply when accepting salvation and joining the kingdom of God. It is not possible to secure the benefits that come with joining the body of Christ if there is a lack of dedication and commitment to the righteousness that is manifest in the Person of Christ.

When in Matthew 17:15-20 the disciples were shown to be unable to heal the son of the frantic father, it appears that this was because of a lack of commitment by the disciples to the cause of Christ. This conclusion is confirmed by the words of Jesus in verse 21 where He is recorded as saying: *"Howbeit this kind goeth not out but by prayer and fasting."*

Thus faith and belief can be equated with commitment that will increase by walking daily with Christ.